Blockchains in 6G

A Standardized Approach to Permissioned Distributed Ledgers

RIVER PUBLISHERS SERIES IN COMMUNICATIONS AND NETWORKING

Series Editors:

ABBAS JAMALIPOUR
The University of Sydney, Australia

MARINA RUGGIERI
University of Rome Tor Vergata, Italy

The "River Publishers Series in Communications and Networking" is a series of comprehensive academic and professional books which focus on communication and network systems. Topics range from the theory and use of systems involving all terminals, computers, and information processors to wired and wireless networks and network layouts, protocols, architectures, and implementations. Also covered are developments stemming from new market demands in systems, products, and technologies such as personal communications services, multimedia systems, enterprise networks, and optical communications.

The series includes research monographs, edited volumes, handbooks and textbooks, providing professionals, researchers, educators, and advanced students in the field with an invaluable insight into the latest research and developments.

Topics included in this series include:-

- Communication theory
- Multimedia systems
- Network architecture
- Optical communications
- Personal communication services
- Telecoms networks
- WiFi network protocols

For a list of other books in this series, visit www.riverpublishers.com

Blockchains in 6G
A Standardized Approach to Permissioned Distributed Ledgers

Editors

Mischa Dohler
Work done at King's College London, UK
(Now at Ericsson Inc., Silicon Valley, USA)

Diego R. Lopez
Telefónica, Spain

Chonggang Wang
InterDigital Inc., USA

River Publishers

Routledge
Taylor & Francis Group
NEW YORK AND LONDON

Published 2024 by River Publishers
River Publishers
Alsbjergvej 10, 9260 Gistrup, Denmark
www.riverpublishers.com

Distributed exclusively by Routledge
605 Third Avenue, New York, NY 10017, USA
4 Park Square, Milton Park, Abingdon, Oxon OX14 4RN

Blockchains in 6G / by Mischa Dohler, Diego R. Lopez, Chonggang Wang.

Routledge is an imprint of the Taylor & Francis Group, an informa business

ISBN 978-87-7004-094-5 (hardback)
ISBN 978-87-7004-178-2 (paperback)
ISBN 978-10-4009-031-2 (online)
ISBN 978-10-0349-813-1 (master ebook)

While every effort is made to provide dependable information, the publisher, authors, and editors cannot be held responsible for any errors or omissions.

To all blockchains, for proving that even a chain of blocks can be more exciting than a chain of hotels.

Mischa Dohler

To my three girls and their near to infinite patience,an essential ingredientin the brewing of this book.

Diego R. Lopez

To my family for their constant inspiration and support.

Chonggang Wang

Contents

Preface

Blockchain technologies are fascinating! They are technically simple yet ingenious; they power a wide gamut of applications yet struggle with adoption beyond cryptocurrencies.

To this end, we believe that standards can play a critical role in ensuring a wider uptake of this emerging tech, especially in mature industries like telecommunications. This is why some key industry and academic stake-holders have established the ETSI Industry Specification Group (ISG) on permissioned distributed ledgers (PDLs).

This book summarizes key findings of the years long ETSI PDL standards work. It positions the output with respect to other related standards initiatives as well as pertinent prior art. Importantly and central to our book, we suggest possible blockchain applications in emerging 6G networks.

After a more in-depth introduction to the field, we proceed in Part I with some basic principles of blockchains and distributed ledgers; we include an exposure about different blockchain types, their underlying consensus protocols, the foundations of smart contracts, as well as more advanced topics like scalable and interoperable blockchains.

The wider ecosystem is extremely critical for a successful development and deployment of new technologies, such as blockchains. Part II thus covers the blockchain ecosystem, which includes blockchain governance standards, blockchain technical standards, blockchain alliances, blockchain regulation and compliance, and some example research projects on blockchain and distributed ledger technologies.

The focus of Part III is on the ETSI PDL contributions. Specifically, we commence with an exposure on the reference architecture and then proceed to discuss advanced operational issues like data management, offline operations, and interoperability.

Part IV is dedicated to 6G. We commence with a short introduction to the industry timelines of 5G Advanced and 6G, and then proceed discussing possible applications of blockchains in the emerging 6G tech landscape. Of course, these applications are indicative only since – at the time of publication of this book – 6G is still years away.

No book on blockchains in 2023 (and with one of the authors sitting in Silicon Valley) can be without the mention of the metaverse. We thus include a section on this emerging technology and show how blockchains play a fundamental role in the uptake of the metaverse.

We hope that you as a reader get excited about blockchain technologies and see its (solid) potential beyond (volatile) cryptocurrencies.

We would like to thank all our colleagues who supported the writing of this book, most notably those being part of the ETSI PDL ISG.

Prof Mischa Dohler
Ericsson Inc.
Silicon Valley, USA

Diego R. Lopez
Telefonica
Seville, Spain

Dr Chonggang Wang
InterDigital Inc.
Princeton, USA

List of Figures

List of Tables

List of Abbreviations

3GPP	3rd Generation partnership project
5G	Fifth generation
6G	Sixth generation
ABBs	Architecture building blocks
ACL	Access control list
AD	Administrative-domain
ADRF	Analytics data repository function
AF	Application function
AI	Artificial intelligence
AIOTI	Alliance on IoT innovation
AMF	Access and mobility function
AML	Anti-money laundering
ANSI	American national standards institute
APIs	Application programming interfaces
AR	Augmented reality
AS	Autonomous system
ATIS	Alliance for telecommunications industry solution
ATW	Asynchronous time wrap
BCA	Blockchain client application
BCN	Blockchain node
BDTI	Big data test infrastructure
BEAT	Blockchain-enabled accountable and transparent
BGP	Border gateway protocol
BLK	IEEE blockchain initiative
BMC	Blockchain messaging client
BMS	Blockchain messaging server
BNA	Blockchain network application
CAs	Certificate authorities
CCF	Connecting capability fund

CDMA	Code division multiple access
CEF	Connecting europe facility
CEN	European committee for standardization
CENELEC	European committee for electrotechnical standardization
CFT	Counter-financing of terrorism
CFTC	Commodity futures trading commission
CI/CD	Continuous integration and continuous delivery
CN	Core network
CP	Control plane
CRUE	The Council of university rectors
CSA	Coordination and support action
CT	Core network and terminals
CU	Central unit
DAOs	Decentralized autonomous organizations
dApps	Decentralized applications
dBFT	Delegated Byzantine fault tolerance
DCCF	Data collection coordination function
DCE	Data collection enabler
DCs	Data consumers
DDoS	Distributed denial of service
DeFi	Decentralized finance
DG CNECT	Directorate-general for communications networks, content and technology
DIN	Decentralized Internet infrastructure
DINRG	Decentralized internet infrastructure research group
DL	Download/downlink
DL/UL	Uplink/downlink
DLT	Distributed ledger technology
DNS	Domain name system
DoC	Denial-of-capability
DOs	Data owners
DPoS	Delegated proof of stake
DPs	Data providers
DSL	Domain-specific language
DSP	Digital signal processing
EBP	European blockchain partnership

EBSI	European blockchain services infrastructure
EC	European commission
EEA	Enterprise ethereum alliance
EECTI	The spanish national strategy for science, technology and innovation
EIC	European innovation council
EIF	European interoperability framework
EIRA	European interoperability reference architecture
EIS	European interoperability strategy
EIT	European institute of innovation and technology
ELIS	EIRA library of interoperability specifications
EP	ETSI project
EPP	ETSI partnership project
EPSRC	The engineering and physical sciences research council
ERA	European Research Area
ESO	European Standards Organization
FAIR	Forwarding accountability for internet reputability
FCA	Financial conduct authority
FCC	Federal communications commission
FDDSS	Federated data discovery and sharing service
FDM	Federated data management
FDS	Federated discovery service
FG	Focus group
FinCEN	Financial crimes enforcement network
FL	Federated learning
FPP	FDM-PDL proxy
GDPR	General data protection regulation
GSMA	GSM association
HD	High-definition
HEIF	Higher education innovation fund
HEP	Higher education providers
HMDS	Head-mounted displays
HNT	Helium network tokens
HPN	Home PDL-network
HTLC	Hash time-locked contract
IA	Innovation action

IAB	Internet architecture board
IBC	Inter-blockchain communication
I-Corps	Innovation corps
ICOs	Initial coin offerings
ICT	Information and communication technology
IEEE	Institute of electrical and electronics engineers
IETF	Internet engineering task force
IIC	Industrial internet consortium
IIoT	Industrial internet of things
IMSI	International mobile subscriber identity
INATBA	International association for trusted blockchain applications
INEA	Innovation and networks executive agency
INNOSUPSME	Innovation support for SME
IoT	Internet of things
IP	Intellectual property
IPSec	Internet protocol security
IRPs	Interface reference points
IRS	Internal revenue service
IRTF	Internet research task force
ISG	Industry specification group
ISO	International standards organization
ISPs	Internet service providers
IT	Information technology
ITU	International telecommunication union
KPIs	Key performance indicators
KYC	Know your customer
LOD	Level of detail
LSS	Ledger storage service
LTE	Long-term evolution
LTE-A	LTE-advanced
MAC	Medium access control
MANO	Management and orchestration layer
MEC	Multi-access edge computing
MEs	Micro-enterprises
MIMO	Multiple input, multiple output
ML	Machine learning
mmWave	Millimeter wave

MPC	Multi-party computation
MVP	Minimum viable product
NAS	Network attached storage
NDAs	Non-disclosure agreements
NEF	Network exposure function
NeTS	Networking technology and systems
NF	Network function
NFTs	Non-fungible tokens
NGA	Next G Alliance
NGMN	Next generation mobile networks alliance
NIFO	National interoperability framework observatory
NSB	Network slice broker
NSF	National science foundation
NWDAF	Network data analytics function
OMA	Open mobile alliance
OOB	Out-of-band
OOP	Once-only principle
OS	operating system
OTT	Over-the-top
P2E	Play-to-earn
P2P	Peer-to-peer
pBFT	Practical Byzantine fault tolerance
PCF	Policy control function
PCP	Pre-commercial procurement
PDL	Permissioned distributed ledger
PDLF	PDL function
PFDs	Packet flow descriptions
PKI	Public key infrastructure
PoA	Proof of authority
PoC	Proof of coverage
PoC	Proof of concept
PoET	Proof of elapsed time
PoI	Proof of importance
PoS	Proof of stake
PoW	Proof of work
PQC	Post-quantum cryptography
QKD	Quantum key distribution
RA	Reference architecture

RAN	Radio access network
RIA	Research and innovation action
RIC	RAN intelligent controller
RSU	Roadside unit
RTT	Round-trip time
SA	Systems aspects
SAT	Solution architecture template
SaTC	Secure and trustworthy cyberspace
SATP	Secure asset transfer protocol
SBI	Service-based interface
SBIR	Small business innovation research
SC	Special committee
SCITT	Supply chain integrity, transparency, and trust
SDKs	Software development kits
SDM-O	Software-defined mobile network orchestrator
SDO	Standards development organization
SEC	Securities and exchange commission
SLA	Service level agreement
SME	Small and medium enterprise
SMS	Short message service
SSH	Secure shell protocol
STTR	Small business technology transfer
TADIM	Trust anchors for DLT-based identity management
TC	Technical committee
TLS	Transport layer security
TOOP	Trustful online interoperability platform
TPS	Transactions per second
TSAG	Telecommunication standardization advisory group
UDM	Unified data management
UDR	Unified data repository
UDSF	Unstructured data storage function
UE	User equipment
UL	Uplink
UN	United nation
UPF	User plane function
VMs	Virtual machines

VPN	Virtual private network
VR	Virtual reality
W3C	World wide web consortium
WCDMA	Wideband CDMA
WEF	World economic forum
WGs	Working groups
WRC	World radiocommunication conferences
XR	Extended reality
ZKP	Zero knowledge proof

1

Introduction

In this introduction, we give a short overview of important aspects of blockchains and their applications. We start with a very intuitive introduction to the technology and an abridged history of all things about blockchains. We then give some early indications on why blockchains matter in telecoms and how they are being used in first industry-driven applications. We also give a rundown on the importance of standards, which sets the tone for the remainder of the book on standards-related blockchain developments.

1.1 Intuitive Introduction to Blockchains

To understand the fundamental problem blockchains solve, let us go back in time to the medieval period around 1300. Double-entry bookkeeping of financial information had just been invented by the Italian Giovanno Farolfi. He ran a company of Florentine merchants headquartered in Nîmes and acted as a moneylender to the Archbishop of Arles [1]. Financial transactions were kept in a physical book of financial accounts.

This book containing financial transactions was and still is referred to as a "ledger."

Other ledgers appeared slowly, such as the ledgers in churches that kept records of who was born, when, and to whom. The subsequent evolution of ledgers included ledgers on cash, accounts receivable, inventory, fixed assets, debt, equity, revenue, salaries, etc. and culminated in the introduction of the spreadsheet, which is now able to keep track on any digitizable item imaginable.

The main problem of a ledger is that one can never be sure if the information is truthful.

Indeed, one has to trust the person making the original ledger entry; and one has to trust the person keeping an eye on the ledger so that nobody could change the content of the original ledger entry. For instance, if the original ledger entry confirmed that Bob owed Alice $100, Bob could get hold of the ledger and either modify the entry to $10 or rip out the entire page.

This is where digital blockchains come in: each physical ledger page is translated to a digital page we call a block; rather than paginated, each block is cryptographically chained to the previous block; and the entire chain of blocks is copied onto many spatially distributed devices.

If Bob wanted to "rip out" a digital page to erase any proof that he owes money to Alice, he would first need to modify all the cryptographic chains connecting all previous blocks; and then he would need to do this on every single device on which the chain is stored. It is not impossible, but practically infeasible.

And that is really the essence (and magic) of blockchains aka distributed ledgers: the ability to store information that is immutable, i.e., once on the chain it cannot be modified.

The immutability of data creates peace of mind and trust, even if the parties writing onto and reading from the ledger do not know or trust each other. It underpins a seismic shift in anything operational! For instance: one does not need to pay lawyers to negotiate lengthy non-disclosure agreements (NDAs) to establish trust; or pay bankers to keep an eye on our money; or pay large governmental administrations to validate the proof of our identity.

Above is, of course, a simplification that is further illustrated in Figure 1.1. It serves well to illustrate the philosophy and workings of a blockchain. Throughout the book, we will substantiate our understanding of distributed ledgers and also learn about major shortcomings which need to be considered when evaluating business and performance tradeoffs.

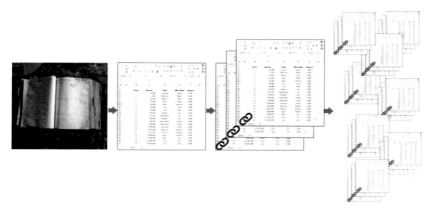

Figure 1.1 Illustration of the blockchain roadmap from traditional book ledgers to digital files, to cryptographically linked digital files, to linked and spatially distributed files.

1.2 Short History of Blockchains

Most of us would have heard about Bitcoin - the most prominent digital currency based entirely on blockchains - for the first time a few years ago. However, the underpinning technologies and large parts of the ecosystem have been in making for several decades.

The progress on distributed ledgers can be grouped into five distinct phases [2, 3] that are also illustrated in Figure 1.2: Phase 1 - emergence of early mathematical, cryptographic, and technology enablers; Phase 2 - focus on financial transactions; Phase 3 - focus on smart contracts; Phase 4 - focus on applications; and Phase 5 - emergence of the metaverse. These are now discussed in more detail below. Note that the given timelines only indicate the period of appearance and growth; all of the phases are still pertinent today.

1.2.1 Phase 1 - enablers [1979-2008]

One of the important ingredients of most blockchains is Merkle trees. They were invented by computer scientist Ralph Merkle in his 1979 Stanford University Ph.D. thesis on public key distribution and digital signatures. The Merkle tree provides a data structure for verifying individual records.

Three years later, in 1982, David Chaum obtained his Ph.D. degree from Berkeley. University of California, advocating for a "vault system for establishing, maintaining and trusting computer systems by mutually suspicious groups." It laid the foundation for digital money; and, indeed, in 1989, he founded the DigiCash Corporation.

Another milestone contribution was made by Stuart Haber and Scott Stometta in 1991 by introducing the concept of timestamping digital documents, and thereby preventing anybody from backdating or forward-dating

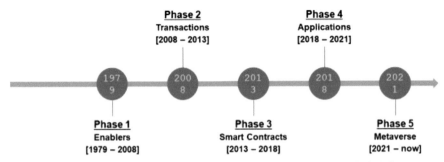

Figure 1.2   Illustration of the five phases in the short history of blockchains.

electronic documents. The goal was to maintain complete privacy of the document itself, without requiring record-keeping by a timestamping service. A year later, they updated the design to natively include Merkle trees. This facilitated several document certificates to live on the same block.

In 1996, the cryptographer Nick Szabo introduced the concept of a smart contract. He referred to "a set of promises, specified in digital form, including protocols within which the parties perform on these promises. "It laid the foundation for smart contracts used today.

Last but not least, an approach to require computational efforts, and thereby deter cyberattacks was introduced around 1997. Upon that idea, Adam Back introduced Hashcash in 1997 to limit email spamming by requiring computational tasks to be executed by the sender. This laid the foundation for the concept of proof-of-work (PoW). an approsch used in Bitcoin mining today.

Above all are fundamental mathematical, cryptographic, and computer science concepts. However, the role of the computing and networking industry should not be forgotten: notably, computers became smaller, storage more performant, and networks more reliable. Napster, now defunct, pioneered the concept of peer-to-peer (P2P) networks (even though it used a hybrid approach after all).

1.2.2 Phase 2 - transactions [2008-2013]

With the foundations in place, Bitcoin emerged as a first transactional application. It was documented by Satoshi Nakamoto in his whitepaper as an electronic P2P system based on the foundations discussed above [4]. The identity of Nakamoto is still disputed; it could be an individual or a group of people - indeed an interesting twist given the focus on privacy by blockchain technologies.

He/they formed the Bitooin genesis block, i.e., the very first block in the blockchain, to which other blocks were attached to over time to become one of the largest and widely distributed blockchain. Each block acts like a spreadsheet listing a set of financial Bitcoin transactions.

Ever since, a myriad of cryptocurrencies appeared - each with its own characteristics. However, in essence, they all replicate the same operating principles in that a block contains a list of financial transactions which is then cryptographically linked to the previous block and distributed across many devices/participants.

1.2.3 Phase 3- smart contracts [2013-2018]

A visionary of his time, Vitalik Buterin, learned from the earlier work of Nick Szabo and observed that the trusted construct of a blockchain could be expanded from financial transactions to actual financial contracts and later to general contracts. A contract is a piece of logic, i.e., actual programming code, sitting on the blockchain and being executed automatically following some triggers.

He also realized that the way the Bitcoin blockchain had been constructed would not suffice for his purposes and - after his requests for amending the Bitcoin blockchain had been rebuffed - he created his own blockchain from scratch: Ethereum.

This extended the capabilities of Ethereum from being a mere cryptocurrency to being a full-fledged platform for developing automated smart contracts, including contracts for bespoke tokens. This enabled a secondary economy to be developed on top of the blockchain, and surely contributed to the popularity of Ethereum.

1.2.4 Phase 4 - applications [2018-2021]

The initial applications of blockchains gravitated around initial coin offerings (ICOs). Using the ability to create tokens bespoke to given purposes, start-up entrepreneurs used the ICO as a means to raise capital for their blockchain ventures, similarly like an IPO would do so for traditional businesses. Here, investors - private and institutional would pay for tokens with real-world fiat currencies in exchange for the token to gain value over time due to the "exciting application" being funded. The total money raised from ICOs until today is billions of dollars globally. Since the space was entirely unregulated, not surprisingly, ICOs become a fertile ground for scams.

More mature applications appeared over time, notably those focusing on the need to have a marketplace where untrusted parties could conduct business in one form or another. Binding the value of the used tokens to a real-world utility proved the best way to ensure growing value for the underlying token. Working out the value details were often not trivial, which is why the economic branch of tokenomics appeared.

With a growing amount of tokens and cryptocurrencies, another useful set of applications that emerged were exchanges. These are digital exchanges, /similar to the forex market, where cryptocurrencies and tokens can be interchanged; later, the option to exchange with fiat currencies also appeared. Given the volatility of the cryptomarket, exchanges like Binance or Coinbase suffer when there is a downturn. However, the usefulness of blockchain-based finances seems to have been proven so exchanges will very likely remain intact as an important application.

Yet another class of applications is $dApps$, i.e., decentralized applications. These are applications that reside entirely on the blockchain through a smart contract logic.

Popular blockchains supporting such applications are EOS and Ethereum.

1.2.5 Phase 5-metaverse [2021-now]

The term metaverse was coined by Neal Stephenson in his 1992 novel "Snow Crash." It remained buried deep under the snow for several decades, until Facebook announced a virtual reality (VR) powered metaverse to be the next big thing [5]. So big, that this once trillion-dollar company rebranded to Meta. The Internet, device, and connectivity ecosystems have been in frenzy ever since.

The concept of metaverse does not belong to Meta, of course. It means different things depending on who you ask [6]. Important to note, however, is that it is accelerated through novel technologies, like Web3.0, blockchains, non-fungible tokens (NFTs), fifth generation (5G), digital twins, artificial intelligence (AI), and extended reality (XR) devices, just to name a few.

It is important to understand that the metaverse could probably exist without most of these tech ingredients, but uptake and scale would be seriously hampered. Given the importance of blockchain and Web3.0 for the metaverse, we have dedicated an entire chapter to it.

1.3 Why Blockchains Matter in Telecoms

We will not cover the full application space of blockchains in telecoms, mainly because it is an evolving field. However, a few prime application classes stand out and we would like to discuss them at the beginning of the book already. We will substantiate some of the findings in later chapters.

1.3.1 Simply more telco traffic

While a challenge to enable, telco systems have thrived under exponentially increasing traffic loads. Curiously, we always start designing a generation 10 years ahead of the use case. For instance, we started designing 3G when the internet was not really around; we started designing 4G when the iPhone was not invented yet. 5G and shortly sixth generation (6G) are thus awaiting their main application, and it may indeed be the metaverse.

Market projections on the uptake of VR but mainly augmented reality (AR) devices will enact a steep increase in traffic going over the mobile networks over the next years to come. AR/VR devices will bring to life various blockchain-powered metaverse applications of the future. This has an important implication onto radio and radio access network (RAN) configurations, such as radio bearers, sessions, and slice configurations[1]. Thus, a unique opportunity for vendors and telcos alike to benefit from the proliferation of the metaverse and the underlying blockchains.

1.3.2 Supply chain trust

As stated above and substantiated in subsequent chapters, an important characteristic of the blockchain is to establish trust between parties which either do not know or do not trust each other. The supply chain in telecoms is hugely complex and very vast.

Therefore, a useful blockchain application is to ensure a more scalable trust between different telco hardware and software vendors. For example, a piece of software - for instance an application (i.e., rApp) running on the non-realtime RAN intelligent controller (RIC) in O-RAN to manage/configure/automate the RAN [7] - can be properly authenticated if residing on or authenticated by a blockchain.

The same principle can be extended to spectrum, indeed a scarce resource that is difficult to monitor and manage in the GHz and THz bands. Blockchains could offer a viable and scalable alternative to centralized spectrum databases typically maintained by the national regulator.

1.3.3 Telco tokenomics

One can also imagine emerging telco business models that profit from the tokenization approach among untrusted parties. Ideal applications are consumer-driven and feature one form or another of a market place where an exchange of telco goods happens.

---

[1]A network slice is generally defined as a set of network services, running on a shared and virtualized infrastructure that can be managed and consumed as a separate network, providing specific and bespoke features.

Examples include: the exchange of data among consumer third parties; the establishment of spectrum and wireless access communities; the support of roaming in a foreign country; etc. A few of these examples have actually become commercial products and are briefly discussed below.

1.3.4 OTT applications

Over-the-top (OTT) applications, of course, remain an attractive income source for monetizing services that utilize specific features of the telecommunications infrastructure.

For instance, with respect to the rApp discussed above, it could also run on a blockchain in form of a dApp. Another example opportunity pertains to the metaverse, where a telco vendor or operator could offer its own metaverse, which in turn can be monetized.

1.4 Blockchain Telco Business Examples Today

The focus of this section is to introduce a few commercial blockchain projects in the telco industry. This is only a small sample set but serves the purpose to show the versatility of distributed ledgers.

1.4.1 Improving telco business processes

With further details given in [8], an interesting application of blockchains is to improve the business processes in telecoms. Indeed, business processes are at the center of any company and are instrumental to the success of any business execution.

A business process is defined as a series of interlinked steps which are assigned to every stakeholder for specific work to deliver a product or service to a third party (for example, a business partner, client, or supplier).

Each stakeholder or group of contributors is expected to perform specific task(s) to achieve a concrete goal. These steps are often repeated many times by multiple users in a standardized and optimized way, following the policy (a set of pre-defined rules) of the business process. Examples here include hiring processes, supply chain operations, product development, and product/service delivery.

Business processes today run in silos from one step to the next, from one organization to the next, from a company to its partners and clients. This is even more evident for processes running across companies, where the lack of trust between the parties prevents true and transparent integration in all steps of the process. This also includes organizations within the same company, where more often than not, they pursue different objectives and goals. For the big corporates, they can even have different or separate legal entities.

This can cause faulty or inconsistent outcomes and consequently the need to rework, fault-detect, and correct the business outcomes. The result is inefficiency! That inefficiency can be quantified in terms of direct and indirect costs and the time it takes to validate the rules of the underlying processes.

The following flaws in a business process can thus be recognized:

- **Lack of data integration and integrity:** The data layer supporting above processes are often "broken" due to lack of integration between the parties. Integrating a data layer in a process is not only a technical and costly challenge, but a very hard task to enforce across organizations with different objectives. The resulting lack of data layer integration prevents data consistency across the process, which can cause inconsistency, inefficient and ineffective replication of data when available, as well as critical flaws.
- **Poor standardization and compliance:** Local regulations, country laws, or cultural attitudes prevent a common standardized way of working between the parties running the process. Turning to a local adaptation on the execution of a process can deviate from a common governance and a straight path to reach a common goal. Moreover, in such recurrent scenarios, compliance is often highly affected, heading to costly consequences during audits.
- **No step-by-step rule validation:** A simple fault of a task occurring in a single step of the process without preventative controls may have devastating chain reaction effects on the result of the whole process execution. No matter how detailed the instructions of the steps in the process procedure are, a small error may have drastic consequences in the process execution, and would require rework to find the errors, correct them, and execute all again.

As detailed in [9], above flaws can be addressed through blockchains. The siloed approach of many current business processes can be "broken" through the blockchain forming a "common source of truth." Whilst being physically distributed, the ledger is logically centralized (i.e., "the common source of truth"), securing integrity of the underlying data, integration and confidentiality (also known as "transparency on a need to know basis") between involved and possibly untrusted parties.

Moreover, the policy and related procedure of the process can be coded into smart contracts, ensuring high compliance and the standardization of the process. It can also prevent any unauthorized member to access or execute a process that is not in accordance with the predefined procedures and their rules. Validation happens step-bystep, preventing any potential flaw in the process.

Above approach to using blockchains facilitates creating zero-fault business executions and digitalized end-to-end automation and integration with legacy systems

Ericsson has made this commercial with focus on inter-company invoicing and covering more than 180 countries in which Ericsson operates. In contrast to other implementations which "shadow" the traditional approach and are thus running in parallel, Ericsson's implementation is stand-alone and successfully serving the advanced business logics. Upcoming global implementations pertain to the end-to-end supply chain and actual network assets which will prove useful in private networks and neutral host deployments in the setting of smart cities, industry 4.0 and other enterprise applications.

By leveraging blockchains, Ericsson was able to prevent above-mentioned issues upfront, rather than fixing them afterwards. Today, it is fully automated and involves minimal human intervention. This means tedious manual jobs are avoided, and a common way of working between all the parties involved has been enforced. This ensures a high efficiency and positive return of investment.

1.4.2 Decentralized wireless networks

An interesting approach to giving a virtually centralized ownership structure to a decentralized telco infrastructure is the Helium Network [10, 11]. It was launched in 2019 by Amir Haleem, CEO and cofounder of Helium, and his team.

The focus has initially been on the Internet of Things (IOT), which needs very little bandwidth but high range and little power consumption. The Helium blockchain network enables a decentralized global network of IoT hotspots, which act as both the wireless access points and token miners.

The Helium hotspots can be deployed by anyone and enable individuals to earn Helium's native Helium network tokens (HNT) coins in exchange for providing connectivity to Helium-enabled IoT devices. It uses the LoRaWAN technology family that is the license-exempt equivalent to licensed cellular implementations such as NBIoT [12]. However, the decentralized blockchain-based approach allows the loT connectivity infrastructure to scale more rapidly compared to traditional approaches.

The Helium ecosystem is growing and is powering a variety of loT use cases around the world, such as remote wildfire sensors, environmental data collection, smart pet collars, scooters, and bikes that are being tracked across smart cities.

To reward users for participating in the Helium network, a proof of coverage (PoC) is used that verifies coverage at a given location. Hotspots are also given tests to cryptographically prove that they are indeed providing radio coverage in a particular place and a particular time. They can also earn HNTs by transferring data from attached loT devices to the Internet.

In terms of tokenomics, as of summer 2022, it has 120 million HNT tokens in circulation with a maximum supply of 223 million. New blocks are being produced every 60 seconds with rewards distributed approximately every 30 blocks. HNT's coin emissions rate began at five million HNT per month and halves every two years.

From an end-user point of view who wants to connect his/her loT devices, data credits are needed since each device using the Helium network is required to pay in data credits for internet access. Data credits are fixed in value and - somehow counterintuitively - tied to individual users and thus not transferable.

As of summer 2022, more than half a million Helium-powered LoRaWAN hotspots have been deployed [13]. That is, in about two years, a global network fabric has been created for loT applications. For Helium to survive and grow, all will depend on how much traffic will actually be sent over the network: the network cannot sustain itself on the economics of HNTs but really needs the data credits that are paid in fiat currency. Another issue is that many participants and/or traders will be using the HNT as an investment that makes it susceptible to the general crypto market volatilities.

What about other applications beyond the loT? At the time of writing this book (summary 2022), DISH - the US operator - has started to integrate Helium into parts o its 5G networks. It is being used with customers deploying their own 5G hotspots. The crypto volatility, however, will make DISH cautious in integrating Helium deeply into its operating model.

1.4.3 Metaverse Ifland

Korean operator SK Telecom has launched a metaverse platform called "Ifland," summer 2021. It is mainly targeting Millennials and Generation Z, and is aimed to be a "new tolerant space" for people to spend time in. The experience is purely virtual and embodied through avatars engaging in a truly high-quality graphics environment. An example is shown in Figure 1.3.

The different spaces created in Ifland include conference halls, outdoor stages, rooftops, nature places, etc. Once a room is selected, users are able to customize the environment including weather, time of day, flooring materials, room color/wallpaper, and scenery outside the room [14].

An interesting feature of Ifland is that it allows users to share PDF documents and MP4 files, which makes it popular with organizations to host conferences and trainings. The education and tourism industries are also utilizing the Ifland metaverse to host student orientations and exhibits.

By the end of 2021, Ifland had more than 1 million monthly users. The average time nearly doubled to one full hour by the end of 2021, compared to the summer 2021 launch date. The growth in monthly users and increase in usage time are impressive and indicate a shift from a 2D to a 3D internet to be imminent.

Note that South Korea has created a Metaverse Alliance in May 2021 [15] to foster the development of VR and AR platforms. The alliance includes telecom carriers like SKT, Korea's web giant Naver, researchers from various universities and private sectors, and multiple industrial giants including Hyundai.

The interesting aspect of Ifland, however, is that at inception it did not use any cryptocurrency or blockchain. It is not the only metaverse not to do so; other examples are Fortnite, Minecraft, and Roblox. However, Ifland

Figure 1.3   Example illustration generated by DALL.E symbolizing the Ifland metaverse.

has announced that a tokenomics based on a blockchain will be introduced shortly where assets can be traded, bought, and exchanged. Depending on the choice of the blockchain, assets could be interchanged with other metaverses, such as Decentraland, and assets listed on asset exchange platforms, such as OpenSea.

References

[1] https://en.wikipedia.org/wiki/History_of_accounting
[2] https://101blockchains.com/history-of-blockchain-timeline/
[3] https://www.techtarget.com/whatis/feature/A-timeline-and-history-of-blockchain-technology
[4] https://en.wikipedia.org/wiki/Satoshi_Nakamoto
[5] https://about.fb.com/news/2021/10/facebook-company-is-now-meta/
[6] https://www.ericsson.com/en/blog/2022/4/why-metaverse-needs-5g
[7] https://www.ericsson.com/en/ran/intelligent-ran-automation/intelligent-automation-platform/rapps
[8] https://www.ericsson.com/en/blog/2021/4/blockchain-technology
[9] https://www.ericsson.com/en/blog/2021/4/blockchain-technology
[10] https://www.nytimes.com/2022/02/06/technology/helium-cryptocurrency-uses.html
[11] https://www.gemini.com/cryptopedia/helium-network-token-map-helium-hotspot-hnt-coin#section-introduction-to-the-helium-network
[12] https://www.ericsson.com/en/blog/2019/10/what-is-nb-iot
[13] https://www.coindesk.com/markets/2022/02/17/helium-network-passing-half-million-hotspots-could-fire-up-hnt-price/
[14] https://medium.com/all-things-metaverse/sk-telecom-launches-new-metaverse-platform-ifland-5573ed4bfe7c
[15] https://thediplomat.com/2021/11/south-koreas-approach-to-the-metaverse/

Part I

Blockchain Enablers

2

Primer on Blockchains

Part I of the book is dedicated to an intuitive and historical introduction to blockchains. Not all aspects can be covered but the most important modern issues will be explained such that subsequent sections can be easily understood.

In this chapter specifically, we focus on a technical introduction to blockchains, how the cryptographic linkage works and how the various proofs and validations are used to create a trusted infrastructure. We will also dwell on some issues which have not been resolved over past years, as well as new emerging issues which require solutions over the years to come.

2.1 Technical Introduction

A blockchain is a digital ledger of transactions that is distributed across a network of computers. Each block in the chain contains a number of transactions, and each block is linked to the previous block through the use of cryptography. This creates a chain of blocks that cannot be altered, providing a secure and tamper-proof record of all transactions.

One of the key advantages of blockchain technology is its ability to provide a secure and tamper-proof record of transactions. This is achieved through the use of cryptography, which ensures that once a block is added to the chain, it cannot be altered or deleted. Additionally, the decentralized nature of blockchain networks makes them resistant to attacks and ensures that no single point of failure can bring the entire system down.

As a result, blockchain technology has the potential to revolutionize a wide range of industries by providing a secure and tamper-proof way to record and transfer digital assets. It also has the potential to reduce costs and increase efficiency by eliminating the need for intermediaries. Let us dive into some of the technical details of blockchains!

Blockchains are based on ledgers. A ledger is a database. A distributed ledger is thus a distributed database that is consensually shared and synchronized across multiple sites or nodes (e.g., people's computers). The database is typically used through three main interactions:

1. *submit* (content from a client/user onto the ledger);
2. *validate* (and write onto the ledger the submitted content through a consensus protocol); and
3. *read* (the stored content from the ledger).

The content itself has evolved over past years. Initially, only ledger entries could be stored, such as financial transactions, ownership association, etc. However, with the introduction of Ethereum in 2015, execution logic in form of programming code could be stored too. This has led to the emergence of *smart contracts* and, as of late, decentralized applications (dApps). The role of distributed ledgers is thus evolving from distributed databases that only store data, to distributed contracts which can take programmatic action on stored or submitted data, to distributed applications that can interface with the clients/users when submitting/reading data.

The *writing of content* onto the ledger typically happens in blocks which are cryptographically linked and, once validated, distributed to all nodes across the entire ledger. The cryptographic linkage and spatial distribution, along with a properly designed validation protocol, make the data written onto the ledger immutable. The distributed nature of the ledger ensures that no central authority can alter content, thus making this technology useful in the context of non-trusted parties interacting with each other.

At the core of each distributed ledger technology (DLT) is the *consensus* protocol, which is being carried out by the validators. It has many roles but mainly ensures that a specific ledger entry cannot appear more than once (thus, e.g., preventing the double-spend problem). Different consensus protocols have emerged over past years, such as proof of work (PoW), proof of stake (PoS), proof of elapsed time (PoET), or practical Byzantine fault tolerance (pBFT). They differ in energy efficiency, scale, and speed of transactions, among other factors.

Another important aspect is the notion of *public vs. private* ledger. It commonly refers to the degree of anonymity of the validators but also typically extrapolates to the access rights in general, i.e., who can write to and read from the ledger. In the case of a public ledger, validation and access can be done anonymously and by anybody wishing to participate in the ledger. In the case of a private ledger, validation and/or access is restricted to a closed user group such as a consortium (e.g., 10 companies).

Another point to consider is the difference between *permissionless vs. permissioned* ledgers. It defines the degree of trust in the validators which execute the consensus protocol. In a permissionless ledger, anyone can participate in the consensus mechanism; whereas, in a permissioned ledger, only those fulfilling certain requirements can take part in the consensus mechanism. Not all consensus protocols are suitable to all scenarios; for example, permissionless ledgers (such as Bitcoin) would use protocols such as PoW while permissioned ledgers (such as Hyperledger Fabric) may use protocols such as pBFT.

2.2 Cryptographic Hash

Hashing is *defined* as a single or set of cryptographic functions that convert a digital input of any length into a unique output of fixed length. For instance, for the same cryptographic hashing function, the short input letter "*a*" would produce a hash of the same length to the input being the entire *Encyclopedia Britannica*; however, whilst the length is the same, the hash itself is different. This means that no matter what combination of characters are used as input, the output will (almost) always be unique and of the same length.

The foundations of hashing were laid in Diffie and Hellman's 1976 seminal public key cryptography paper identifying the need for a one-way mathematical function. The first functional hash functions were developed over a timespan of several decades: Ronald Rivest invented the MD4 hash in 1990, and later the MD5 and MD6 functions; the National Security Agency (NSA) designed the SHA-1 (Secure Hash Algorithm 1) in 1995 and SHA-2 in 2001.

With this cryptographic based in place, more advanced hashing functions were developed, such as SHA-256, SHA-512 or Keccak256. They are being used in many applications ranging from digitally signing documents and emails to helping secure the operations of blockchains.

The main *properties* of cryptographic hashes can be summarized as follows:

1. Fixed length: It will always produce a fixed-length output from any input. For instance, a SHA-256 hash is 256 bits long that is represented as 64 symbols comprised of numbers 0–9 and letters A–F. Independent of the input, the output of SHA-256 will be 64 symbols.
2. Deterministic output: The same input has to always produce the same output. If one uses SHA-256 to generate several hashes from the same document, the output will always be the same. However, changing the smallest detail will produce a completely different hash.
3. One-way function: A stringent requirement is that – with current compute power – it ought to be infeasible to determine what the input

was from any given hash output. Reversing the hash function is today only possible via brute force approaches; in the future, we need to pay attention to quantum algorithms which might be able to efficiently reverse the hash output.

4. Resistant to collisions: A collision occurs when a hashing function yields the same output for two different inputs. Whilst this is not impossible, the probability of collisions is minuscule. It is possible because an arbitrary-length input is mapped onto a finite-length input. For instance, if more than 2^{256} inputs are fed into SHA-256, there will certainly be a collision. Luckily, 2^{256} is a gargantuan large number! A well-designed hashing should thus be resistant, but will never be immune, to collisions.

Why do hashes and their properties matter to blockchains? The *purpose is immutability*! Indeed, they provide the cryptographic "chains" in blockchain. Illustrated in Figure 2.1, a hash is created from the *i*th block of information which is added in the header of the subsequent block $(i + 1)$; then, a hash is created from the $(i + 1)$st block and added to block $(i + 2)$; etc. If a malicious actor was to compromise a set of information in a given block, the hash of the subsequent block would not match and would thus require changing too; this, in turn, would make the hash of the subsequent block mismatch, etc. Therefore, to change information in a cryptographically linked blockchain is extremely difficult. This is complicated further by distributing the entire blockchain across many (often millions of) nodes – a topic discussed in the subsequent section.

The *exact process* of hashing is fairly elaborate. Explained in great detail in, e.g., [1], we only outline the high-level details:

1. String-to-binary: The first step is to convert the input – whether a single letter or an entire encyclopedia – from string to binary [2].
2. Padding to block length: Modern hashes operate in blocks of input (not to be confused with the output length!); note that the notion of "blocks of input" here is obviously different from "blocks" in blockchains. For instance, both SHA-224 and SHA-256 work in blocks of 512 bits, whereas SHA-512 works in blocks of 1024 bits. If above string-to-binary conversation yields a length which is not modulus block length, then hash-specific padding has to be performed until the length is modulus of the hash's block processing length.
3. Convert to hexadecimal: A block of information is then split up into groups and converted to hexadecimal. For instance, in the case of SHA-256, the 512 bits are grouped into sixteen 32-bit words; let us label them W_0 to W_{15}. They are subsequently converted into hexadecimal.

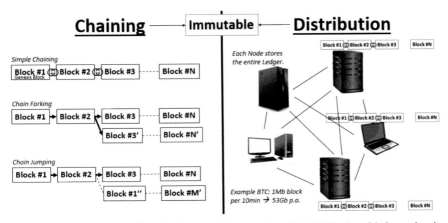

Figure 2.1 Illustration of how hashes are being used to "chain" blocks of information in blockchains; and how distribution of the blockchain to several spatially distributed nodes creates the distributed ledger.

4. Feed through scrambling rounds: These hexadecimal words are then fed through several rounds using algebraic operations, with more details provided in [3]. Important to note is that the forward operations of converting arbitrary input into an output hash might be laborious but are by nature trivial to execute; whilst the inverse operation of obtaining the input from the hash is virtually impossible.

Modern blockchains use above mechanisms, along with more optimized implementations. For instance, content on the Bitcoin blockchain is hashed using Merkle Trees [4] which allows for a more efficient implementation and thus an efficient validation if a transaction has been successfully included in an existing block.

2.3 Distribution of the Blockchain

An important aspect of blockchains is the distribution of the chain to many independent nodes, which is why we refer to *distributed* ledgers. A public blockchain may have millions of nodes, whilst a permissioned ledger may have tens to hundreds of nodes. Said nodes could be computers or virtual machines, or any other compute and storage instances.

The *operational mechanisms* are trivial: once a block has been established, it is simply copied across the nodes of the blockchain; see illustration in Figure 2.1. It further strengthens the case of immutability: if a malicious actor wants to compromise the content, then not only the hashes of all subsequent blocks would need to be modified but also the content across millions of nodes.

Clearly, there is a *trade-off* between immutability and operational efficiency! Replicating millions of blockchain blocks across the network is costly in terms of networking infrastructure, compute and storage; yet, it provides resilience!

2.4 Validation Process

So far, we have covered the mechanics of the blockchain in terms of cryptographic hashing and spatial distribution. An important aspect however is how the content of a specific block is validated.

Because the blockchain is immutable, it is important to ensure that content is unique and correct. Without it, one could double-spend a given amount of cryptocurrency, e.g., Bitcoin; or several people could claim ownership to the same NFT.

Several validation mechanisms have thus been introduced over past decades, with the most important summarized below:

- Proof of work (PoW): In a PoW system, participants – sometimes referred to as "miners" – compete to solve a complex mathematical problem. For instance, in the case of Bitcoin, the miner has to find a nonce such that the corresponding hash inserted into the block has a certain amount of zeros in it. The first miner to "solve" the problem (through brute force attempts) gets to create a new block and add it to the blockchain. This block contains a record of recent transactions, and the miner is rewarded with a certain number of coins or tokens for their work.

  The complex mathematical problem that miners need to solve is designed to be difficult to solve, but easy to verify. This ensures that only those miners who have put in a significant amount of computational effort are able to create new blocks.

  PoW is considered to be a secure way of validating transactions and adding blocks to the blockchain because it ensures that no single miner or group of miners can take control of the network. Additionally, it ensures that the blockchain is resistant to certain types of attacks, such as a 51% attack, where a group of miners could potentially control the majority of the network's computational power and manipulate the blockchain.

- Proof of stake (PoS): In PoS, instead of using computational power to validate transactions and create new blocks, the validation process is based on a participant's stake, or the amount of coins or tokens that they hold. In a PoS system, validators (sometimes referred to as stakers) are randomly or deterministically chosen to create a new block and validate transactions based on the amount of coins they hold and agree to "lock up" as collateral. The more coins a validator holds and stakes, the higher their chances of being selected to validate a block.
  Once a block is validated, the staker is rewarded with a certain number of coins or tokens. Unlike PoW, in PoS there is no competition among validators to be the first one to validate a block and validators are chosen by the protocol.
  PoS is considered to be more energy-efficient than PoW as it does not require as much computational power to validate transactions and create new blocks. Additionally, it tends to be more decentralized as it does not require specialized hardware and is more accessible to a wider range of participants.
- Delegated proof of stake (DPoS): This is a variation of PoS where token holders vote for a set of validators, who then validate transactions and create new blocks. It aims to provide a balance between decentralization and scalability, as only a group of validators are chosen to validate transactions.
- Delegated Byzantine fault tolerance (dBFT): This is a consensus mechanism used by the NEO blockchain. It uses a combination of PoS and BFT (Byzantine fault tolerance) to achieve consensus. Validators are elected by the community, and the consensus process is deterministic, making it more efficient and faster than PoW.
- Practical Byzantine fault tolerance (pBFT): This is a variation of BFT, where a group of validators reach consensus through a series of messages exchanged between them. This method is highly fault-tolerant and can be used in private or consortium blockchains.
- Proof of authority (PoA): This consensus mechanism is used in private or consortium blockchains, where a set of pre-approved and known identities are chosen as validators. This method is ideal for use cases where the participants are known and trust is already established.
- Proof of elapsed time (PoET): This is a consensus mechanism used in Hyperledger Sawtooth, which uses a random leader election process that is based on the amount of time a node has been waiting. It relies on the assumption that waiting for a longer period of time is indicative of a more trustworthy node.

- Proof of importance (PoI): This is a consensus mechanism used in the NEM blockchain, where nodes are assigned an importance score based on their overall support of the network, including the amount of their stake, the number of transactions they make, and the number of other users they support.

All these alternatives have their own advantages and disadvantages, and the choice of the most suitable consensus mechanism depends on the specific requirements of the blockchain network and its use case.

2.5 Blockchain Challenges

Blockchain is a relatively new and untested technology. Many challenges thus remain to be solved over the coming years, such as:

- Energy cost: Blockchains using PoW – such as Bitcoin – remain very popular. The energy cost associated with such blockchains is extremely large. Some chains, such as Ethereum, migrated to a more energy efficient PoS protocol; however, more needs to be done to lower the extremely large energy consumption.

- Technology cost: The spatial distribution of the blockchain in regular intervals is extremely costly from a networking, computing, and storage point of view. Networks need to be powered too, thus adding to the energy cost.

- Speed and scalability: Compared to most centralized implementations enabling (financial) transactions, blockchains are relatively slow. For instance, compare the Visa's 24,000 transactions per second with Bitcoin's handful transactions per second. New chains have emerged which address the issue of speed and scalability, but they are nowhere as popular as Bitcoin or Ethereum.

- Regulation: Arguably the largest issue is regulation, or lack thereof. Whilst regulators are catching up, many aspects of blockchains remain unregulated. Due to the distributed nature of blockchains, establishing a responsible owner is impossible. Another – and often overlooked – issue is around data privacy regulations, such as Europe's GDPR, where the "right to be forgotten" cannot be reconciled with the immutable nature of blockchains.

- Volatility: The weak regulation has many consequences, including illegal activities, financial scams, and volatilities. At the time of writing of this book, several blockchain projects went into liquidation, such as FTX. This is not helping the confidence in this powerful technology!

In addition to above challenges, some other interesting issues have been unearthed recently. The most notable is:

- Unintended technical centralization: Making a fascinating read, report [5] focuses on possible sources of centralization and their unintended consequences.

  ○ Sources of centralization:

    - Authoritative centrality: What is the minimum number of entities necessary to disrupt the system?
    - Consensus centrality: To what extent is the source of consensus centralized? For instance, does a single entity (like a mining pool) control an undue amount of the network's hashing power?
    - Topological and network centrality: How resistant is the consensus network to disruption? Are the nodes sufficiently geographically dispersed such that they are uniformly distributed across the internet?
    - Software centrality: To what extent is the safety of the blockchain dependent on the security of the software on which it runs?

  ○ Important findings [6]:

    - Every widely used blockchain has a privileged set of entities that can modify the semantics of the blockchain to potentially change past transactions: Four for Bitcoin and two for Ethereum – worryingly low!
    - The vast majority of Bitcoin nodes appear to *not* participate in mining and node operators face no explicit penalty for dishonesty.
    - Of all Bitcoin traffic, 60% traverses *just* three ISPs.
    - Tor is now the largest network provider in Bitcoin, routing traffic for about half of Bitcoin's nodes. A malicious Tor exit node can modify or drop traffic similarly to an ISP.
    - 21% of Bitcoin's nodes were running an old version of the Bitcoin Core client that is known to be vulnerable as of June 2021.

- Investor centralization: Another important issue is related to ownership behind specific crypto projects. Currently, a large swath of crypto companies is in the hands of a few selected investors. Whilst it does not impact operations of the underlying blockchains, the way tokens are being issued, controlled, and liquidated can be influenced by shareholders with decision rights.

Overall, however, the benefits of blockchain technology can outweigh the remaining issues as will become apparent in the latter part of this book.

References

[1] https://www.comparitech.com/blog/information-security/what-is-sha-2-algorithm/
[2] https://www.rapidtables.com/convert/number/ascii-to-binary.html
[3] https://www.comparitech.com/blog/information-security/what-is-sha-2-algorithm/
[4] https://www.investopedia.com/terms/m/merkle-root-cryptocurrency.asp
[5] https://assets-global.website-files.com/5fd11235b3950c2c1a3b6df4/62af6c641a672b3329b9a480_Unintended_Centralities_in_Distributed_Ledgers.pdf
[6] https://assets-global.website-files.com/5fd11235b3950c2c1a3b6df4/62af6c641a672b3329b9a480_Unintended_Centralities_in_Distributed_Ledgers.pdf

3

Smart Contracts

In this chapter, we focus on smart contracts [1, 2, 3, 4, 5]. They are an important aspect of distributed ledger technologies as they enable the automation of processes among non-trusting entities.

3.1 Introduction to Smart Contracts

A smart contract is a computer program or a transaction protocol that is intended to automatically execute, verify, or enforce the negotiation or performance of a contract. Smart contracts allow the automation of the execution of a contract, making the process faster, more efficient, and more secure.

Smart contracts are self-executing contracts with the terms of the agreement written directly into lines of code. They are stored on a blockchain network, which allows them to be executed automatically when certain conditions are met. Because smart contracts are stored on a blockchain, they are transparent, immutable, and secure.

Smart contracts can be used to automate a wide variety of processes, such as the transfer of assets, the execution of financial transactions, the management of supply chains, and the execution of legal agreements. They can also be used to create decentralized autonomous organizations (DAOs), which are organizations that are run mostly by code rather than by people.

For example, a smart contract could be set up to automatically transfer ownership of a digital asset from one person to another upon the payment of a certain amount of cryptocurrency. Once the payment is made, the smart contract would automatically execute the transfer of ownership without the need for a third-party acting as intermediary.

In summary, smart contracts are digital agreements that can be programmed to automatically execute once certain conditions are met, they are transparent and secure, and they can be used to automate a wide variety of processes, making the process faster, more efficient, and more secure.

3.2 Short History of Smart Contracts

The concept of smart contracts was first introduced in the 1990s by computer scientist Nick Szabo. Szabo recognized that many legal and financial agreements could be formalized as a set of rules and conditions in a computer program, and that these rules could be automatically enforced by the computer code. He called this concept *"smart contracts."*

Szabo's early work on smart contracts focused on digital contracts and digital legal systems, and he proposed the use of digital signatures and digital timestamps to ensure the security and integrity of these contracts.

The first practical implementation of smart contracts came in the form of "Formalized Contracts" and "Contract Languages" developed using a Ricardian contract by Ian Grigg in 1995 and 1996.

However, it was not until the emergence of blockchain technology and the creation of Bitcoin in 2008 that smart contracts began to gain widespread attention. The blockchain, with its ability to securely and transparently record and execute transactions, provided the perfect platform for the implementation of smart contracts.

In 2013, Ethereum was launched, a blockchain platform that was specifically designed for the creation and execution of smart contracts. Ethereum's smart contract capabilities have been used to create a wide variety of decentralized applications, including decentralized finance (DeFi) platforms, prediction markets, and gaming platforms.

Today, smart contracts are being implemented on various blockchain platforms, and they are being used in a wide variety of industries, including finance, supply chain management, and real estate. Additionally, several enterprise-grade blockchain platforms are being developed to support smart contract functionalities to cater to the need of different industries.

In summary, smart contracts were first proposed by Nick Szabo in the 1990s, they were first implemented using a Ricardian contract by Ian Grigg in the mid-1990s, the real potential of smart contracts was unlocked with the emergence of blockchain technology and the launch of Ethereum in 2013, and now they are being implemented on various blockchain platforms and used in various industries.

3.3 How Smart Contracts Work

Smart contracts work by encoding the terms of an agreement into lines of code. These contracts are stored on a blockchain network, such as Ethereum, which allows them to be executed automatically when certain conditions are met.

Here is an example of how a smart contract works on the Ethereum blockchain:

1. A developer creates a smart contract using the Solidity programming language, which is specifically designed for the Ethereum blockchain.
2. The developer then deploys the contract to the Ethereum blockchain. This involves sending a transaction that includes the contract code to the network, where it is verified and added to the blockchain.
3. Once the contract is deployed, it exists as a unique address on the Ethereum blockchain and can be interacted with by anyone with the contract address.
4. Users can then interact with the contract by sending transactions to its address. These transactions contain data that is used by the contract's code to execute its logic and make decisions.
5. For example, let us say the smart contract is a simple escrow contract that is used to facilitate the sale of a digital asset. The contract includes rules for the buyer to send the payment and for the seller to release the asset to the buyer once payment is confirmed.
6. Once the contract is deployed, the seller can share the contract address with the buyer. The buyer can then send the payment to the contract address, which triggers the contract's code to execute.
7. The contract's code checks that the payment has been received and verifies that it is the correct amount. If the payment is correct, the contract's code releases the digital asset to the buyer.
8. The smart contract also records the transaction on the blockchain, making the transaction transparent and tamper-proof.

In this example, the smart contract acts as an intermediary, automating the process of transferring ownership of the digital asset once payment is received, without the need for a third-party intermediary. This makes the process faster, more efficient, and more secure.

It is worth mentioning that smart contracts are not limited to just simple escrow contracts, they can also be used to create complex decentralized applications with multiple functionalities, such as decentralized exchanges, prediction markets, and lending platforms.

3.4 Smart Contract Use Cases

The applicability of smart contracts is very versatile. A few examples use cases are given below:

- Banking and finance: Smart contracts can be used to automate financial transactions, such as the issuance of loans and the settlement of trades.
- Healthcare: Smart contracts can be used to securely and transparently store and share medical records, as well as to automate the processing of insurance claims.
- Government: Smart contracts can be used to automate and streamline government processes, such as the issuance of licenses and the collection of taxes as well as procurement.
- Supply chain management: Smart contracts can be used to automate and streamline supply chain processes, such as tracking goods as they move through the supply chain and automatically releasing payments when certain conditions are met.
- Real estate: Smart contracts can be used to automate the process of buying and selling real estate, including the transfer of ownership and the payment of taxes and fees.
- Insurance Smart contracts can be used to automate the claims process and make it more efficient.
- Decentralized finance (DeFi): Smart contracts have been used to create decentralized finance platforms that provide financial services, such as lending and borrowing, without the need for traditional intermediaries.

In summary, smart contracts can be used to automate a wide range of processes and transactions, resulting in increased efficiency, security, and trust.

3.5 Open Challenges

Smart contracts have the potential to revolutionize the way that a wide range of industries and applications operate, but – similarly to the underlying blockchains discussed earlier – there are a number of open challenges that need to be addressed before they can be widely adopted. Some of these challenges include:

1. Complexity: Smart contracts are often complex and difficult to understand, which can make it difficult for non-technical users to interact with them.

2. Scalability: The current infrastructure for blockchain-based smart contracts is not able to handle a large number of transactions, which limits their scalability.

3. Security: Smart contracts are vulnerable to hacking and other types of attacks, and there have been several high-profile cases of smart contract vulnerabilities being exploited.

4. Interoperability: Different blockchain platforms use different languages and protocols, which can make it difficult for smart contracts on different platforms to interact with each other.

5. Usability: Smart contracts are still not user-friendly enough and require a technical background to interact with them, which limits their adoption.

6. Oracles: Smart contracts rely on external data to function and validate the rules, hence the need for oracles or external data providers, this can be a point of failure or a security vulnerability if the oracle is compromised.

7. Regulation: Smart contracts operate outside of traditional legal frameworks, which can make it difficult for regulators to oversee them and ensure compliance with laws and regulations.

8. Governance: Smart contracts, especially those running on public blockchains, need a governance model to handle disputes and upgrade the smart contract.

Addressing these challenges will require ongoing research and development in areas such as blockchain scalability, security, and governance, as well as collaboration between industry, government, and academia.

References

[1] https://smartcontract.com/
[2] https://ethereum.org/
[3] https://solidity.readthedocs.io/
[4] https://consensys.net/
[5] https://www.hyperledger.org/

4

Scalability and Interoperability

In this chapter, we focus on two important aspects of blockchains, i.e., how to make them more scalable and also how to ensure interoperability.

4.1 Improving Scalability

Whilst blockchains offer an enormous amount of advantages, one of the important drawbacks is the lack of throughput due to its inability to natively scale. A few proposals have been made in the past to overcome the scalability issues:

1. Sharding: This approach involves breaking the blockchain into smaller, more manageable pieces (shards) that can be processed in parallel. This can significantly increase the number of transactions that can be processed per second.
2. Off-chain transactions: This approach involves moving some of the transactions off the blockchain and into a separate, off-chain system. This can reduce the load on the blockchain and increase its scalability.
3. Layer-2 approaches: This approach involves building additional layers on top of the blockchain that can handle some of the transactions and data storage. These layers can be used for different types of transactions, such as micropayments or high-frequency trading.
4. Optimizing consensus: Some consensus mechanisms like proof of stake (PoS) are more scalable than others like proof of work (PoW).
5. Reducing block size: Increasing the block size can help to increase the number of transactions that can be included in a block, but it also increases the amount of data that needs to be stored and processed.
6. State channels: They are off-chain payment channels, where two parties can transact without broadcasting all the transactions to the blockchain. This reduces the load on the blockchain and increases scalability.
7. Compression: Using compression techniques to reduce the size of the data stored in the blockchain can help to increase the scalability of the network.

No single approach is likely to address all issues. The most effective scalability solutions will likely involve a combination of several of these techniques. Additionally, research and development in areas such as blockchain scalability is ongoing and new solutions are being proposed and developed constantly.

4.2 Scalability through Sharding

One of the most important solutions proposed to improve scalability is sharding [1, 2, 3, 4, 5]. It refers to a way of distributing the data stored on a blockchain network across multiple devices or nodes, instead of having all the data stored on a single node.

Sharding is used to increase the scalability of a blockchain network by allowing it to process more transactions at a faster rate. In a blockchain network that uses sharding, the network is divided into smaller groups, called shards. Each shard contains a subset of the network's nodes and is responsible for processing a specific subset of the network's transactions. This allows for parallel processing of transactions, which can significantly increase the overall throughput of the network.

Sharding can be applied to different layers of a blockchain infrastructure, for example, it can be applied to the data layer, where each shard would store a different subset of the network's data; or to the network layer, where each shard would be responsible for validating a specific subset of the network's transactions.

There are different sharding methods, such as transaction sharding, where each shard processes a specific set of transactions and state sharding, where each shard stores a specific set of state data.

Sharding is considered a promising solution to address scalability issues in blockchain networks, but it is still a research topic and is not widely used yet. It is important to note that sharding also introduces new challenges such as the need for cross-shard communication, the need for a new consensus mechanism and the risk of increased centralization.

4.3 Enabling Interoperability

Blockchain interoperability is hugely important. It ensures that there is no customer lock-in, and that assets of value can be transferred and used across different ecosystems. Blockchains have not been designed with interoperability in mind; however, a few important solutions have emerged in the past:

1. Atomic swaps: Atomic swaps are a technique that allows for the exchange of cryptocurrencies between different blockchain networks without the need for a centralized intermediary. This is achieved through the use of smart contracts and hash time-locked contracts (HTLCs) that ensure that the exchange of assets is atomic, i.e., either both parties receive the assets they agreed to or the transaction is rolled back.

2. Cross-chain communication protocols: Cross-chain communication protocols, such as Cosmos' inter-blockchain communication (IBC) protocol and Polkadot's Relay Chain (described in more detail below), allow for the transfer of assets and information between different blockchain networks. These protocols use a layer-2 scaling solution to enable communication between different networks, allowing for interoperability.

3. Tokenization: Tokenization is the process of creating digital tokens that represent assets on one blockchain, and can be used to represent the same assets on other blockchains. Tokenization allows for the transfer of assets across different blockchain networks, and enables interoperability.

4. Sidechains: Sidechains are separate blockchain networks that are connected to a main blockchain network (the parent chain). They can be used to transfer assets between different blockchain networks, and can also be used to scale the parent chain by moving some of the transactions to the sidechain.

5. Hybrid solutions: Hybrid solutions combine the features of different blockchain networks in order to achieve interoperability. For example, a hybrid blockchain network can be used to connect a public blockchain network with a private blockchain network, allowing for the transfer of assets and information between the two networks.

6. Interoperability standards: Interoperability standards, such as ISO TC 307, aim to develop common standards for different blockchain networks, allowing for better communication and integration between different networks.

With the increasing demand for interoperability, the interoperability ecosystem is growing:

1. The interoperability alliance [6]: It is a global alliance of organizations and individuals working to promote interoperability in blockchain and

other distributed ledger technologies. They have a lot of educational resources on their website.

2. Cosmos [7]: Cosmos is an ecosystem of interconnected blockchains. Their website provides a lot of technical information on how they are implementing interoperability in their ecosystem.

3. Polkadot [8]: Polkadot is a blockchain network that allows for interoperability between different blockchain networks. Their website provides a lot of technical information on how they are implementing interoperability in their network.

4. Aion [9]: It is a blockchain network that provides interoperability between different blockchain networks. Their website provides a lot of technical information on how they are implementing interoperability in their network.

5. Wanchain [10]: Wanchain is a blockchain network that provides interoperability between different blockchain networks. Their website provides a lot of technical information on how they are implementing interoperability in their network.

6. Interoperability.tech [11]: This platform provides information and resources on blockchain interoperability, including articles, research papers, and case studies.

These methods and approaches are still under active development and research, and it is important to note that interoperability remains a challenging task, as each blockchain network has its own unique characteristics and protocols.

References

[1] https://ethereum-magicians.org/t/ethereum-sharding-research-compendium/3412
[2] https://chainguardian.com/blockchain-sharding/
[3] https://consensys.net/blog/ethereum-scaling/sharding/
[4] https://dfinity.org/
[5] https://github.com/ethereum/sharding-research
[6] https://interoperabilityalliance.org/
[7] https://cosmos.network/
[8] https://polkadot.network/
[9] https://aion.network/
[10] https://wanchain.org/
[11] https://interoperability.tech/

5

Permissioned Distributed Ledgers (PDLs)

In this chapter, we offer a short introduction to the ledgers that are focus of this book, i.e., permissioned distributed ledgers (PDLs).

5.1 A Short History of PDLs

Permissioned ledgers, also known as private blockchains, have evolved from the early days of blockchain technology. The first permissioned ledger was created by a consortium of banks called R3CEV in 2015, in order to explore the potential of blockchain technology in the financial industry.

However, the concept of permissioned ledgers predates the creation of blockchain technology. In the early 2000s, companies such as IBM and Microsoft developed distributed ledger technology (DLT) solutions for specific industries, such as supply chain management and healthcare. These solutions were based on traditional centralized databases and were not truly decentralized like what we currently understand to be a blockchain.

The term "permissioned ledger" started to gain popularity after the launch of R3CEV's Corda platform, which is a permissioned blockchain platform designed specifically for financial services. Since then, many other companies and consortiums have developed their own permissioned ledger solutions, such as Hyperledger, which is an open-source project supported by the Linux Foundation that aims to advance cross-industry blockchain technologies.

The main motivation behind the development of permissioned ledgers is to take advantage of the benefits of blockchain technology, such as increased security and transparency, while addressing some of the limitations of public blockchains, such as scalability and regulatory compliance.

Permissioned ledgers have been widely adopted in industries such as finance, supply chain management, and healthcare, and it is expected that their adoption will continue to grow in the future as more industries realize the potential benefits of this technology.

5.2 Introduction to PDLs

Permissioned ledgers, also known as private blockchains, are a type of distributed ledger technology that is restricted to a specific group of participants. They are different from public blockchains, such as Bitcoin and Ethereum, which anyone can join and participate in.

A permissioned ledger is essentially a blockchain network that is controlled by a central authority, who is responsible for granting access to the network to specific participants. These participants are identified, authenticated, and authorized by the network administrator, ensuring that only trusted entities can join the network.

In a permissioned ledger, the network administrator is responsible for maintaining the network's integrity, by making sure that all participants follow the network's rules and protocols, and by removing any participants who do not comply.

Permissioned ledgers use consensus mechanisms, such as proof of stake (PoS) or practical Byzantine fault tolerance (pBFT), to validate the transactions and reach consensus, but the participants in these mechanisms are pre-selected by the administrator.

Permissioned ledgers can be used in a wide range of industries, such as finance, supply chain management, and healthcare. They are often used in situations where the need for increased security, compliance, and privacy is high, and where the participants are known and trusted entities.

Some examples of permissioned ledgers are:

- Corda, developed by R3CEV consortium, is designed for financial services.
- Hyperledger, an open-source project supported by the Linux Foundation, aims to advance cross-industry blockchain technologies.
- Quorum, an Ethereum-based permissioned ledger, is designed for enterprise use cases.

Permissioned ledgers have the potential to revolutionize the way that many industries operate, by providing increased security, transparency, and efficiency, but they also have limitations, such as a lack of decentralization, which can make them less trustless.

5.3 Pros and Cons of PDLs

Advantages of permissioned ledgers include the following:

1. Increased security: Since access to the network is restricted, permissioned ledgers can be designed to be more secure than public blockchain networks. This is particularly useful in cases where the network deals with sensitive information such as personal data or financial transactions.
2. Greater control: Permissioned ledgers allow for a higher degree of control over the network and its participants. This is important in certain use cases such as in financial services or healthcare where regulatory compliance and data privacy are crucial.
3. Faster processing: Permissioned ledgers typically use a more centralized or high-throughput consensus mechanism, which allows for faster processing of transactions as compared to public blockchain networks.
4. Better scalability: Permissioned ledgers can be designed to be more scalable than public blockchain networks, as the number of participants is limited and the network can be optimized for specific use cases.
5. Compliance with regulation: Permissioned ledgers can be designed to comply with regulations, which is important in certain industries such as finance and healthcare.

Some disadvantages of permissioned ledgers include:

1. Limited accessibility: Since access to the network is restricted, permissioned ledgers are not as accessible as public blockchain networks. This can be a disadvantage in cases where accessibility is important, such as in decentralized applications.
2. Centralization: Permissioned ledgers are typically more centralized than public blockchain networks

In summary, PDLs are a promising technology which trade well the advantages of blockchains with the challenges to obey regulation. They thus form the central part of this book.

Part II

Blockchain Ecosystem

6

Governance Blockchain Standards

Part II of the book is dedicated to the telco-related blockchain ecosystem. We will not revisit the entire blockchain and crypto ecosystem and rather focus on standards, alliances, regulatory issues as well as R&D projects.

In this chapter specifically, we focus on standards that study and describe high-level architecture designs and governance issues. Said governance standards play an instrumental role in harmonizing vocabulary and use cases. That allows then a technical community to execute deep technical standards.

6.1 Blockchains as General Purpose Technology

Before diving into specific governance standards initiatives, it is helpful to understand that blockchains are a general-purpose technology which can be applied in a myriad of societal applications.

As such, distributed ledgers can provide benefits to a large number of applications across many industries. Applications that use distributed ledger technologies benefit from distributed trusted databases with recorded verifiable transactions which can be automated to increase efficiency and reduce costs.

Typical applications, commoditized and emerging, may be divided into horizontal applications which provide common functions, and vertical applications that serve a more specific industry application typically leveraging one or more horizontal application. Some examples are given in Table 6.1.

The downside of blockchains being applicable to many use cases is that market fragmentation is emerging which many in the industry attribute to a lack of standards. The emergence of below governance and technical standards are thus paramount to the long-term success of distributed ledger technologies in industries at large, and telecoms specifically.

Table 6.1   Example areas of PDL application domains.

HORIZONTAL DOMAIN	VERTICAL DOMAIN
Identity management: Individuals, objects, legal entities and processes	eGovernment: Properties, benefits records
Data management: Data sharing	Healthcare: Health records, prescriptions
Logistics and supply chain	Industries: Manufacturing distribution
Security management	Automotive and IoT: Supply chain, data integrity, autonomous vehicles
Digital evidence	Commerce, digital evidence admissible in court
Invoicing management	Finance: Securities trading, trade finance, micro-credits and remittance, insurance
Crypto-structures and DAO	Utilities: Share records and trading, energy sector, smart-metering, smart-grids, telecommunications, water and waste management
Contract management: Smart contracts	Media and social media: Intellectual properties management, e-Sport, culture, art, advertisement
Commodity management	Yield management, agriculture
Decision management: AI-decision traceability	Education: e-Learning, diplomas validation
Privacy management	Healthcare, automotive and IoT, commerce, finance-securities trading, utilities
Infrastructure management	ICT: Internet resource management, trust infrastructure (e.g., PKI), network security

6.2 International Standards Organization (ISO)

The International Standards Organization (ISO) has formed a technical committee (TC) on blockchains, also known as ISO/TC 307 "Blockchain and Distributed Ledger Technologies [1]." It was established in 2016, and has more than 40 participating members and more than 10 observing members.

It has liaisons committees to/from ISO/TC 307. It is also highly relevant to the Joint Working Groups ISO/TC46/SC11/JWG1 with title "Joint ISO/TC46/SC 11-ISO/TC 307 WG: Blockchain." Furthermore, there are liaison organizations, such as the European Commission, the Enterprise Ethereum Alliance Inc, the IEEE, ITU, OECD, SWIFT, UNECE, and the International Federation of Surveyors.

There are several active projects which – at the time of writing in summer 2022 – are illustrated in Figure 6.1 and can be summarized as:

- Blockchain and distributed ledger technologies – Use cases (ISO/PRF TR 3242)

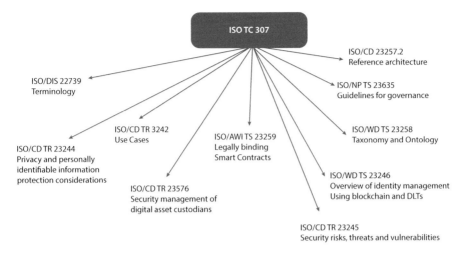

NOTE: ISO/TR 23455:2019 overview of and interactions between Smart Contracts and DLT systems is published already.

Figure 6.1 ISO TC307 standards under development (as of end 2022).

- Blockchain and distributed ledger technologies – Identifiers of subjects and objects for the design of blockchain systems (ISO/DTR 6039)
- Blockchain and distributed ledger technologies – Data flow model for blockchain and DLT use cases (ISO/WD TR 6277)
- Decentralized identity standard for the identification of subjects and objects (ISO/AWI 7603)
- Blockchain and distributed ledger technologies – Vocabulary (ISO/CD 22739)
- Blockchain and distributed ledger technology – interoperability framework (ISO/AWI TS 23516)
- Blockchain and distributed ledger technologies – Overview of smart contract security good practice and issues (ISO/WD TR 23642)
- Blockchain and distributed ledger technologies – Overview of trust anchors for DLT-based identity management (TADIM) (ISO/DTR 23644)

6.3 European Committee for Standardization (CEN/CENELEC)

An important European Standards Development Organization (SDO) is CEN-CENELEC. It is composed of European Committee for Standardization

(CEN) and European Committee for Electrotechnical Standardization (CEN-ELEC). They are recognized by the EU and EFTA as Europe's SDO responsible for developing standards at European level.

These standards set out specifications and procedures in relation to a wide range of materials, processes, products and services. The members of CEN-CENELEC are the National Standardization Bodies and National Electrotechnical Committees of 34 European countries. European Standards and other standardization deliverables adopted by CEN-CENELEC are accepted and recognized in all these countries.

Its Focus Group on Blockchain and Distributed Ledger Technologies has identified specific European needs in 2019 and released a new version of its technical white paper for the successful implementation of blockchain and DLT in Europe [2].

There are numerous standards under development within CEN-CENELEC and the strategic approach is to focus on i) digital transformation; ii) international cooperation with countries around the world, such as the Gulf, India, Japan, China, and Africa; and iii) seminars and workshops.

Some of the noteworthy standards under development are:

- For *digital society*, CEN/WS 084 Self-Sovereign Identifier for Personal Data Ownership and Usage Control, CEN/CLC/WS SEP2 Industry Best Practices and Industry Code of Conduct for Licensing of Standard Essential Patents in the field of 5G and Internet of Things, CLC/TC108X Safety of electronic equipment within the fields of Audio/Video, Information Technology and Communication Technology, CLC/TC 209 Cable networks for television signals, sound signals and interactive services.
- For *mechanical and machinery* mainly focus for safety and segments like entertainment technology and amusement park machinery and structures.
- For *services*, CEN/TC 445 Digital Information Interchange in the Insurance Industry, CEN/TC 278 Intelligent transport systems.

Recently CEN-CENELEC has approved liaison with ETSI Industry Specification Group (ISG) PDL [3] and a new TC will act as mirror with ISO/TC 307 [4]. Last but not least, it should be noted that the focus group has decided to continue as a technical committee CEN/CLC JTC19 [5].

6.4 International Telecommunications Union (ITU)

The ITU Focus Group (FG) for Distributed Ledger Technologies (DLTs) was established in May 2017 and concluded in August 2019. The parent group is Telecommunication Standardization Advisory Group (TSAG).

The deliverables of the FG-DLT can be found at [6]. The deliverables have been transferred to SG16 and SG17, which have established new work items for further study of DLT. Note that the ITU has embarked on several blockchain-related standards initiatives, which are illustrated in Figure 6.2.

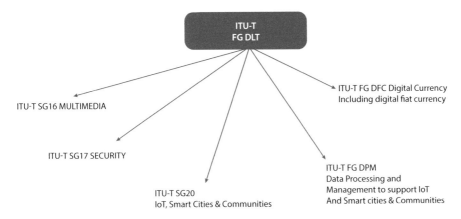

NOTE: There are other Study Groups which are related to DLTs like SG 13 of ITU-T about Future Internet, the Work Item is Decentralized Network Infrastructure. The interaction with the SG 16 about Multimedia has launched three new areas of exploration for the ITU-T FG DLT.

Figure 6.2   Blockchain-related ITU standards.

References

[1] https://www.iso.org/committee/6266604.html
[2] ftp://ftp.cencenelec.eu/EN/EuropeanStandardization/Sectors/ICT/Block chain%20+%20DLT/FG-BDLT-White%20paper-Version1.2.pdf
[3] https://www.etsi.org/committee/1467-pdl
[4] https://www.iso.org/committee/6266604.html
[5] https://www.cencenelec.eu/areas-of-work/cenelec-sectors/digital-societ y-cenelec/emerging-technologies/
[6] https://www.itu.int/en/ITU-T/focusgroups/dlt/Pages/default.aspx

7

Technical Blockchain Standards

In this chapter, we focus on technical standards. These standards typically feed off the governance standards discussed in the previous chapter. We will commence by highlighting why technical standards matter, and then give a high-level overview of the most important technical standards that currently work on embedding blockchains into their technologies (i.e., ETSI, 3GPP, the IEEE, and the IETF).

It is interesting to note already here that technical standards bodies – which are recognized by governments around the world as SDOs – do not exist for blockchains themselves. That is clearly a disadvantage and has repercussions in applications, like the metaverse, non-fungible tokens (NFTs), cryptocurrency, but also with respect to regulation, oversight, and business ethics.

7.1 The Importance of Technical Standards

Standards are important! Indeed, it is because of standards that one can buy a smart phone in the USA and a SIM card in the UK and be in South America whilst calling a friend in Australia who got the phone in Africa and the SIM card in Asia.

Standards ensure interoperability between vendors, and thus scale use that comes along with significant price decreases for consumers. The downside of standards is that the process takes long since all parties at the table need to agree to common frameworks.

Recognizing the importance of standards, the European Commission (EC) has heavily promoted research in distributed ledger technologies and the projects have individually seen the importance of contributing to the (international) standardization ecosystems, in order to:

- promote interoperability of solutions and "future-proof" solutions in the market place;

- improve the reliability of services;
- improve transparency of operations for service providers and ultimately for consumers;
- offer verifiable proof or benchmarking of features such as privacy or tamper-proofing;
- ensure fair procurement by means of transparent reference to best-of-breed technological solutions (according to World Trade Office recommendations);
- improve the results of "due diligence" investigations for government and private services;
- build efficient ecosystems (and avoid vendor "lock in").

7.2 European Telecommunications Standards Institute (ETSI)

The European Telecommunications Standards Institute, also known as ETSI, is an independent, not-for-profit, standardization organization in the field of information and communications [1]. ETSI supports the development and testing of global technical standards for ICT-enabled systems, applications and services.

Located in Sophia-Antipolis, in the south of France, it was set up in 1988 by the European Conference of Postal and Telecommunications Administrations (CEPT) following a proposal from the European Commission. ETSI is the officially recognized body with a responsibility for the standardization of information and communication technologies (ICTs). It is one of the three bodies, the others being CEN and CENELEC (see above), officially recognized by the European Union as a European Standards Organization (ESO).

The role of the European Standards Organizations is to support EU regulation and policies through the production of harmonized European Standards and other deliverables. The standards developed by ESOs are the only ones that can be recognized as European Standards (ENs).

ETSI's standardization activities are organized around sectors: Home & Office, Better Living with ICT, Content Delivery, Networks, Wireless Systems, Transportation, Connecting Things, Interoperability, Public Safety, and Security. Technical activities are carried out in the different ETSI technical groups such as the Technical Committee (TC), ETSI Project (EP), ETSI Partnership Project (EPP), Industry Specification Group (ISG), and Special Committee (SC).

Today, ETSI has more than 900 member organizations worldwide from 65 countries and five continents. Its community is diverse and includes all the key stakeholders of the ICT sector: private companies, research entities, academia, government, and public bodies as well as societal stakeholders. Small and medium enterprises (SMEs) and micro-enterprises (MEs) represent more than a quarter of ETSI's total membership.

The ETSI ISG on permissioned distributed ledger (PDL) [2] analyzes and provides the foundations for the operation of permissioned distributed ledgers, with the ultimate purpose of creating an open ecosystem of industrial solutions to be deployed by different sectors, fostering the application of these technologies, and therefore contributing to consolidate the trust and dependability on information technologies supported by global, open telecommunications networks.

The group puts its focus on addressing infrastructure and operational aspects that had not been covered by previous or parallel standardization activities, and forms the cornerstone of this book.

The ISG PDL started from already available experiences in the field of permissioned distributed ledgers, seeking for the definition of open and well-known operational mechanisms to validate participant nodes, support the automation of the lifecycles of the ledger and individual nodes, publish and execute operations regarding the recorded transactions through smart contracts, improve security of ledgers during both their design and operation, and establish trusted links among different ledgers using these mechanisms.

After an initial phase where the goals of PDL activities have been delimited and the general (and prolific) DLT landscape analyzed in PDL001 [3], different reports on salient issues have been produced, including:

- The implications of the conduits used to feed data to distributed ledgers, and how regulatory aspects for data infrastructures can be satisfied.
- The analysis of application scenarios, with special emphasis on as-a-service paradigms, and PDL infrastructure governance aspects.
- The proposal of an architecture and functional framework for smart contracts, their planning, coding, and testing.
- A reference architecture highlighting PDL platform services has been developed, listing services where some are seen as mandatory and others optional; this enables the use of PDL to ensure certain networks and provide data and application integrity tracking and non-repudiation.
- A framework for technology assessment and demonstration via proofs of concept has been established as well.

The ISG has established a strong connection with research activities, especially the collaborative research projects within the Horizon 2020 program, with specific work items focused on this coordination.

The ISG PDL plans to evolve current reports into normative specifications, addressing early feedback coming from operational experience, and ensure the adaptation of its principles and work items to new application environments, especially those enabled by the emergence of next-generation networking infrastructures, such as those related to resource trading at all levels, from compute nodes to spectrum, as well as new industrial scenarios.

The ISG PDL works in tight coordination with other groups in ETSI and elsewhere, including open-source initiatives and PDL is committed to produce deliverables of three different natures:

- informative (studies and recommendations for further work);
- normative (specifications); and
- demonstrative (in the form of proof-of-concept reports and interoperability assessment events).

A full list of related specifications in the public domain is accessible via the PDL committee page [4], and can be searched through the ETSI web search interface. The ISG has an open policy for document access in order to facilitate the interaction with research and industry, and early versions of working drafts are publicly available at the document open area.

7.3 The 3rd Generation Partnership Project (3GPP)

The 3rd Generation Partnership Project (3GPP) was established in December 1998 with the goal of developing standards specifications for a 3G mobile phone system as an evolution from the 2G Global System for Mobile Communications (GSM) system.

Today, it comprises a number of SDOs that develop protocols for mobile telecommunications [5], namely seven national or regional telecommunication standards organizations as primary members ("organizational partners") and a variety of other organizations as associate members ("market representation partners").

The 3GPP organizes its work into different streams, i.e., radio access networks (RANs), services and systems aspects (SA), and core network and terminals (CT). It is mainly known for the development and maintenance of:

- GSM and related 2G and 2.5G standards, including GPRS and EDGE

- UMTS and related 3G standards, including HSPA and HSPA+
- LTE and related 4G standards, including LTE Advanced and LTE Advanced Pro
- 5G NR and related 5G standards, including 5G-Advanced
- Emerging 6G standardization approaches

The standardization work is contribution-driven, i.e., the more than 700 companies participate through their membership with specification work being done within working groups (WGs) and Technical Specification Groups (TSGs):

- 3GPP WGs hold several meetings a year (over Covid-19, all was done remotely). The WGs discuss change requests against 3GPP specifications.
- 3GPP TSGs hold plenary meetings quarterly. The TSGs can "approve" the change requests that were agreed at WG level. Importantly, once approved, the change requests are incorporated into 3GPP specifications.

Following the ITU-T Recommendation I.130, the 3GPP follows a three-stage standardization methodology:

- Stage 1: specifications define the service requirements from the user point of view;
- Stage 2: specifications define an architecture to support the service requirements; and
- Stage 3: specifications define an implementation of the architecture by specifying protocols in details.

Importantly, 3GPP does not operate in "generations," such as 4G or 5G; but rather in Releases. That is, specifications are grouped into releases with each consisting of a set of internally consistent set of features and specifications.

5G, for instance, is composed of five releases. Three have already been finalized ("frozen"), i.e., Release 15, 16 and 17; one is under current design (summer 2022), i.e., Release 18; and one yet to be designed, i.e., Release 19. The finalized and active releases are shown in Table 7.1. Note that 6G is expected to commence with Release 20.

Blockchains and distributed ledgers are (for the time being) tangential within the 3GPP. However, first contributions start to appear and we expect parts of the standards work being done in ETSI, IEEE, IETF, W3C, as well as the ITU and ISO, to eventually spurn an avalanche of study items on blockchains.

Table 7.1   Finalized as well as active 3GPP releases which define 5G [6].

Release 15	2018 Q2	First 5G NR ("New Radio") release which includes the support for 5G vehicle-to-x service, IP Multimedia Core Network Subsystem (IMS) and future railway mobile communication system.
Release 16	2020 Q3	5G Phase 2 release which includes 5G enhancements, NR-based access to unlicensed spectrum (NR-U), satellite access, among many other advanced features.
Release 17	2022 Q1	It includes enhanced support of non-public networks, industrial Internet of Things, low complexity NR devices, edge computing in 5G, access traffic steering, switch and splitting support, network automation for 5G, network slicing, advanced V2X service, multiple USIM support, proximity-based services in 5GS, 5G multicast broadcast services, unmanned aerial systems (UAS), satellite access in 5G, 5GC location services, multimedia priority service, among many other features.
Release 18	2023 Q4	It is the first release referred to as 5G-Advanced. It introduces machine-learning based techniques at different levels of the wireless network, edge computing, evolution of IMS multimedia telephony service, smart energy and infrastructure, vehicle-mounted relays, low power high accuracy positioning for industrial IoT scenarios, enhanced access to and support of network slicing, satellite backhaul in 5G, among many other features.

One example of current work is the China Unicom and China Mobile contribution to 3GPP TSG-SA WG6 Meeting which took place remotely in May 2020 [7]. The tabled proposal was entitled "Study on Blockchain support in Application Layer for 5G Verticals," with potential target into Release 18 (R18).

The objectives of the study were outlined to be:

1) Analyze use cases/service requirements from existing vertical related TS and identify for which blockchain can be used to fulfill the requirements from application perspective.

2) Develop key issues, corresponding architecture requirements and solution recommendations to enable the blockchain in application layer support for 5G vertical.

3) Analyze the re-use of functionalities from SA6 specifications for the solutions, where applicable.

4) Identify deployment models to facilitate tight integration with the underlying 3GPP system architecture.

5) Study potential application layer APIs.

The rationale to engage within the 3GPP were because "blockchain is a promising technology to enhance [...] industry applications (e.g., traceability applications, credential applications, etc.) and is an important component in the application layer over 3GPP network."

It was noted that "blockchain is a promising technology/capability at the application layer to be utilized to fulfil the general vertical requirements, e.g., data integrity, distributed identify, traceability, etc."

To define the application layer architecture and to enable its binding to 3GPP networks, it was proposed that SA WG6 undertake a study to identify the supporting application layer architecture and corresponding solutions to enable blockchain applications in 5G/6G verticals over 3GPP networks.

7.4 Institute of Electrical and Electronics Engineers (IEEE)

The Institute of Electrical and Electronics Engineers (IEEE) is a non-profit association for electronic engineering and electrical engineering with its operations center being in Piscataway, New Jersey, USA [8].

As of 2018, it is the world's largest association of technical professionals with more than 400,000 members in over 160 countries around the world. Whilst its objectives are fairly broad – i.e., educational and technical advancement of electrical and electronic engineering, telecommunications, computer engineering and similar disciplines – it is mainly known for having standardized the popular technologies Ethernet, Wi-Fi, and Bluetooth. It also is the central point for academic publications across a wide variety of technical disciplines [9].

An initiative related to this book is the IEEE Blockchain Initiative [10]. This came about because the IEEE Future Directions Committee, represented by the societies of the IEEE, has approved the formation of the IEEE Blockchain Initiative (BLK) in January 2018. The BLK is the hub for all IEEE Blockchain projects and activities. It currently encompasses a comprehensive set of projects and activities supported by the following core subcommittees: Pre/Standards, Education, Conferences and Events, Community Development and Outreach, Publications, and Special Projects.

The IEEE rightly recognized blockchain as a new and emerging technology family positioned on the leading edge of the technology hype curve. It also recognized that the blockchain technical community is highly fragmented and badly needs what the IEEE can deliver; a stabilizing think space of seasoned professionals specifically trained and positioned to make a difference. Blockchain is by far the most forward thinking, impactful, and disruptive emerging technology family that the Future Directions Committee and the IEEE has sought to embrace.

As said above, core to the activities of the IEEE are standards. Not surprisingly, it has published already a large list of blockchain standards:

- 2140.1-2020 – IEEE Standard for General Requirements for Cryptocurrency Exchanges
- 2140.2-2021 – IEEE Standard for Security Management for Customer Cryptographic Assets on Cryptocurrency Exchanges
- 2140.5-2020 – IEEE Standard for a Custodian Framework of Cryptocurrency
- 2142.1-2021 – IEEE Recommended Practice for E-Invoice Business using Blockchain Technology
- 2143.1-2020 – IEEE Standard for General Process of Cryptocurrency Payment
- 2144.1-2020 – IEEE Standard for Framework of Blockchain-based Internet of Things (IoT) Data Management
- 2418.2-2020 – IEEE Standard Data Format for Blockchain Systems
- 2418.7-2021 – IEEE Standard for the Use of Blockchain in Supply Chain Finance
- 2418.10 – IEEE Approved Draft Standard for Blockchain-based Digital Asset Management
- 3801-2022 – IEEE Standard for Blockchain-based Electronic Contracts

An even larger list of standards is currently (Summer 2022) under development, with more information available from [11].

7.5 Internet Engineering Task Force (IETF)

The Internet Engineering Task Force (IETF) is responsible for the technical specifications that run the global internet today [12]. It was initially supported by the federal government of the United States but since 1993 has operated under the auspices of the Internet Society, an international non-profit organization. As a result, it is not strictly speaking an SDO but is generally recognized to have the same impact as traditional SDOs. Important to note is that it has no formal membership roster and all its participants are volunteers that represent themselves rather than their companies.

The IETF is organized into working groups and "birds of a feather" informal discussion groups, each dealing with a specific topic. The IETF operates bottom-up through its working groups, where each working group has an appointed chairperson; a charter that describes its focus. Since there are no formal voting procedures like in 3GPP or the IEEE, consensus is the primary basis for decision making. Since the majority of the work is done via mailing lists, meeting attendance is not required for contributors.

The working groups are organized into areas by subject matter with current areas being: applications, general, internet, operations and management, real-time applications and infrastructure, routing, security, and transport. The most important but not the only contribution by the IEFT is today's Internet protocol suite (TCP/IP).

In terms of blockchain specifications, several important initiatives are gaining momentum [13]. The following ones are worth mentioning:

- Interoperability Architecture for DLT Gateways [14]
- Blockchain Gateways: Use-cases [15]
- BGP Blockchain [16]
- Blockchain Transaction Protocol for Constraint Nodes [17]
- Supply chain integrity, transparency, and trust (SCITT) [18]
- Secure asset transfer protocol (SATP) [19]

For instance, the *"Interoperability Architecture for DLT Gateways"* notes that there is currently little technical interoperability between decentralized ledger technology networks. This results in the difficulty in transferring or exchanging virtual (digital) assets from one network to another directly.

The existing solutions involve a third party that mediates the transfer. This mediating third party is typically an asset-exchange entity (i.e., crypto-exchange) operating in a centralized hub-spoke fashion. This reliance on a third party leads to delays in transfers and also in the need for asset owners to have a business relationship (e.g., open accounts) at the mediating third party. Many of these solutions centralize control at the hands of the mediating party, thereby diminishing the autonomy of blockchains and DLT networks, and limits their scalability.

The *"Interoperability Architecture for DLT Gateways"* contribution [20] thus proposes an interoperability architecture based on blockchain distributed gateways, which are points of interconnection between networks. There are several services that may be offered by a gateway, one of which being the direct transfer of a digital asset from one network to another via pairs of gateways without a mediating third party. A given network may have one or more gateways to perform a unidirectional direct transfer of digital assets to another network possessing one or more compatible gateway. Similar to the notion of border gateways in interdomain routing (e.g., running the BGPv4 protocol), a gateway belonging to an origin network is said to peer with another gateway is a destination network. Both gateways must implement an asset transfer protocol (referred to as secure asset transfer protocol (SATP) [21]) that must satisfy certain security, privacy and atomicity requirements.

Another example is the "*Blockchain Transaction Protocol for Constraint Nodes*" contribution [22]. It assumes sensors/actuators that are powered by micro-controllers comprising about 10 KB of RAM and 100 KB of non-volatile memory. The node electronic board may include a radio system-on-chip (SoC) or the micro-controller can be part of the SoC. The radio chip manages IP connectivity with another device, typically acting as a controller, which provides a full internet access with standard computing resources.

A constraint node driving sensors and/or actuators may deliver critical data dealing with safety (e.g., fire detection) or other applications (e.g., pollution). A supporting blockchain infrastructure provides important features in an Internet of Things (IoT) context:

- authentication of data in P2P context where blockchain signed transactions are checked by numerous nodes;
- information publication where transactions are stored in duplicated and distributed databases; and
- date stamping information where transactions are dated during the mining process.

The goal of the blockchain transaction protocol for constraint nodes is thus to enable the generation of blockchain transactions by constraint nodes, according to the following design principles:

1) Transactions are triggered by controllers. Needed blockchain parameters are included in provisioning messages.
2) Binary encoded transaction messages are returned by constraint nodes. A node has the ability to compute the transaction signature.

Whilst the IETF focuses on the shorter term issues of engineering and standards making, the long-term research issues related to the Internet are within the scope of the Internet Research Task Force (IRTF) [23]. The IRTF is a parallel organization to the IETF, both of which are overseen by the Internet Architecture Board (IAB).

A research group has been in formation in the IRTF on the topic of decentralized internet infrastructure (DIN) [24]. The Decentralized Internet Infrastructure Research Group (DINRG) is investigating open research issues in decentralizing infrastructure services such as trust management, identity management, name resolution, resource/asset ownership management, and resource discovery. The focus of DINRG is on infrastructure services that can benefit from decentralization or that are difficult to realize in local, potentially connectivity-constrained networks. Other topics of interest are the investigation of economic drivers and incentives and the development and operation of experimental platforms. DINRG will operate in a technology- and solution-neutral manner, i.e., while the RG has an interest in distributed ledger technologies, it is not limited to specific technologies or implementation aspects.

The IETF/IRTF work is in progress, but we expect important blockchain-related networking standards to become operational over the coming years.

References

[1] https://en.wikipedia.org/wiki/ETSI
[2] https://www.etsi.org/committee/1467-pdl
[3] https://www.etsi.org/deliver/etsi_gr/PDL/001_099/001/01.01.01_60/gr _PDL001v010101p.pdf
[4] https://www.etsi.org/committee/1467-pdl
[5] https://en.wikipedia.org/wiki/3GPP
[6] https://en.wikipedia.org/wiki/3GPP
[7] https://view.officeapps.live.com/op/view.aspx?src=https%3A%2F%2 Fwww.3gpp.org%2Fftp%2Ftsg_sa%2FWG6_MissionCritical%2FTSG S6_037-e%2FInbox%2FDrafts%2F9_FutureWork%2FS6-200699_R ev2-New%2520SID%25EF%25BC%259AStudy%2520on%2520Blo ckchain%2520in%2520Application%2520Layer%2520support%252 0Verticals%2520over%25205G%2520network.doc&wdOrigin=BR OWSELINK
[8] https://en.wikipedia.org/wiki/Institute_of_Electrical_and_Electronics _Engineers
[9] https://ieeexplore.ieee.org/Xplore/home.jsp
[10] https://blockchain.ieee.org/
[11] https://blockchain.ieee.org/standards
[12] https://en.wikipedia.org/wiki/Internet_Engineering_Task_Force
[13] https://datatracker.ietf.org/
[14] https://datatracker.ietf.org/doc/html/draft-hardjono-blockchain-interop- arch-03

[15] https://datatracker.ietf.org/doc/draft-sardon-blockchain-gateways-usec
      ases/

[16] https://datatracker.ietf.org/doc/draft-mcbride-rtgwg-bgp-blockchain/

[17] https://datatracker.ietf.org/doc/draft-urien-core-blockchain-transaction
      -protocol/

[18] https://datatracker.ietf.org/wg/scitt/about/

[19] https://datatracker.ietf.org/wg/satp/about/

[20] https://datatracker.ietf.org/doc/html/draft-hardjono-blockchain-interop-
      arch-03

[21] https://datatracker.ietf.org/wg/satp/about/

[22] https://datatracker.ietf.org/doc/draft-urien-core-blockchain-transaction
      -protocol/

[23] https://irtf.org/

[24] https://datatracker.ietf.org/rg/dinrg/about/

8

Blockchain Alliances

In this chapter, we focus on blockchain alliances. They differ from standards organizations in that they are not acknowledged by governments as standards-setting organizations. Alliances mainly represent industry interests but have an important role to play in that technical approaches, operational principles, and business models are often aligned among the leading industries in the specific domain.

Many telco-related blockchain alliances have emerged over past years. We will mainly focus on those which are well established and have blockchain at their founding principles. At the very end, we also list various alliances which have started to use blockchains in their wider industry settings.

8.1 World Wide Web Consortium (W3C)

World Wide Web Consortium (W3C) [1] is a well-known international community where a diverse set of members deploy together web standards. Between other initiatives within this organization, the last version about Verifiable Credentials Data Model [2] is published, which is a standardization effort with relevant commonalities for identity management on distributed ledger technologies. There is also an open GitHub repository for technical specifications at [3].

8.2 Hyperledger – Linux Foundation

Hyperledger is a well-organized charter by Hyperledger Linux Foundation [4] with the aim to:

- create an enterprise-grade, open-source distributed ledger frame-work, and code base, upon which users can build and run robust, industry-specific applications, platforms, and hardware systems to support business transactions;

- create an open source, technical community to benefit the ecosystem of Hyperledger solution providers and users, focused on blockchain and shared ledger use cases that will work across a variety of industry solutions;
- promote participation of leading members of the ecosystem, including developers, service and solution providers, and end users; and
- host the infrastructure for Hyperledger, establishing a neutral home for community infrastructure, meetings, events and collaborative discussions and providing structure around the business and technical governance.

Today, Hyperledger [5] is the leader of private permissioned distributed ledger initiatives with Hyperledger Fabric, but it is also a combination with other tools and functionalities which are impacting for interoperability with permissionless distributed ledgers and public permissioned distributed ledgers.

Hyperledger got a variety of projects available which incubates and promotes for a business blockchain technologies industry, in permissioned distributed ledgers:

- Burrow, which is a for permissible smart contract machine,
- Fabric with a range of use cases from finance to supply-chain, Indy for a decentralized identity management,
- Iroha a consensus with multi-signature support, or
- Sawtooth with a proof of elapse time with the aim of a minimal resource consumption.

8.3 Enterprise Ethereum Alliance (EEA)

The Enterprise Ethereum Alliance (EEA) is a member-driven alliance whose charter is to develop open blockchain specifications that facilitate harmonization and interoperability for business and consumers worldwide.

It is a community with key players in the industry cooperating on specifications under working groups and some of their publications pertain to telecommunications use cases, real estate use cases, and a token taxonomy initiative flyer.

8.4 International Association for Trusted Blockchain Applications

The International Association for Trusted Blockchain Applications (INATBA) [6] was founded in April 2019 and is organically under coordination and establishment of various Working Groups and liaisons with Standards Developing Bodies.

It is well organized and closely connected to the European Commission's European Blockchain Observatory and Forum [7] as well as the European Blockchain Partnership [8]. It is actively promoting the dialogue with policy makers and public administrative bodies, and connected the private sector envisioned for the European Blockchain Service Infrastructure.

8.5 GSM Association (GSMA)

The GSMA published a white paper on "Blockchain - Operator Opportunities" [9] in July 2018. It pointed out that blockchain technology can help to reduce the need for trust between stakeholders, build a secure value exchange system, streamline business processes across multiple entities, and increase record transparency and ease of auditability, in three dimensions: higher efficiencies due the removal of "trusted" third parties, new business models triggered and supported by blockchain technologies, and better customer engagement thanks to incentives provided by blockchain systems. It has been predicted in this white paper that business opportunities in using blockchain for operators are diverse and extensive, but in the near future blockchain may be mainly used to improve roaming, billing, payments, data distribution, and network capabilities in telecom networks.

In 2022, the GSMA established a working group – Distributed Ledger Technology Group [10]. One objective of this group is to develop and maintain common framework and standards for telecom use cases (e.g., payments, identity, wholesale settlement, supply chain, fraud and security, and blockchain as a service), which should be agnostic of a particular ledger technology.

8.6 Other Blockchain Alliances

Blockchain Alliances*Alastria* [11]: It is a non-profit association that promotes the digital economy. It is a framework for networks based on public permissioned distributed ledgers. Public and private sector and governmental administrative bodies are composing a whole economic coverage on distributed ledger initiatives which compete and cooperate between their members to help the harmonization of standards and regulation with their use cases. The Association has presented at UNE a proposal of "de-facto" standard implemented on Alastria, the new work item was accepted and it is under revision by UNE CTN 71/SC 307/GT1 for a decentralized model of identity.

Alliance on IoT Innovation (AIOTI) [12]: It is an industrial partner of the European Commission. The alliance is representing the European industry around the Internet of Things, fostering research and innovation from within its 14 working groups [13]. The AIOTI working group on distributed ledger technologies is working on mapping current DLT and blockchain implementations on IoT, rate the models toward legal compliance (including GDPR), assist existing AIOTI WG's on the development of sustainable ecosystems across verticals while including startups and SMEs, gather evidences and market obstacles for DLT as enabling technology on the digital single market and assist to shape research and innovation policy to foster experimentation, replication and deployments.

Dutch Blockchain Coalition [14]: The efforts of this Dutch private public partnership is to build a reliable blockchain infrastructure in Netherlands, the coalition contains Banks, supervisory bodies such as Netherlands Authority for Financial Markets and Royal Dutch Association of Civil-law Notaries, government ministries, legal organizations, knowledge institutions and Academic Institutions. At the European level the coalition holds talks with EU and at country level with Belgium, Luxemburg, and Germany.

Industrial Internet Consortium® [15]: It is a global not-for-profit partnership of industry, government, and academia, which was founded in March 2014 to bring the organizations and technologies necessary to accelerate the growth of the industrial internet by identifying assembling, testing, and promoting best practices. Recently, propositions were made to use blockchain to detect and deter denial of service attacks.

OASIS [16]: It is a non-profit consortium that drives the development, convergence, and adoption of open standards for the global information society. The consortium has more than 2000 participants representing over 600 organizations and individual members in more than 65 countries. Existing OASIS standards projects with e-commerce applications are being applied to define blockchain-based serialization methods, as alternative representations of their content (such as e-invoices).

Open Mobile Alliance (OMA^{TM}*)* [17]: It deploys specification and promoting standards in mobile and Internet of Things technology development, in particular APIs it is a part of components with DLT's scenarios.

oneM2M^{TM} [18]: It deploys standards for machine-to-machine and the Internet of Things, and has almost 200 members. The purpose and goal are to develop technical specifications which for a common M2M Service Layer that can be embedded within various hardware and software, and relied upon to connect the devices in the field with M2M application servers worldwide.

OpenTimestamps [19]: This is a relevant jointly initiative for a Timestamping Proof Standard, accordingly with their focus to prove that some data existed prior to some point in time. OpenTimestamps defines a set of operations for creating provable timestamps and later independently verifying them. The exploration of this open-source initiative is bringing to a key attribute for trust on the DLT system which is very easily compatible for hybrid and permissioned distributed ledger systems, a variety of tools on Java, Rust, Python, and JavaScript.

Metaverse Standards Forum [20]: It provides a venue for cooperation between standards organizations and companies to foster the development of interoperability standards for an open and inclusive metaverse, and accelerate their development and deployment through pragmatic, action-based projects. It does not only focus on blockchain technologies but they play a central role in most working groups.

References

[1] https://www.w3.org/
[2] https://www.w3.org/TR/vc-data-model
[3] https://github.com/w3c/vc-data-model/issues
[4] https://linuxfoundation.org/tools/hyperledger/
[5] https://www.hyperledger.org/
[6] https://inatba.org/
[7] https://www.eublockchainforum.eu/
[8] https://digital-strategy.ec.europa.eu/en/policies/blockchain-partnership
[9] https://www.gsma.com/newsroom/wp-content/uploads/IG.03-v1.0_W hitepaper.pdf

[10] https://www.gsma.com/aboutus/workinggroups/distributed-ledger-technology-group
[11] https://alastria.io/en/
[12] https://aioti.eu/
[13] https://aioti.eu/working-groups/
[14] https://dutchblockchaincoalition.org/en
[15] https://www.iiconsortium.org/
[16] https://www.oasis-open.org/standards
[17] https://www.openmobilealliance.org/wp/API_Inventory.html
[18] http://www.onem2m.org/
[19] https://opentimestamps.org/
[20] https://metaverse-standards.org/

9

Regulation and Compliance

In this chapter, we focus on regulatory and compliance issues. We first dwell on regulatory challenges, which mainly stem from the fact that blockchain is a nascent field. We then detail general regulatory aspects before diving into the positions of the European Union, the USA, and the UK.

9.1 General Regulatory Challenges

Regulating blockchain technology and cryptocurrency poses a number of challenges for regulators. Some of the main challenges include:

- *Understanding the technology*: Blockchain technology is a relatively new and complex technology, and regulators may struggle to fully understand it and its potential implications. This can make it difficult for regulators to develop effective regulations that address the risks without stifling innovation.
- *Jurisdictional issues*: Blockchain technology is decentralized and operates on a global scale, making it difficult for any single regulator to fully control or regulate it. This can lead to regulatory arbitrage, where companies and individuals can simply operate in jurisdictions with less strict regulations.
- *Lack of transparency*: The decentralized and anonymous nature of blockchain transactions can make it difficult for regulators to track and monitor suspicious activity, such as money laundering or fraud.
- Balancing innovation and risk: Regulating blockchain technology and cryptocurrency can be a delicate balancing act between protecting consumers and investors from potential risks and allowing the technology to continue to innovate and evolve.
- *Keeping pace with rapid developments*: Blockchain technology and cryptocurrency are rapidly evolving, and regulators may struggle to keep pace with the changes and developments in the space.

- *Compliance*: Blockchain and cryptocurrency companies may have a hard time to comply with regulations and laws, as they are still in development, and the technology may not be ready for it yet.

Regulators are actively trying to address these challenges by working together, sharing information and collaborating with industry participants. This is to ensure that suitable mechanisms are found to control privacy, safeguard minors, ensure compliance, among many other challenges. It is a work in progress as blockchain technology is still in its early stages and the regulatory landscape is still evolving.

9.2 Current Regulatory Aspects

At the time of writing this book, a number of laws are enacted that are applicable to DLT. Examples are know your customer (KYC) and anti-money laundering (AMl) requirements.

At the same time, there are initiatives from countries to include exemptions or benefit to startups using DLT; an example is Switzerland with her sandbox rule in Swiss banking law. France and Germany proposed to introduce a uniform regulation of DLT in 2018 at the G20 summit but did not convince the G20 to embrace suitable legislation.

A number of countries are receiving recommendations from their central banks and other regulatory authorities which increases the need for a legal framework, thus ending a decade of uncertainty.

For countries which pioneered DLT-specific legislation, focus is more on initial coin offerings (ICOs) and counter-financing of terrorism (CFT). The latter involves investigating, analyzing, deterring and preventing sources of funding activities for political achievement, religious or ideological goals through violence.

In the realm of telecoms, Directive 2000/31/EC defines the liability of intermediary service providers in Section 4, article 12:

"Mere conduit": Where an information society service is provided that consists of the transmission in a communication network of information provided by a recipient of the service, or the provision of access to a communication network, Member States shall ensure that the service provider is not liable for the information transmitted, on condition that the provider:

a) *does not initiate the transmission;*

b) *does not select the receiver of the transmission; and*
c) *does not select or modify the information contained in the transmission.*

In trade and logistic, UN/CEFACT is highly relevant which has prepared a White Paper on blockchain. Furthermore, UNCITRAL is ideal to a conferred multijurisdictional approach.

Furthermore, government services are increasingly utilizing DLT to provide trust services. E-government initiatives are enhancing their frameworks to make use of DLT. For instance, in Europe, the Trustful Online Interoperability Platform (TOOP) is a pilot for interoperability. It is important to enable a new design with policy enforcement points that are distributed among the governed network. These areas can harmonize data minimization and limitation of data use.

Regulation on electronic identification and trust services is an important aspect to consider. There are a number of laws for digital signatures, electronic certificates, and identification which sometimes are not neutral or converge to a common denominator globally. The electronic identification, authentication, and trust services (eIDAS) framework is extensively improving these aspects.

Smart contracts enforceability is another backbone in permissioned distributed ledger systems. These contracts play a significant role in ensuring that the parties involved in a transaction are held accountable.

Competition law and anti-trust policies are also relevant for regulatory areas and policy makers. These laws ensure that there is fair competition in the market, and that consumers are protected from anti-competitive practices.

Conformance and compatible chip-sets and other components are also in compliance needs for multijurisdictional frameworks. Hybrid ecosystems bring new challenges in this sense, where multiple actors with different components can interoperate between them.

The emergence of experimental testing sandboxes in different countries is important. It enables a secured testing environment for discover ability and improving the legal innovation and experimentation. These sandboxes provide a safe environment for companies to test their products and services, while also allowing regulators to monitor and evaluate their performance.

9.3 Ecosystem and the EU-Market Aspects

European Blockchain Partnership (EBP) [1] was launched on 10 April 2018, with the aim to develop a trusted, secure and resilient European Blockchain

Services Infrastructure (EBSI) meeting the highest standards in terms of privacy, cybersecurity, interoperability, and energy efficiency, as well as fully complaint with the EU law.

The EBP develops a set of guiding principles and specifications for the EBSI to enhance and recognize a reference for development of blockchain infrastructures and will propose a model to describe the overall policy and technical governance of the EBSI.

EBSI currently has four use cases which are: self-sovereign identity, diploma, verification, and trusted data sharing. In the future, this is likely to increase. The goal of the EBSI is on cross-border interactions, to make national projects interoperable, and to enhance identity frameworks (e.g., eIDAS). Pilot developments had started in 2019 with large scale implementations following in 2022.

Some pilots are in deployment with various organic development for managing different aspects like European Interoperability Reference Architecture (EIRA) and European Self-Sovereign Identify Framework (ESSIF).

ICT Standardization priorities for the digital single market are an indicator to overview the EU-Market development [2]. eIDAS regulation is the framework of preeminent success in Europe and an intrinsic part of the European Ecosystem.

9.4 Regulation of Blockchains in the USA

In the United States, the regulation of blockchain technology and cryptocurrency is handled by a number of different agencies and regulatory bodies at the federal and state level. The main regulatory agencies that handle blockchain and cryptocurrency regulations are:

- *The Securities and Exchange Commission (SEC)*: The SEC is responsible for regulating securities and investment products, including ICOs and security tokens. The SEC has issued guidance stating that many ICOs and tokens are considered securities and are subject to federal securities laws.
- *The Commodity Futures Trading Commission (CFTC)*: The CFTC has jurisdiction over derivatives and commodities, including Bitcoin and other cryptocurrencies. The CFTC has stated that it views cryptocurrencies as commodities and has taken action against firms for fraud and manipulation in the cryptocurrency markets.
- *The Financial Crimes Enforcement Network (FinCEN)*: FinCEN is responsible for enforcing AML and CFT regulations. FinCEN has issued

guidance stating that businesses involved in cryptocurrency transactions, including exchanges and wallets, are subject to AML/CFT regulations.

- *The Internal Revenue Service (IRS)*: The IRS has issued guidance stating that cryptocurrencies are considered property for tax purposes and are subject to capital gains taxes.

Additionally, many states have also implemented their own regulations and licensing requirements for businesses operating in the blockchain and cryptocurrency space.

Regulatory requirements for blockchain and cryptocurrency companies in the USA may include obtaining licenses, registering with regulatory agencies, complying with AML and KYC regulations, and filing regular reports. Additionally, companies that are involved in the sale of securities, including ICOs, must comply with federal securities laws and regulations.

It is important to note that regulations are dynamic and may change over time, it is always best to check the latest guidance from the regulatory bodies.

9.5 Regulation of Blockchains in the UK

The UK's Financial Conduct Authority (FCA) has issued guidance on the regulatory treatment of crypto assets and ICOs to help firms understand whether their activities fall within the FCA's regulatory remit.

According to the FCA, crypto assets can be split into three categories:

1. exchange tokens,
2. security tokens, and
3. utility tokens.

Exchange tokens, such as Bitcoin, are not regulated by the FCA, but firms involved in their exchange may be subject to money laundering regulations. Security tokens, which have similar characteristics to traditional securities and give holders a right to a share of profits or assets, are regulated by the FCA. Utility tokens, which give holders access to a current or prospective product or service, are generally not regulated by the FCA.

For ICOs, the FCA has stated that whether or not an ICO falls within their regulatory remit will depend on the nature of the token being offered and the rights it gives holders. If the token is a security, then the FCA's regulations will apply, including the need to be authorized by the FCA, to publish a prospectus, and to comply with the FCA's rules on the promotion of financial products.

Furthermore, The FCA also has published a guidance on the use of DLT, including blockchain, for firms operating in the financial markets. The guidance explains the FCA's approach to the use of DLT and highlights the key regulatory issues that firms should consider when developing and implementing DLT projects.

References

[1] https://ec.europa.eu/digital-single-market/en/news/european-countries-join-blockchain-partnership
[2] https://ec.europa.eu/digital-single-market/en/news/communication-ict-standardisation-priorities-digital-single-market

10

Blockchain R&D Projects

In this chapter, we provide a horizon scanning on blockchain R&D projects. We first provide an overview of the European funding mechanisms; and then highlight some important blockchain projects as part of the European Union R&D framework as well as specific countries like the UK and the USA.

10.1 Overview of European R&D Funding Landscape

In Europe, research and innovation has a high priority. The EU provides funding for research projects in Europe within the EU Framework Programmes for Research. These programs have been established since 1984 with the overall objective to strengthen the competitiveness and growth of the European market.

Horizon 2020

Horizon 2020 is the 8th EU Framework Programmes for Research and Innovation. Reflecting on the growing importance of innovation from previous EU Framework Programmes for Research, the Horizon 2020 Framework Programme has a strong focus on Innovation. In particular, Horizon 2020 has implemented instruments for scaling-up the ICT innovation ecosystem in Europe.

Support for ICT innovation plays a central role in Horizon 2020 together with the creation of better framework conditions for innovation in Europe through ICT standardization. The ICT innovation strategy is to ensure that the rapidly changing ICT technology directly transforms into substantial benefits for European citizens and society.

Horizon 2020 is funding research projects covering the whole innovation chain from foundational research toward the preparation of market-ready products. With a total budget of about 80 billion euros over a runtime of seven years, i.e., from 2014 to 2020, Horizon 2020 has been one of the largest research and innovation funding programs worldwide. It is structured into the three research and innovation program priorities:

1. excellent science;
2. leadership in enabling and industrial technologies; and
3. societal challenges.

Horizon Europe

Horizon Europe is the successor of Horizon 2020 and will be the largest EU Research and Innovation Framework Programme following up on the implementation and maintenance of well-established programs from Horizon 2020 with a budget of around 95.5 billion Euros over a runtime of seven years from 2021 until 2027.

Horizon Europe is set out to strengthen research and innovation in Europe further and to drive the digital transformation for supporting the creation of innovative services and new markets and to provide more targeted solutions to global and societal challenges. Horizon Europe has the objective to create impact more effectively through a clear mission orientation and a strategy toward active engagement and involvement of society and citizens as well as stronger dissemination and exploitation of research and innovation results.

With an exclusive focus on civil applications the specific program implementing Horizon Europe is structured into the three priority areas:

1. excellent science;
2. global challenges and European industrial competitiveness; and
3. innovative Europe.

The "Excellent Science" work program comprises "European Research Council (ERC)," "Marie Skodowska-Curie," and "Research Infrastructures" actions set up to strengthen excellent European science and technology through more investments into individual and highly skilled researchers and leading-edge innovations.

The "Global Challenges & European Industrial Competitiveness" work program is set up to advance the industrial competitiveness and innovation capacities of the EU. It encompasses funding of research activities through clusters relating to global challenges (i.e., "Health," "Culture, Creativity and Inclusive Society," "Civil Security for Society," "Digital Industry and Space," "Climate, Energy and Mobility," and "Food, Bio Economy, Natural Resources, Agriculture and Environment") and also includes support activities by the "Joint Research Centre" for policies.

The "Innovative Europe" work program is grouped into "European Inno-vation Council (EIC)," "European Innovation Ecosystems," and "European Institute of Innovation and Technology (EIT)" activities. The Horizon Europe Research and Innovation Programme is based on the widening participation and strengthening the European Research Area (ERA).

Other Blockchain-related Programs

The Connecting Europe Facility (CEF) run by the European Commission's Innovation and Networks Executive Agency (INEA) is a fund for European infrastructure investments in transport, energy as well as digital projects lever-aging not only intra- but also cross-border connectivity within and between the EU member states. CEF funding and grants are organized through calls for proposals are particularly set out to support the adoption of the CEF Building Blocks.

CEF Building Blocks are most commonly needed digital services based on European legislation and standards helping to implement the development and adoption of the required digital infrastructures in a more efficient way by using existing technologies and synergies. The European Commission's Directorate-General for Communications Networks, Content and Technology (DG CNECT) is responsible for managing the digital agenda and is defining the CEF Building Blocks.

Among the currently available CEF Building Blocks including eID, eDelivery, eInvoicing, eSignature, Context Broker, eArchiving, eTransla-tion, and the Big Data Test Infrastructure (BDTI), in the context of DLT-related research and innovation programs the CEF Building Block European Blockchain Services Infrastructure (EBSI) needs to be highlighted. The goal of the CEF EBSI is to provide cross-border pan-European public services using blockchain technology with the highest standards of security and privacy.

In November 2020, the EC launched a call for tenders on EU Blockchain Pre-Commercial Procurement (PCP) for novel, innovative distributed ledger or blockchain solutions helping to establish the future European Blockchain Services Infrastructure for the European Citizens in compliance with the EU legal framework (i.e., GDPR, eIDAS, and NIS Directive).

In particular, the PCP call is set out to support a number of new types of use cases with high-volume and high-velocity requirements improving inter-operability, security, robustness and sustainability of EBSI. The European Blockchain PCP will award research and development service contracts to a number of blockchain solution providers for the development of innovative solutions covering all phases from design, prototyping toward installation and testing.

Among others these solutions should provide for identification and traceability of objects, and the management of their data, automation of tasks through smart contracts, also relevant interfaces for the exchange and interoperability with external solutions (e.g., IoT and AI), improving scalability and providing security levels addressing new cyber threats, addressing potential use cases like digital product passport within the circular economy, tracking of digital records, and associated rights or other IoT use cases.

10.2 EC Blockchain Projects

A fairly comprehensive (yet not exhaustive) list of EU Horizon 2020 Projects related to DLT and blockchain can be found in the Annex A of [1].

The majority of the projects is funded under the research and innovation action (RIA) schemes, followed by the small- and medium-sized enterprise (SME) instrument funding schemes, then by the innovation action (IA) schemes and finally the coordination and support action (CSA) funding schemes.

The PDL Application Domain or Field of Research of the Horizon 2020 projects related to blockchain and DLT is distributed as shown in Figure 10.1.

In more detail, within the EC European Research Council 2021 Work Programme, there are three dedicated research topics with thematic focus on blockchain. Within these three blockchain research topics, seven H2020 grants with a total volume of around 32.8 million euros have been awarded by the EU. These seven blockchain projects relate to three thematic priorities/pillars of the H2020 Programme:

1. Information and communication technology (ICT);
2. Innovation support for SME (INNOSUPSME); and
3. Health (HEALTH).

Finally, the very wide span of topics influenced by DLT and PDL can be seen by analyzing the Annex A of [2] in the form of a mind map which is illustrated in Figure 10.2.

10.3 Example EC Project: 5GZORRO

5GZORRO [4] is a recently finished joint research project, funded by the European Commission within its Horizon Europe program, and focused,

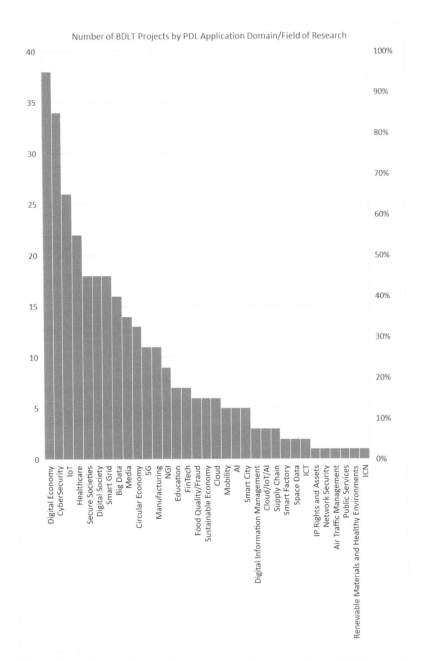

Figure 10.1   Blockchain related projects by application domain or field of research.

Table 10.1 EC H2020 blockchain research topics.

Topic Code	Research Topic	Thematic Priority	H2020 Projects	H2020 EU Contribution
ICT-54-2020	Blockchain for the Next-generation Internet	ICT	3	€ 20 066 094
INNOSUP-03-2018	Blockchain and distributed ledger technologies for SMEs	INNOSUPSME	3	€ 4 493 900
IMI2-2018-15-02	Blockchain-enabled healthcare	HEALTH	1	€ 8 290 694
Total	3/147		7	€ 32 850 688

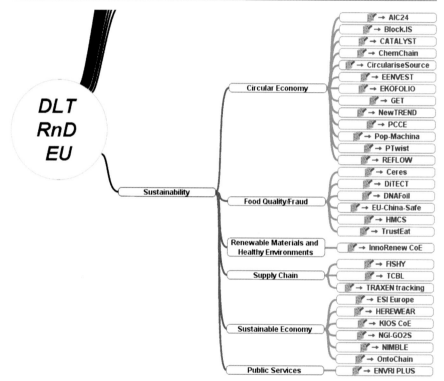

Figure 10.2 Mind map of Horizon 2020 blockchain projects summarized in Annex A of [3].

among other goals, on the use of trustworthy data sources to facilitate zero-touch network management.

Data about different aspects of networking – from infrastructure metrics to the information provided by network functions, measurements of any nature and accounting records – have been collected and utilized for different purposes since the first telecommunications were deployed. The evolution of data technologies has made it possible to increase the number of sources, quality, volume, and detail of data. However, data-enabled network operation and management in multi-party environments such as 5G is not possible without establishing proper roots of trust and enabling secure interoperability when applying data technologies for any particular purpose.

Current trends in the telecommunication industry call for advancements in data-enablement technologies to support zero-touch management, autonomous network operations and the application of AI algorithms, and require a novel operational data platform that is:

- *Open*, so different data sources, processors, and consumers can collaborate on this platform.
- *Dynamic*, so sources, processors and consumers can be added, activated, suspended or deleted on demand.
- *Distributed*, to support the geographical and management span of current networks.
- *Elastic*, to accommodate the vast amount of raw and derived data, alerts and insights.
- *Secure*, properly controlling access according to participant roles and supporting third-party independent audits, while preserving privacy of all participating entities, and especially of end users.
- *Reliable*, to ensure data is trustworthy and relevant, and disallowing fraud data injection into the system.

The 5GZORRO project addresses these requirements by combining three major technology trends: data lakes, AI-based operations (AIOps), and blockchains as a basis for creating its operational data platform.

The Telefónica Group has several companies providing different infrastructure services, both to third parties and internally to support all ICT activities, and it has already identified a growing interest in blockchain-mediated and smart discovery to enhance their IaaS or even PaaS. This also includes disintermediation aspects related to service level conflict resolution, extended auditability and more agile business models.

There are two initiatives that can be considered directly related to the provisioning of trusted data and the explicit application of DLTs in a networking environment. The *Mouseworld* [5] is a framework for the generation of synthetic data to be used in the development and validation of data-enabled network management applications (AI, analytics, etc.), committed to preserve privacy and to guarantee reproducibility and repeatability. *TrustOS* [6] is an abstraction layer for blockchain access built with the aim is of simplifying the development and deployment of blockchain-enhanced edge applications.

10.4 Blockchain Projects in EU Countries

Germany

In 2019 the Federal Government of Germany adopted a comprehensive "Blockchain – Strategy" to strengthen and advance an innovative blockchain ecosystem in Germany further.

The blockchain strategy of the German federal government comprises 44 measures in five priority areas of action to foster the development and scaling of blockchain applications. It entails related strategic investments in these areas to be launched by the end of 2021.

With its blockchain strategy, the German federal government aims to exploit the opportunities offered by the blockchain technology and intends to activate its potentials for driving the digital transformation.

National public funding programs for research projects related to blockchain and DLT have been established among others by the German Federal Ministry of Education and Research [Bundesministerium für Bildung und Forschung (BMBF)]. The BMBF is funding research on blockchain-based verification of university education certificates (blockchain in education).

A recent research funding program of the BMBF, announced in January 2021, is the research funding framework program "Insight – Interdisciplinary perspectives of the societal and technological change" formerly also known as "ITA – Innovations – and Technologies Analysis."

The Insight research framework program is a strategic instrument and has the objective to analyze and evaluate the perspectives and challenges of new societal and technological developments and innovations in order to produce research results relevant for shaping politics and future strategies and policies.

The Insight research program has a holistic approach toward research and the funding comprises besides the scientific and technological aspects of research also ethical, social, legal, economic, and political aspects in order to allow for an impact as well as potential risk assessment of innovative solutions in several dimensions. The Insight program also has a focus on communication and direct participation and involvement of citizens.

The funding is directed toward multi-perspective scientifically interdisciplinary research projects, in order to develop several alternative solution options and recommendations for action, addressing future challenges as well as opportunities of technological and social innovations. In particular, the BMBF will be funding research projects on innovation, with thematic topics application of blockchain, digital education, hydrogen, and impact assessment of social innovation scenarios.

Spain

In Spain, the Government, regulators and prominent entities in the business field have been active to create an ecosystem since around 2017, while avoiding or warning against certain risks on several occasions, e.g., initial coin offerings and digital currencies.

The Spanish National Strategy for Science, Technology and Innovation (EECTI) for the 2021–2027 defines a set of strategic lines, grouped in six wider areas, as the framework for the actions of the Spanish Government to support research and technology development. Two of these areas, titled "Security for Society" and "Digitalization," include mentions to DLT and its applications as matters for research, specifically in three strategic lines: "Cybersecurity," "Artificial Intelligence and Robotics," and "Next-generation Internet."

The Council of University Rectors (CRUE) started in 2019 project BLUE, in collaboration with the public entity for the promotion of the Information Society (Red.es) and the academic network (RedIRIS). The project is focused on the applications of DLT within the academic sector, with special emphasis on academic certifications and lifelong learning support.

The project started by producing a survey on the applicability of these technologies in the university environment and continued with several development projects that are consolidating into a first field trial involving three universities, integrated within the EBSI early adopters program, and planning cross-border pilots before the end of 2021.

The blockchain observatory provided by the business intelligence [7] lists 13 active projects working on DLT, addressing matters related with fintech, energy, legal and compliance, logistics and transportation, documents and traceability, and health.

Alastria, the non-profit association promoting the development of decentralized ledger technologies and participant in ISG PDL, hosts a "project counter" [8] to support research and development initiatives in these areas.

United Kingdom

UK Research Projects on application of PDL/DLT/blockchain/smart contract enabling IoT adoption include the following: The Engineering and Physical Sciences Research Council (EPSRC) [9] is a British Research Council that provides government funding for grants to undertake research and postgraduate degrees in engineering and the physical sciences, mainly to universities in the United Kingdom. EPSRC Projects include: "Accountable Just-in-Time Resource Reservation with Smart Contracts." For instance, King's College London, UK has contributed a paper under this project, on "AJIT: Accountable Just-in-Time Network Resource Allocation with Smart Contracts" [10], which was presented at the MobiArch – 15th Workshop on Mobility in the Evolving Internet Architecture (London, UK, September 25, 2020) [11].

Research England's Connecting Capability Fund (CCF) [12] complements Higher Education Innovation Fund (HEIF) by supporting Higher Education Providers' (HEPs) collaboration in commercialization through competitive projects and formula funds. The CCF aims to share good practice and capacity internally across the higher education sector, forge external technological, industrial and regional partnerships, and deliver the Government's Industrial Strategy priorities. The CCF funds among other projects the Pitch-In "Connecting Capabilities for the Internet of Things" project [13], a research collaboration project between the Universities of Cambridge, Newcastle, Oxford, and Sheffield, UK, which is connecting capabilities to enable the Internet of Things adoption.

BEAT, blockchain-enabled accountable and transparent infrastructure sharing in 6G [14]: BEAT introduces an end-to-end accountable and transparent infrastructure sharing architecture based on blockchains and smart contracts. BEAT enables multi-vendor and multi-operator operations by solving the challenges of a transparent sharing of infrastructure and network resources by means of PDL and smart contracts. A PDL is formed among consortium members owning or wanting access to networking resources. In BEAT, service level agreements (SLAs) are recorded as smart contracts, which automatically record any networking and API flow details to monitor and enforce the SLAs between the consortium members.

AJIT, accountable just-in-time network resource allocation with smart contracts: with the surge in demand for network resources, operators need to cope with this grown demand. In future, more devices are expected to request network services and more often than before, this means operators need an automated system to accommodate these requests. Moreover, the requirement for differentiated services adds an additional challenge. Operators need to rethink current resource allocation methods and should introduce more flexible, short-term, and tailor-made service offerings considering their coverage and capacity, and if and only if they can guarantee the SLA promised.

Providing flexible, dynamic network connectivity along with strict and guaranteed SLAs for millions, probably billions, of devices is not an easy task. This approach will cause substantial management overheads, and customers will need to contact operators more frequently for new service contracts, causing additional staff and operating expenses. Another problem is that SLAs are often opaque to the customer, making it difficult for them to detect an infringement.

AJIT exploits the inherent transparency, automation, and immutability properties of DLT to solve the issues above. Service contracts are deployed as smart contracts on a PDL that records all the service provisioning and can provide an impartial record for SLA accountability. AJIT provides an end-to-end system architecture for dynamic resource provisioning with smart contracts and side channels.

10.5 Blockchain Projects in the USA

Table 10.2 shows an example list of selected ongoing blockchain-related projects in the United States (US), which have been funded by the National Science Foundation (NSF). These projects were funded through various NSF programs such as Faculty Early Career Development (CAREER), Innovation Corps (I-Corps), Networking Technology and Systems (NeTS), Secure and Trustworthy Cyberspace (SaTC), Small Business Innovation Research (SBIR), and Small Business Technology Transfer (STTR).

These projects cover broad technical areas from core technologies (e.g., inter-ledger communications, payment channel networks, scalability, and smart contract) to vertical domains (e.g., cybersecurity, digital economy, digital information management, fintech, healthcare, IoT, and media).

The projects related to blockchain core technologies were funded before the projects about blockchain-enabled vertical domains.

Table 10.2 Example US NSF projects with focus on or related to blockchains.

US NSF AwardProject Name	US NSF Project Starting Date	US NSF Award Factsheet	ISG PDL classification Core Technologies and/or Vertical Domain
Measurement, Analysis, and Novel Applications of Blockchains	2017-02-15	https://www.nsf.gov/awardsearch/showAward?AWD_ID=1651938	Core Technology Applications
Making Blockchains Scale Privately and Reliably	2017-08-15	https://www.nsf.gov/awardsearch/showAward?AWD_ID=1719196	Core Technology Scalability
Towards Privacy and Availability of Inter-blockchain Communication	2019-02-15	https://www.nsf.gov/awardsearch/showAward?AWD_ID=1846316	Core Technology InterLedger
Reducing Claims Denials in Healthcare Through Blockchain and Machine Learning	2019-07-01	https://www.nsf.gov/awardsearch/showAward?AWD_ID=1914203	Vertical Domain Healthcare
The Use of Distributed Ledger Technology in Climate Governance	2019-08-15	https://www.nsf.gov/awardsearch/showAward?AWD_ID=1932220	Vertical Domain Climate
Toward Enforceable Data Usage Control in Cloud-based IoT Systems	2019-10-01	https://www.nsf.gov/awardsearch/showAward?AWD_ID=1916902	Vertical Domain IoT
Blockchain Architectures for Resource-Constrained Devices	2019-10-01	https://www.nsf.gov/awardsearch/showAward?AWD_ID=1937357	Vertical Domain IoT, Healthcare
Network Architecture and Routing Protocols for Payment Channel Networks	2019-10-01	https://www.nsf.gov/awardsearch/showAward?AWD_ID=1910676	Core Technology Payment Channel Networks
Blockchain-Backed Financial Services for Refugees and Migrants	2020-02-01	https://www.nsf.gov/awardsearch/showAward?AWD_ID=1946229	Vertical Domain FinTech

Table 10.2   (Continued.)

US NSF AwardProject Name	US NSF Project Starting Date	US NSF Award Factsheet	ISG PDL classi-fication Core Technolo-gies and/or Ver-tical Domain
Blockchain-backed System that Establishes the Provenance of Digital Images and Videos	2020-06-01	https://www.nsf.gov/awardsearch/showAward?AWD_ID=2011744	Vertical Domain Media
Distributed Ledger Technology as a Security and Tracking Mechanism for Online Gaming	2020-07-01	https://www.nsf.gov/awardsearch/showAward?AWD_ID=2038357	Vertical Domain Media
Automated Support for Writing High-Assurance Smart Contracts	2020-07-01	https://www.nsf.gov/awardsearch/showAward?AWD_ID=1801369	Core Technology Smart Contract
Blockchain-Enabled Machine Learning on Confidential Data	2020-08-01	https://www.nsf.gov/awardsearch/showAward?AWD_ID=2026404	Vertical Domain Digital Information Management
Secure blockchain communication for federal benefit assessments during COVID-19	2020-09-01	https://www.nsf.gov/awardsearch/showAward?AWD_ID=2031813	Vertical Domain Healthcare
Self-Adaptive Cyber Risk Management via Machine to Machine Economy Supported by Blockchain and Smart Contracts Technology	2020-10-01	https://www.nsf.gov/awardsearch/showAward?AWD_ID=2000792	Vertical Domain Digital Economy
Blockchain-based Mechanisms for Timed Data Release and Timed Transactions	2020-10-01	https://www.nsf.gov/awardsearch/showAward?AWD_ID=2020071	Vertical Domain Digital Information Management

US NSF AwardProject Name	US NSF Project Starting Date	US NSF Award Factsheet	ISG PDL classification Core Technologies and/or Vertical Domain
Self-Adaptive Cyber Risk Management via Machine to Machine Economy Supported by Blockchain and Smart Contracts Technology	2020-10-01	https://www.nsf.gov/awardsearch/showAward?AWD_ID=2000792	Vertical Domain Cyber Security

Table 10.2   (Continued.)

References

[1] https://www.etsi.org/deliver/etsi_gr/PDL/001_099/008/01.01.01_60/gr_PDL008v010101p.pdf

[2] https://www.etsi.org/deliver/etsi_gr/PDL/001_099/008/01.01.01_60/gr_PDL008v010101p.pdf

[3] https://www.etsi.org/deliver/etsi_gr/PDL/001_099/008/01.01.01_60/gr_PDL008v010101p.pdf

[4] https://www.5gzorro.eu/

[5] https://torsec.github.io/shield-h2020/documents/scientific-papers/CyberTIM2018_NFV_ML_training.pdf

[6] https://ledgerinsights.com/telefonica-blockchaineuropean-start-ups-free-ai-iot/

[7] https://blockchainintelligence.es/en/map/

[8] https://alastria.io/en/mesa-de-proyectos/

[9] https://epsrc.ukri.org/

[10] https://dl.acm.org/doi/pdf/10.1145/3411043.3412506

[11] http://cosafe.org.uk/mobiarch2020.html

[12] https://re.ukri.org/knowledge-exchange/the-connecting-capability-fund-ccf/

[13] https://pitch-in.ac.uk/

[14] https://ieeexplore.ieee.org/document/9768191

Part III

PDL Blockchain Standards

11

PDL and Application Governance

Part III is central to this book and is specifically dedicated to the standardization approach of ETSI PDL [1]. All chapters in this part of the book exclusively detail the various contributions made by the ETSI PDL Industry Specification Group (ISG) over the years, ever since the inception of the ISG in November 2018. Note that copyright permissions were obtained from ETSI on all content reproduced in this book.

In this chapter, we focus on applications which profit from using permissioned distributed ledgers (PDLs) rather than a non-blockchain or public-ledger implementation. We also discuss important governance issues which need to be addressed and adhered to if applications were to run successfully with PDLs.

11.1 PDL Application Examples

11.1.1 Short recap of PDLs

Given the focus in this part of the book on PDLs, we shall briefly recap the most important concepts from the previous part of the book on blockchain enablers.

As said before in the book, in the most general case, a ledger is a database. A distributed ledger is thus a distributed database that is consensually shared and synchronized across multiple sites, or nodes. The database is typically used through three main interactions:

- *submit* (content from a client/user onto the ledger);
- *validate* (and write onto the ledger the submitted content through a consensus protocol); and
- *read* (the stored content from the ledger).

The content itself has evolved over past years. Initially, only ledger entries could be stored, such as financial transactions, ownership association, etc.

However, with the introduction of Ethereum in 2015, execution logic in form of programming code could be stored too. This has led to the emergence of *smart contracts* and, as of late, decentralized applications (dApps). The role of distributed ledgers is thus evolving from distributed databases that only store data, to distributed contracts which can take programmatic action on stored or submitted data, to distributed applications that can interface with the clients/users when submitting/reading data.

The *writing of content* onto the ledger typically happens in blocks that are cryptographically linked and, once validated, distributed to all nodes across the entire ledger. The cryptographic linkage and spatial distribution, along with a properly designed validation protocol, make the data written onto the ledger immutable. The distributed nature of the ledger ensures that no central authority can alter content, thus making this technology useful in the context of non-trusted parties interacting with each other.

At the core of each distributed ledger technology (DLT) is the *consensus* protocol, which is being carried out by the validators. It has many roles but mainly ensures that a specific ledger entry cannot appear more than once (thus, e.g., preventing the double-spending problem). Different consensus protocols have emerged over past years, such as proof of work (PoW), proof of stake (PoS), proof of elapsed time (PoET), or practical Byzantine fault tolerance (pBFT). They differ in energy efficiency, scale, speed of transactions, among other factors.

Another important aspect is the notion of *public vs. private* ledger. It commonly refers to the degree of anonymity of the validators but also typically extrapolates to the access rights in general, i.e., who can write to and read from the DLT. In the case of a public ledger, validation and access can be done anonymously and by anybody wishing to participate in the ledger. In the case of a private ledger, validation and/or access is restricted to a closed user group such as a consortium (e.g., 10 companies).

Another point to consider is the difference between *permissionless vs. permissioned* DLTs. It defines the degree of trust in the validators which execute the consensus protocol. In a permissionless ledger, anyone can participate in the consensus mechanism; whereas, in a permissioned ledger, only those fulfilling certain requirements can take part in the consensus mechanism. Not all consensus protocols are suitable to all scenarios; for example, permissionless ledgers (such as Bitcoin) would use protocols such as PoW while permissioned ledgers (such as Hyperledger Fabric) may use more energy-efficient protocols such as pBFT.

Initially, solely PDLs were considered as part of ETSI's PDL standard-ization efforts. Subsequent application scenarios, architectures and protocols all pertain to the permissioned mode of running the distributed ledgers.

11.1.2 Industrial PDL applications

Figure 11.1 illustrates an example of a PDL reference use-case scenario, which had been introduced in [2]. The scenario pertains to an agricultural application, which is explained in more detail below.

Consider a farmer of a large set of disaggregated land claiming to only be using natural and organic substances, without any chemical and/or genetically modified substances. To prove these credentials, and thus boosting sales, the farmer decides to join a Bio Certification Alliance. The alliance offers bio certification using a PDL, so as to increase transparency to its alliance governance players, to its farmers and to the end consumer wishing to validate the truthfulness of the bio certificate.

At the farmer's side, this is enabled through a set of Internet of Things (IoT) sensors measuring chemical and other pollution throughout the growth and production process. These sensors have their trusted certification and unique digital identity. They constitute the *client nodes*, which transmit information into the PDL for validation. Said validation is done by means of *validator nodes*. Once validated, the information is immutably written onto the ledger and stored by means of the *ledger nodes*.

The accuracy of the measurements, and thus the credibility of the bio credentials, depends on the quality and accuracy of the IoT devices and the sampling process. This is referred to as "the last mile" problem. It is beyond the scope of ETSI PDL to discuss or solve the last mile problem, but embedding the trusted certification of such IoT devices in the PDL may increase users' trust in the data that these devices collect and store in the PDL.

In the context of a PDL, the validator and ledger nodes typically belong to a consortium where each member may own a prior agreed set of these nodes. Furthermore, each member or a subset of members may offer a set of applications. For instance, a part of the alliance members jointly offers the bio certificate, as long as the sensors in the field support the bio credentials. Another alliance member may offer a smart irrigation service which controls the irrigation system in each of the disaggregated land areas.

Above is enabled through *smart contracts* residing in the PDL. Notably, the logic of the smart contract will issue a positive certification flag only when all sensors from each of the fields report adherence to bio credentials.

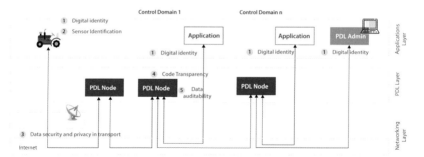

Figure 11.1   Example of a PDL reference use-case scenario in an agricultural setting [3].

The logic can be programmed to perform that check at regular intervals, or be updated when new data from the sensors in the field arrives. Equally, the irrigation smart contract will trigger the water valves to be opened when moisture falls below a certain level across a prior agreed set of nodes. Other interesting conditions can be baked in, such as only switching on irrigation when the water price is below a certain threshold (unless irrigation is critical to the survival of the crop). Note that such conditions may be specific for bio credentials (e.g., detection of chemicals) while others may be general (e.g., water cost optimization).

11.1.3 Retail and wholesale PDL applications

PDL-based *retail applications* are offered to end users who may be employees of a company using the application to perform their day-to-day job or individuals using the application for their own personal use. Retail PDL applications may be made available to end users through a wholesale supply chain or by a single supplier. The users would typically access and communicate with the application through a graphical user interface.

The application will typically communicate with the PDL platform through the API and tooling abstraction layer, though it may as well interface with the PDL platform directly. A PDL-based mobile wallet would be the immediate example of a retail application. On the backend such wallet will use the PDL to store value/balance of users' accounts and may also serve to identify users through KYC. On the front-end, the wallet applications will allow the user to view their balance, initiate and approve transactions, as well as perform other user facing capabilities.

Wholesale applications, on the other hand, are offered and used by wholesale stakeholders as part of a supply chain, forming an alliance of organizations/entities participating in the PDL platform. In a wholesale environment, the participating entities may use the APIs and tooling layer to manage the PDL platform and run decentralized applications eliminating the need for a top-level orchestrator/intermediator. PDL serves as a trusted source of truth eliminating the need of a top-level "honest broker." PDL may also serve to exchange value between entities simplifying the complex bank-based fiat transactions, and eliminating the costs associated with Society for Worldwide Interbank Financial Telecommunications (SWIFT) settlements.

In certain scenarios, a PDL may also be used to eliminate the loss of goods as it will immediately identify where in the supply chain goods recorded as delivered from one entity to another are not recorded as received by the other party.

A wholesale application may serve retail applications and may do so in a manner that is transparent to the retail customer. An example would be supply chain management of a mobile shopping web site, where the retail customer interface hides the wholesale supply chain through which the goods are offered and the payment routes for such goods. Goods may be sold through a third party but appear to the consumer as though they are being sold locally. Additionally, the retail customer may be roaming internationally but may still enjoy a shopping experience as if they were shopping on their home network. On the wholesale side – the supply chain handles the resell of goods between vendors and the exchange and distribution of funds received from the retail customer. A wholesale application should also handle commercial aspects of supply chain management such as mark-up, invoicing and settlement.

One example would be the decentralized trustworthy network infrastructure (a work item developed as part of ITU-T SG13), where Internet service providers (ISPs) participate in the ledger to manage trustworthy Internet resource (including IP address, autonomous system (AS) number, and domain name) ownership, and resource mapping [e.g., IP-to-AS mapping for border gateway protocol (BGP) security, and domain-name-to-IP mapping for domain name system (DNS) security]. This consistent trustworthy data on the ledger is then distributed to other components in the network. In the BGP case, the IP-to-AS mapping data is directly downloaded to BGP routers, which is not aware of the ledger. In the DNS case, since the DNS client may not fully trust the DNS resolver, the client may also participate in the ledger (as a lightweight verification client) to verify the resolution result returned by the resolver.

Inter-application *interoperability between retail and wholesale* is important where such interaction does not necessitate that both the retail and wholesale applications use the same PDL, nor does it require that they both use the same PDL-type. It does require, however, that the unit of value being transacted by the retail application matches the unit of value recorded/transacted on the associated wholesale application.

For instance, when a consumer is purchasing 1 kilogram of tomatoes in a grocery store using a PDL-based wallet, the grocer's wholesale supply chain management PDL platform should record that 1 kilogram of tomatoes was sold and should be able to track the route of those tomatoes from the field to the consumer. Such an arrangement may be used to offer the consumer proof of origin of the tomatoes (e.g., organic, or date of picking).

Note that the interface between PDL-based wholesale and retail applications had not been formalized nor standardized at the time of writing this book.

11.1.4 PDL smart contract applications

As explained in Part II of this book, smart contracts provide a mechanism to automate contractual processes, track the contract executions, and provide accountability in the contractual process. There are several ways and solutions where smart contracts can be applied to achieve the goals mentioned above, and some of them are highlighted here.

In the *telecommunications sector*, for instance, there are a number of ways a digital service provider and a customer (business or individual) engage in contracts. For example, home mobile provider and visited mobile provider have contracts for roaming services; the services consumed by the customer in the visited location is recorded and sent by the visited provider to the home provider. Smart contracts can automate this procedure by enabling service providers to create smart contracts for such digital services; as soon as the visiting customer consumes the network services of the visited operator, the corresponding smart contract is activated and enables instant settlement between the host and the visited provider including the availability of the credit and payments.

Furthermore, mobile operators may not offer the same consistent performance; factors such as congestion in the area and day/time impact the performance. This may result in a violation of the SLA between the user and the service provider. In situations where the mobile operators cannot provide the required QoS, possibly due to the congestion, customers may consider getting the services from other operators who offer a service guarantee.

These provisions need automation and transparency: the customer wants to get the services instantly and automatically. In the scenarios where QoS is of paramount importance (e.g., services for life-relying activities such as remote surgery), strict SLAs are expected to be honored. If the violation happens, the customer is notified (transparency) and potentially compensated.

Smart contracts can help to achieve these targets and provide a contractual framework in an untrusted environment. This is achieved through logging of SLA and performance data on a PDL, and applying a smart contract to calculate the actual performance against the targets and automatically calculate the penalties according to the SLA where applicable. Penalties can be automatically reduced from the invoice on the next billing cycle.

Automated machinery such as tractors and solar farms are equipped with sensors; these sensors transmit the device data such as engine readings or battery life to the cloud or command center, where this information is processed to make future decisions such as capacity planning. Such systems are vulnerable to eavesdropping, replication, and man-in-the-middle attack. The attacker can pretend to be a legitimate device and send erroneous or incorrect data to the command center, and the valid user can be blamed for sending false/fake information.

Such attacks can be mitigated using smart contracts which are installed on the ledger. While transmitting the sensor data, the unique identifier of the sensor and the data is recorded as part of smart contract execution, allowing the identity of the sensor to be verified. It is expected that data is sent in a quantum-safe encryption to mitigate man-in-the-middle attack and eavesdropping.

Automated auctions are found in almost every field – for example, telecom regulators auction bandwidths to operators. Smart contracts can help automate this process in such a way that the bandwidth contract is installed on a PDL with predefined parameters. An auction starts and ends with predefined time, and all the bids are recorded in a PDL. This process becomes transparent to all the parties preventing dishonesty, both by the bidder and the auctioneers. These bids can be tailored for specific needs for visibility and automated auctioning.

Smart contracts may be used as a *mechanism for access control*; as by definition, they execute automatically, all the access information (e.g., user credentials) can be recorded in a PDL. For example, a smart contract can be executed when some access rights are granted by a PDL-based certification authority. This may prevent the future disputes of the data breach and provide a record of all the information exchange and key distribution.

In a related example, certificate authorities (CAs) are trusted by the users, and it is possible for malicious parties to act as a CA and issue fake certificates. This can cause users to trust malicious websites and share their personal records and bank information with them. This problem can be mitigated with PDLs by distributing trust between a group of users rather than a single entity and the corresponding system can be compromised only when more than 50% (or any higher threshold set by the governance) nodes are malicious. As soon as user credentials are allocated, the respective smart contract can be executed, and all the relevant information for the certificate is recorded.

These credentials may be used to access the controlled data or records (e.g., PDL data). Since the credentials are issued by the group of users in a PDL and their integrity is backed by a transparent mechanism, they can be trusted. Also, it is difficult for malicious users to act as a CA because PDLs are managed by a group of nodes, and all the records (such as public keys) are transparent. The users can thus verify the integrity of a website with the PDL.

Smart contracts can provide a mechanism for accessing data from a foreign ledger, by distributing authorized keys to the authenticated participants only. In this way, the participants will not need to ask for access keys repeatedly; the key distribution is recorded via smart contract to a PDL enabling the records to be updated automatically and transparent to all PDL members. This facilitates the future audit of access records.

11.2 PDL Governance and Operations

11.2.1 The need for governance

Permissionless ledgers, such as Bitcoin, are governed through the open-source code that runs them. PDLs, on the other hand, may use less stringent verification of transactions, and distribute tokens to participants without the need to spend resources for PoW or PoS. Solid governance is then required in order to manage and operate the PDL.

The functions governance should perform throughout the lifecycle of a PDL would be i) selectively admitting new participants into the platform and granting read/write privileges; ii) managing software development and deployment terms and conditions; and iii) establishing guidance, rules, policies and processes for operating the PDL.

As illustrated in Figure 11.2, a PDL goes through three major lifecycle phases:

1. *Creation of the genesis block and initialization of the PDL*: This is a static phase that happens once. It includes the inception of the governing

Lifecycle Phases of PDLs

Figure 11.2 Illustration of the lifecycle phases of a PDL: Creation & Initialization (left), Dynamic Evolvement (middle), Termination (right).

rules that would then apply to all PDL stakeholders in the respective environment. Such rules can be embedded into the code that runs the PDL or may be added as a smart contract.

2. *Evolvement phase*: This is a dynamic phase through which the blocks are appended to the PDL under the consensus mechanism in convention, the PDL (optionally) forks to sub-chains or side chains, smart contracts are (optionally) added and other. In the event that the consensus mechanism needs to be changed to a new one or other enhancement measures need to take place based on governance requirements, such changes will be agreed upon through consensus.

3. *Termination*: This is a static phase where the PDL is decomposed. In certain cases, termination may require specific actions to be taken, such as surrendering all records to a certain jurisdiction or other actions in compliance with respective regulations.

11.2.2 Governance methods and structure

Governance covers four contexts:

1. *Data*: Governance of the information stored in the PDL that is aligned and adapted to the lifecycle stages of the PDL in compliance with privacy and other regulations.

2. *Protocol*: Governance defines the rules and protocols governing the behavior and alterations of the PDL during the lifecycle of the PDL.

3. *Application*: Governance defines and ensures compliance with the rules for changes, maintenance and how different applications operate and interact with the PDL and guides how applications are terminated.

4. *Institutional*: The governance defines how the PDL co-exists and inter-operates with the organizational functions related to decision rights, accountability and incentives.

As stated in the previous paragraph, permissionless ledgers would typically be managed through publicly known validation rules and the associated (open-source) code. PDLs, on the other hand, are off-chain or on-chain governed.

Off-chain governance requires a governing body that could be: a) a group of selected representatives from the PDL membership (this group may also include *all* members of the PDL); b) an external panel/board of experts; or c) a mix of both.

The governing body may be appointed or elected or may consist of a mix of appointed and elected members. Election of board members can be based on seniority (e.g., senior members' vote weights more) or size (e.g., weight of vote is proportional to turnover or headcount of the voting member), or could be based on a single and equal vote per member.

On-chain governance differs in that IT systems allow to perform certain characteristics and dependencies of the PDL governance on-chain. On-chain governance requires a different approach that governs the adoption of automated functions and associated processes according to the degree of de-centralization. In particular there are dimensions such as decision rights, accountability, incentives, which are perfectly performed on-chain with the properties of immutability, transparency, and administration of the PDL.

11.2.3 Governing the governance

Governance involves the delicate task of both generating the rules and enforcing them. When bootstrapping a PDL based platform, it is recommended that measures are taken to prevent a hostile takeover of the governing body in a manner that can lead to irreversible consequences. Governance, in blockchain and DLT, is in principle affected by three factors:

1. *Governing roles*: Roles that maintain security, robustness, availability, efficiency, continuity and accountability. Management of governing roles could be implemented through automated processes or by an external governing body defining the operational principles of the PDL.

2. *Target audience and developer accountability*: A DLT can be public or private, each of which may separately apply to write privileges (users who may add records to a PDL) and read privileges (users who may only read records already on the PDL). The target audience is

indirectly governed by targeting a specific audience, and methods can be applied to exclude certain (unwanted) audiences. Developer accountability can be governed through unified incident mechanism and auditability principles.

3. *Permission structure*: Governance can be applied through choice of permission structure between permissionless or permissioned. PDL is, by definition, a permissioned environment.

There are also governance mechanisms with hybrid consensus or multi-protocol environments, which in essence inherit principles from above three fundamentals for a particular purpose.

11.2.4 PDL stakeholders

A PDL application may involve one or more of the below stakeholders:

- **End users**:
  - Humans, i.e., individuals or groups of people that use a PDL application.
  - Machines, e.g., an application accessing a PDL without human intervention.

- **Platform operators**:
  - PDL, i.e., a PDL can operate autonomously during certain phases of its lifecycle.
  - Management (e.g., governance, board, etc.), i.e., PDL may be managed through an internal/external governance structure.
  - Auditor/monitor, i.e., PDL may be monitored and audited for purposes.

- **Software vendors**:
  - PDL developers. Software vendors who develop PDLs.
  - Application developers. Software vendors who develop applications that use PDLs.

- **Infrastructure vendors**:
  - Cloud vendors providing cloud infrastructure used to host PDL nodes or store PDL data.
  - Connectivity:
  - Fixed operators providing fixed/physical infrastructure used to convey information between PDL nodes, applications and users.

– Mobile operators providing wireless/mobile infrastructure used to convey information between PDL nodes, applications and users.

• **Regulatory and governance authorities**:

  – Regulator, i.e., an entity or individual that regulates the behavior of a PDL during its lifecycle.
  – Legislator, i.e., an entity or individual that defines the rules and legal terms that a PDL applies to.
  – Auditor/monitor, i.e., an entity or individual that audits/monitors the behavior and activity of a PDL and indicates if a PDL is operating normally or not.
  – Authenticator, i.e., an individual or entity that authenticates validity of actions or other entities/individuals.

• **Business ownership and management**:

  – Standard bodies, i.e., industry associations or collaborative groups that are recognized as standard defining organizations.

11.2.5 General governance considerations

In here, we wish to discuss a few important general governance issues, such as cybersecurity, incentives, identity, etc.

In terms of *cybersecurity*, whilst it can be implemented as an application by itself (e.g., via firewall), very general security aspects need to be considered in the context of PDLs:

• Access control: The ability to restrict access to or use of an application based on criteria such as identity, payment method and balance, and location.
• Transaction security: The ability to preserve confidentiality of information during execution of a transaction and the ability to prevent malicious or unintended execution of a transaction.
• Fraud prevention: The ability to identify and mitigate fraudulent transactions.

Blockchain in general and PDL in particular are considered secure protocols. However, they are not hermetically sealed against fraud or malicious acts. The weak spot with respect to PDLs are the following consensus-based attacks [4]:

1. The 51% attack: There is a risk that nodes that constitute a majority according to the consensus method will collaborate to bias records or

record transaction priority breaching the integrity of the PDL. This is sometimes associated with bribery attacks – trying to buy votes in one's favor [5].

2. Identity theft: If one's access information/details such as private key is acquired or stolen, all the assets this person owns in the PDL will be compromised, and it can be nearly impossible to identify the thief. In PDLs, the information being compromised may include company records of multiple participants in the PDL, across entities. PDLs may not be tamper proof but rather tamper resistant.

3. Impersonation fraud: In absence of sufficient KYC or verification of identity procedures on a PDL, identity can be impersonated, exposing threats similar to those of identity theft or others that could affect the PDL and the network's reputation. Such actions may be considered criminal depending on jurisdiction.

Other concerns pertain to system hacks, i.e., while PDL data may be very difficult to hack and alter, the nodes and the code they execute are vulnerable to hacks and DDoS attacks. In addition to that, PDL data that is transported through public internet is vulnerable to eavesdropping. System security (e.g., mitigations of DDoS attacks through KYC) should be applied to mitigate such threats.

Important to note are illegal activities, notably:

a) It is possible that some participants of PDL issue transactions which are of illegal nature and in breach of certain laws. This problem is not specific to PDL, but the cryptographic nature of blockchains in permissionless environments. Policies and preventive activities implemented in a PDL should identify and mitigate such activities.

b) Different jurisdictions may have different laws. PDLs may be used to execute transactions that may be legal in one country and illegal in another. When PDL nodes span across multiple jurisdiction it is not straightforward to define under which law a PDL operates. Thus, such actions may even be considered a-legal (subject to no law at all) and unregulated.

In terms of *economic incentives*, one of the key benefits of PDL is improved economic management. This is often evidenced in reduction of operational cost (HR, security, gear), acceleration (shortening of identity verification and contract negotiation timelines, automation of processes). However, in many cases it can also be realized through an increase in revenue from existing services/applications and from an ability to yield new revenues through the introduction of new services and applications that would be difficult to realize in absence of PDL technology.

In terms of *operational incentives*, PDL is often implemented as a replacement to complex platforms that may include multiple inter-dependent systems. PDLs provide accountability, i.e., all the transactions are recorded hence, can be verified later. The level and confidentiality details of information to be recorded depend on the consensus mechanism, security and other operational factors.

It has been demonstrated through several proof of concepts (PoCs) that a few lines of code embedded in a smart contract can replace the functionality of entire systems. This ensures cost savings, simplification and acceleration of existing processes.

In terms of *disintermediation*, the industry as a whole and the wholesale supply chain in particular, could benefit from disintermediation. The telecommunications industry, as an example, has a long history of operation in an equal-level playing field of federated operators. Telecom services such as international voice traffic and the public internet operate in absence of a centralized intermediating or controlling entity.

Distributed ledgers, both permissioned and permissionless, operate in a similar self-managed manner with no hierarchy of a top-level entity. There are certain wholesale supply chain applications that rely on intermediaries (e.g., in the telecom world: mobile settlements) and PDL has the potential to replace such intermediaries by establishing trust between parties without the need for a trusted third party.

Last but not least, in terms of *identity sovereignty*, it can be self-declared or obtained through a governed KYC process. KYC processes serve as sufficient proof that the identity of an entity (human, company, machine, etc.) is indeed what it claims to be.

Self-sovereignty is common in permissionless environments but otherwise discouraged or completely forbidden in permissioned environments such as PDLs.

11.3 PDL Reference Framework

11.3.1 PDL reference architecture

In order to provide a basis for discussing various PDL application scenarios, an abstract, simplified, reference framework and functional diagram has been defined in ETSI PDL [6].

Figure 11.3 illustrates the three abstract layers that appear in most PDL implementations. They are discussed here one by one, as well as their relations and dependencies.

The applications and services layer represents the actual customer/consumer facing application, be that an individual consumer accessing the PDL platform through a portal or an application, or another platform/device accessing the PDL platform through an API. Depending on the PDL type, an application can be implemented as a smart contract, as an external code/application (which may be platform or operating system specific; e.g., mobile phone, desktop computer, IoT device, etc.) or as a mix of both.

Note that ETSI PDL does not specify the applications themselves or the methods by which they interface (northbound) with the customer/consumer. Applications would require exchange of information with the PDL platform itself, possibly more than one PDL, through a southbound interface. Such PDLs may be developed and operated by different entities.

APIs and tooling layer allow interaction between the applications/services and the PDLs. This layer is referenced by ISO as the *API layer*. For consistency, ETSI PDL follows the term used by the EU Blockchain Observatory and Forum. This layer allows abstraction of the PDL platform and application layers in a manner that may allow applications to operate on more than one PDL type and vice-versa. This layer consists of consoles, dashboards, and development environments made available to developers, institutional users, auditors and regulators.

The *PDL platform layer* contains the PDL nodes as well as smart contracts, management and governance tools, and other software elements that are embedded into code running on the PDL nodes. The PDL platform may use any of the multitude of PDL types available at the time and may use governance and management tools that are compatible/interoperable with said PDL type.

In certain scenarios, specifically when the application is embedded into the PDL platform (e.g., as a smart contract) and the users interface the PDL platform layer directly, the application and/or API layers may not be required. Some examples are:

1. Scheduled actions taken without external intervention occur on the PDL platform layer and do not require the API and application layers.
2. A smart contract on a PDL platform that can be accessed through an API via a third-party application (e.g., a digital wallet) that is not part of the PDL platform itself.

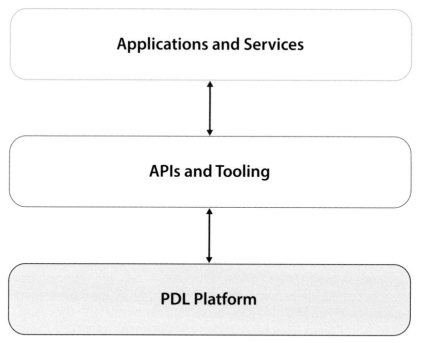

Figure 11.3 Abstract PDL reference framework.

11.3.2 Expanding the PDL reference architecture

The PDL platform architecture discussed above can be enhanced by additional governance and management functionalities as depicted in Figure 11.4.

The major difference between the abstract diagrams depicted in Figures 11.3 and 11.4 is the separation of the infrastructure from the PDL platform, and the addition of a management and governance support functionality. The platform is managed and governed through various methods, which may vary by PDL types, consensus mechanisms, and applications.

Platform management and governance support: This functionality allows the continued operation of the entire platform by ensuring resources are available, governance requirements are met, and the PDL is operating in good order (e.g., no forks, a sufficient number of validating nodes are in operation, etc.).

Governance can be implemented in multiple forms. In certain scenarios it can be implement through a hierarchical structure where a top-level entity governs the behavior of the lower levels. In other scenarios, there may be

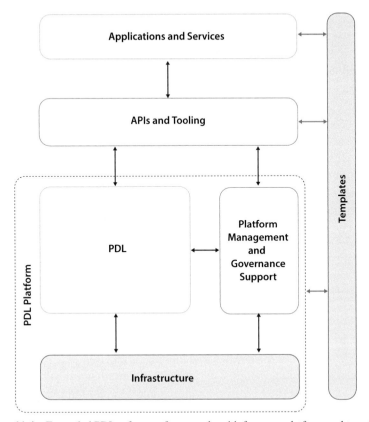

Figure 11.4 Expanded PDL reference framework, with focus on platform and templates.

no hierarchy, and governance is applied through consensus between equal-level entities. There are also hybrid models in existence where a human board of elected or appointed directors defines the rules of operation and the governance structure implements the same.

Infrastructure: PDL platforms require computing, storage and communication infrastructure. The computing resources would typically be off-the-shelf blades, and in most cases can be implemented as virtual machines (VMs) or containers in private or public clouds. It is worth mentioning here that certain permissionless distributed ledgers require that the node is owned and operated in-house by its user. This is not necessarily the case for permissioned distributed ledgers. Such nodes can, subject to regulations and respective policies, be operated in public clouds. Storage requirements depend on the choice of PDL, as well as the requirements of the applications.

PDL platforms today typically use best-effort networks such as the public Internet as the means of communication between nodes and between users to the PDL platform. Future scenarios may introduce the need for managed communications between nodes in order to ensure predictable and secured performance.

Templates: Certain core and common functionalities, such as identity, smart contracts, assurance, are defined as templates that may be re-used and integrated with repetition in multiple instances and aspects. Templates are ready-to-use PDL implementations or functionalities that can be applied as needed. They may be implemented in multiple layers. This is a useful functionality that may serve, in certain scenarios, as a presumption of conformity with certain guidelines, requirements or specifications. Templates are not specific to a given PDL. Examples of templates would be: cybersecurity-type approval for a vehicle, security and privacy specifications for data storage, and commercial reconciliation rules for bilateral settlement. The identity of a person or an entity may be used in multiple applications and will preferably be presented in a common way regardless of the application and ledger.

11.3.3 PDL platform abstraction layers

PDL platform abstraction layers: Most existing PDL implementations are packaged as a bundle that includes all layers. For certain applications this is the preferred approach for various operational and security reasons. Looking ahead, there may be a growing number of PDL implementations that abstract the application from the underlying PDL and allow implementing an application on multiple PDL type. It is obvious that a specific implementation by a specific group of entities will use the same PDL type across all participants; however, a similar implementation of that same application by another group of entities may use a different PDL type.

That is illustrated in Figure 11.5, where the remaining entities will be discussed in subsequent sections.

11.3.4 PDL infrastructure layer

ICT verticals: The PDL infrastructure is built on three vertical families of components. Those verticals are depicted in Figure 11.6. It is beyond the scope of ETSI PDL to discuss the commercial and operational aspects of implementation and integration of those components into a PDL.

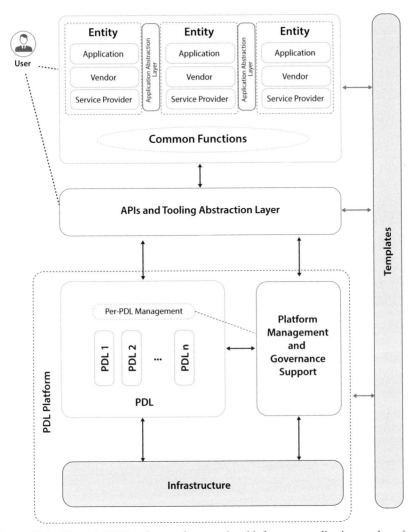

Figure 11.5 Expanded PDL reference framework, with focus on applications and services.

Connectivity vertical: Connectivity provides the ability to move data from place to place. The nodes participating a PDL are typically connected with a peer-to-peer (P2P) network over a secured IP protocol. In its simplest and easiest form, one may choose to use the public internet; however, this raises performance and security concerns. Dedicated connectivity options – such as leased lines or quality-managed virtual private networks (VPNs) – offer a more secure and predictable alternative but introduce commercial

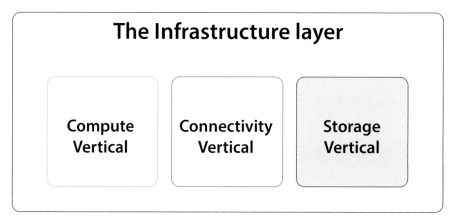

Figure 11.6   The PDL infrastructure layer.

and operational overheads. There are some aspects that the connectivity infrastructure should provide to the ledger:

- *Accessibility*: Once a node is allowed to the ledger (e.g., via access control), the node is able to discover and connect to other nodes.
- *Availability*: The nodes participating in a ledger may locate in a cloud environment (e.g., in a same data center or even in a same local area network), or reside elsewhere and be connected through wide area networks. In either case, the P2P network needs to guarantee the availability for the connectivity.
- *Integrity*: The connectivity infrastructure may encounter malicious behavior, e.g., BGP hijack, DNS hijack, and TCP hijack. The infrastructure needs to continue guaranteeing the integrity of the communication data under these attacks or faults.
- *Confidentiality*: The connectivity may encounter interception. The communication data should be kept confidential under interception.
- *Quality*: Some application scenarios may require high-bandwidth and low-latency connectivity, to accelerate consensus or enhancing throughput of the ledger. To this end, the connectivity can use secure end-to-end protocols [e.g., Internet Protocol Security (IPSec), Transport Layer Security (TLS)] for endpoint authentication, and data integrity and confidentiality. A secure key-exchange mechanism is required in advance. The P2P network should provide robust connectivity, and infrastructure may need to defend against hijack and DDoS attacks and protect

from network faults. Resource reservation may be used for quality of service.

Compute vertical: Compute is the act of performing computations on data. That would be the PDL Nodes and other devices performing management and governance tasks. Computations require a computing device, either a dedicated computer or a virtual resource such as a VM or a container in a cloud. The following issues ought to be considered:

- *Jurisdiction*: Depending on application and regulation, the physical location of a node may be restricted to certain jurisdictions. For instance, certain countries may demand that the nodes that process personal information of its citizens be located within the geographical borders of that country.
- *Privacy and confidentiality*: Certain entities (e.g., banks) would only allow nodes to operate within their own facilities and will not allow use of nodes in the public cloud. Otherwise, encryption may be mandated to avoid data leaks.
- *Availability*: It is expected that the nodes participating in a ledger offer guarantees for availability in a manner that matches or exceeds the requirements of the applications they serve. Certain applications may require a failover device ready for immediate activation.
- *Integrity and security*: The compute infrastructure may encounter malicious behavior, e.g., DDoS attacks. The infrastructure needs to continue guaranteeing the integrity of the compute service under these attacks.
- *Compute device characteristics*: It is expected that the compute device meets or exceeds characteristics (e.g., CPU type, operating system, memory, etc.) required by the application and PDL type.

Storage vertical: Storage may be local, remote, distributed or centralized, and encrypted. PDL is distributed and decentralized by definition. The following ought to be considered:

- *Per-node storage*: Even though each node stores its own copy of the PDL data, the data storage itself does not necessarily need to be on the same node as the compute device. Data may be stored on a directly connected storage device or on a network attached storage (NAS) device.
- *Off-chain storage*: Depending on design and requirements, some chains contain all information always available, others allow off-chain storage of dated information and offer methods to retrieve off-chain information as well as verify its validity when required. Depending on the application

and volume of data processed, as well as the cost of storage and speed of access to off-chain data, one may choose a storage option that fits its purpose.

- *Jurisdiction*: Similar to physical location of compute nodes, depending on application and regulation, the physical location of a storage device may be restricted to certain jurisdictions.
- *Privacy and confidentiality*: Certain entities (e.g., banks) would only allow data to be stored within their own facilities and will not allow data storage in the public cloud.
- *Availability*: It is expected that network storage devices offer guarantees for availability in a manner that matches or exceeds the requirements of the applications they serve.
- *Integrity and security*: The network data storage infrastructure is subject to both device-related and network-related risks. The infrastructure needs to mitigate such risks.
- *Storage characteristics*: Storage is characterized by volume, replication options, transfer rates and speed of access. It is expected that storage devices used in a PDL meet or exceed the requirements of the respective applications.A typical application will use a mix of compute, storage, and connectivity functions to deliver its intended functionality. An example for such a mix would be a PDL application which requires storage, but also requires connectivity to convey data between the nodes as well as between storage facilities, and compute resources in order to manage user credentials, security, consumption, billing, etc. In certain scenarios, the platform management functionality may manage the resources in the infrastructure layer.

11.3.5 Legacy integration issues

This section describes functions and concepts that are common across specific horizontal layers within the architecture defined above. Similarities and differences between a legacy centralized database and a PDL are discussed.

Legacy ledgers: They are centrally managed even though they may be distributed physically and geographically for resiliency purposes. Such legacy ledgers are owned by an entity that may be the same one using the ledger, or a third party operating a ledger used by another entity or entities.

The key feature of a legacy ledger is there is only a single entity operating the ledger and being responsible for the integrity of the information. A PDL, on the other hand, is not only physically and geographically distributed, but it is also managed in a distributed manner. In most cases there is no single entity managing all nodes in a PDL, even though certain entities may each manage more than a single node in a PDL and in certain cases all PDL nodes are managed by a single entity.

The integrity of the information in a PDL is managed through programming all nodes to use the same code, the same software release, and the same smart contracts. A consensus algorithm is expected to detect any node that uses an outdated software release or an outdated smart contract, or contains incorrect data. It is expected to eliminate the use of such nodes until updated and aligned with the consenting majority.

Consensus mechanisms: The most noticeable difference between DLTs is the consensus mechanism used to verify transactions and ensure the integrity of the chain. Consensus mechanisms vary in the algorithm used and in the rigorousness of tests required to verify a transaction.

While in a permissionless distributed ledger the consensus mechanism should be very rigorous and should ensure there is a cost to fraudulent activity that is much higher than the possible gain from such activity, in a permissioned distributed ledger the entities operating the nodes would typically have a common purpose and have a responsibility and an interest to maintain the integrity of the chain and a motivation to avoid malicious activity.

Thus, the consensus mechanisms in such scenarios may use less rigorous methods to reach consensus. As an example, in a permissionless ledger a node has to "prove" it has done work, or has put funds at stake, that it will lose if it acts maliciously. In a PDL, nodes do not necessarily need to put anything at stake and may not be financially penalized if a record is compromised, as it is assumed that there were no malicious intentions. Consensus may then be reached through a reduced list of delegates where most nodes are simply transacting and delegate the consensus management to a select (voluntary or elected) list of validating nodes.

Whilst some consensus mechanisms have been discussed in Part I of this book, it is beyond the scope of ETSI PDL to list all algorithms currently in the market, and new algorithms keep being developed and introduced. Suffice to say that in a PDL there is typically a "double-safety" mechanism as there is the inherent tamper-resistance of the consensus mechanism and the mutual responsibility of the permitted validating nodes for the operation of the PDL; while in a permissionless distributed ledger the consensus mechanism is in fact the only means to prevent tampering with the information since nodes operate under mutual suspicion.

Basic blockchain operations: Basic blockchain operations include:

- *Capture data transactions*: The PDL captures a data transaction, or a group of transactions, or pieces of information, and packages them into a block. The minimal and maximal size of such block varies by PDL type. The data may or may not be encrypted. There is no restriction as to the source of such information or transactions, though the accurate capture of such information, sometimes referred to as "the last mile problem," may have significant influence on the quality and value of the PDL.
- *Hashing the block*: Once a block is generated, a hash is generated from the sum of its contents. Hashes are created using the SHA256 or similar algorithms which are considered to be safe (taking into consideration that some hashes, such as SHA-1, have been compromised).

While it is possible (though with extremely low probability) that two completely different blocks will yield identical hashes, it is even less likely that a change of even only a few bits or bytes of data within a certain block will generate the same hash.

As a result, once a block is hashed its integrity can be easily verified by repeating the hash (no matter if the information in the block is encrypted or not). If the hash produces the same result, then the block can be considered untampered. If the hash produces a different result, one should suspect that the block has been tampered with and may not contain the exact same information that was stored therein when it was originally created and hashed.

- *Chaining blocks*: Blocks are chained to each other by including the hash of one block as part of the data of the next block. This creates a link and a dependency between consecutive blocks in a chain. If a block that is even a few links deep in the chain is tampered with, it will invalidate all subsequent links. Though it is theoretically (and practically) possible to keep altering the data in a tampered block in hope of finding a combination that yields the same hash, or otherwise re-hash all subsequent blocks so as to hide the tampered block, the computational resources and time required to perform such act without being noticed makes blockchains tamper-resistant.
- *Reading data from blocks*: The information stored in blocks can be accessed, read and decrypted by entities that have access to the chain. In a PDL such access is restricted to permitted entities. Encrypted records within a block will require an encryption key that may be provided by the entity that has encrypted that record.

Other blockchain operations: In addition to the basic functions described above, PDLs offer additional functionalities:

- *Smart contracts*: Smart contracts are computer programs stored in a DLT, wherein the outcome of any execution of the program is recorded on the DLT. A smart contract may present terms in a contract in law and create a legally enforceable obligation under the legislation of an applicable jurisdiction. Smart contracts are discussed in a subsequent chapter.
- *Zero knowledge proof (ZKP)*: ZKP is the ability to prove something without having to reveal the information that such proof is based upon. ZKP may require extensive computational resources but is a useful tool in environments where competing entities use a shared resource.
- Forks: See below for a more in-depth discussion on this important topic.

Blockchain forks: Forks are defined by ITU as "creation of two or more different versions of a distributed ledger" [*ITU-T Technical Specification FG DLT D1.1 Distributed ledger technology terms and definitions, Definition number 6.22, "Fork"*]. Forks occur when a blockchain diverges into two potential paths forward. Forks may be intentional or incidental, hard or soft [*ITU-T Technical Specification FG DLT D1.1 Distributed ledger technology terms and definitions, Definition number 6.25, "Hard Fork"*]:

- *Incidental forks*: Incidental forks occur when two entities append a block (each appending a different block) to the chain creating two different chains in the same PDL. The result is that different nodes in the PDL may contain different chains. This is a situation that needs to be avoided.
- *Intentional forks*: Intentional forks are the result of a change in the rules that govern the PDL. Such change of rules could be the result of a software upgrade or a change to a smart contract that governs the behavior of the chain. The result of an intentional fork would be similar to that of an incidental fork: different nodes in the PDL may contain different chains.
- *Hard forks*: Hard forks are such that when a change to the protocol or rules that applies to one branch result in that branch becoming backward incompatible with the other branch of the chain.
- *Soft forks*: Soft forks are such that when a change to the protocol or rules that applies to one branch result in that branch remaining backward compatible with the other branch of the chain.

There are numerous methods to handle forks (intentional and incidental) and it is beyond the scope of ETSI PDL to define this further. Suffice to say that there are two possible solutions: i) one of the chains is continued and the other one is discarded, ending up with a single chain used by all nodes; and ii) the fork becomes permanent generating two separate chains, each used by a subset of the nodes.

Data storage and privacy concerns: Data integrity and privacy are a major concern in any platform used for storage and retrieval of data. The distributed nature of PDL, where data is duplicated in multiple nodes, poses an increased concern from multiple aspects.

- *Competition*: A PDL may be used by competing entities, which results in confidential information of one competitor being stored in a node maintained and owned by another competitor. The solution to such concern would be encryption of the information prior to creating the block, thus preventing unauthorized access. The inherent tamper resistance of PDL ensures an owner of a node cannot tamper information stored on their node. An example would be storage of confidential financial information of an entity in a PDL that has a node operated by a competitor of that entity.

- *Geography*: Certain administrations regulate the geographical spread of information and may not allow nodes to be operated at certain locations. As an example, many countries do not allow personal identification information to be stored or even transported outside the borders of their country. As a result, a PDL that contains such information will be limited to the geographical borders of that country.

- *GDPR*: GDPR and other data protection regulations may regulate processing of personal information in ledgers. It is expected that PDLs that process such data comply with such regulations. Compliance may be achieved by different methods, depending on the specific regulation and type of information. An example would be removing the restricted information prior to creating a block, and possibly, generating a reference to where such information may be obtained in a manner that does not violate such regulations.

- *Storage in the cloud and on-premise*: Regulations may state that certain information can be stored in the cloud while other types of information must be stored on-premise in a private cloud environment, on a device owned and operated bare metal by the entity participating in the PDL. While it is not the intent of ETSI PDL to define or endorse such regulations, it is expected that node operators comply with such regulations and use private and public cloud only in scenarios where they are allowed.

Data interfaces: Data loaded to a PDL by one node will propagate to all PDL nodes with time. The duration of propagation varies depending on factors such as geography (that affects network latency), consensus mechanism, number of nodes and others. It is assumed that the information in all nodes in a properly functioning PDL is identical.

There are three primary data interfaces in a PDL:

- *Application to PDL*: Applications access data in a PDL through an API to one of the nodes that operate the PDL. In the event that the application is running on the same device as the PDL node, then this is an internal API. In the event that the application is running on a different device, then the API will be using a communication protocol that both the PDL node and the application node are subscribed to. In most cases, this will be the IP protocol over the public Internet, but there may be scenarios where a PDL is implemented on an Intranet preventing access to and from the public internet.

  In theory, other communication methods can be used as long as all users and nodes in the PDL are using that method. Examples would be Metro-Ethernet, Frame-Relay, and other OSI Layer-1 to Layer-3 protocols.

  An application may use different methods to communicate with the end-user or edge device that generates or reads the data from the field. For example, a food quality application used by a consumer at a supermarket checking the freshness of food by scanning a barcode on its packaging using a mobile phone. The barcode information is converted by the application into useful data that can be sent to the PDL for processing.

- *PDL node to storage*: A PDL node may use directly attached storage whereby the data interface between the PDL node and its information will be the device's internal bus or peripherals connectivity (e.g., Thunderbolt, SATA). In many cases the PDL node will be using a network attached storage (NAS) in which case the information is accessed through an API or a specific network protocol between the PDL node and the data storage device. NAS can be implemented using any OSI Layer-1 to Layer-3 protocol.

- *PDL node to node*: Nodes would typically exchange information using the IP protocol over either the public internet or an intranet. However, nodes may also exchange information through other protocols, as long as such protocols allow all nodes to communicate with each other.

Data operation and management: The distributed nature of a PDL poses challenges with management and operations of the data stored therein. A PDL allows selective access to its data, through membership management. A PDL also allows governance through a method agreed upon by the members. Such governance may be implemented through regulations imposed by a regulatory body or an external governing board, through a commission that governs software features or through development of specifications that software developers must meet when contributing code (either core or smart contracts) to a PDL. The consensus mechanism used by a PDL should reflect the governance implementation of choice.

- *Membership management*: Membership management is achieved through rules that govern: i) how new members and nodes are added to a PDL; ii) how and under what circumstances membership is revoked; iii) the anonymity/pseudonymity of members; and iv) access rights of members.
- *Governance*: Governance is the method by which a PDL is developed and maintained. The functions being governed include: i) software development; ii) specifications/standards/regulations to follow such as KYC and AML; iii) authoritative teams such as a board or a software-development-advisory; iv) choice of PDL technology; v) choice of vendors; vi) on-going operation and performance of the PDL; and vii) membership management. A reference approach to governance of standards is depicted in Figure 11.7.

Non-permissioned/permissionless ledgers: Though the scope of the book is permissioned distributed ledgers, it is worth mentioning that many of the concepts and implementations of PDLs can also be applied to permissionless ledgers. The reference architecture is one such example, where the abstract layers of a PDL are practically the same as those of a permissionless ledgers and the differences lie in the implementations of membership management and consensus mechanism. Another difference, though not implicit, is the number of nodes, where a PDL will typically be limited to tens or hundreds of nodes, while a permissionless ledger may span thousands and more nodes. The performance would be the reverse of that where a permissionless

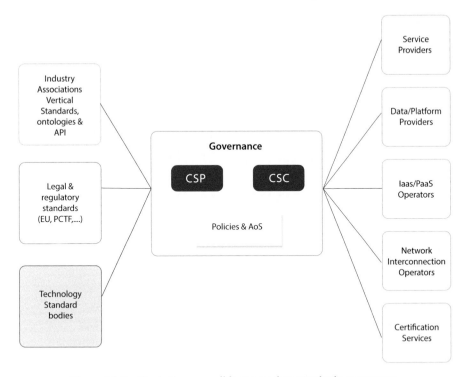

Figure 11.7   Illustrating a possible approach to standards governance.

ledger would typically be limited to roughly 10 TPS (transactions per second) while PDLs may be capable of processing thousands of TPS.

11.3.6 PDL networking and management

Inter-node communications: Inter-node communications are typically handled using the IP protocol, which has intrinsic vulnerabilities. A node may potentially be spoofed and either send a message to, or receive a message from, a bogus/hacked node. There are several approaches to increase the trustworthiness of inter-node communications through methods such as:

- Encryption of the data using public and private keys.
- Using private networks (physical or virtual).
- Requiring the data to be received from multiple sources and comparing them all to ensure integrity.
- Suspecting all data received until verified through other means.

The last two points make up to what is otherwise known as a consensus mechanism.

Node management: A PDL node is a computational device (dedicated node or virtual) that participates in a network of nodes through running an application (software). As such its management can be divided to hardware resource management, software resource management, storage resource management, and governance management as described graphically in Figure 11.5. Policies and certification programs should be developed to describe the below requirements in detail. Such policies should be transparent and available to use by all stakeholders. The policies should be dynamic and development in a collaborative manner. The detailed policies, their development and maintenance are beyond the scope of this book.

- *Hardware resource management*: Resource management for nodes implemented on dedicated devices includes: power continuity – ensuring power is continuous and UPS/generation is available; temperature management – ensuring operational temperature remains within norms; storage safety – ensuring the environment does not pose safety hazards to the surroundings; physical access management – maintaining access control to the device to authorized personnel; diversity management – ensuring diverse device types are available to overcome model vulnerabilities; scalability and extensibility management – ensuring devices can scale in number and resources with anticipated growth in demand or requirements. When a node is implemented on a virtual machine inter-VM it is expected that isolation is maintained on top of the above. CPU resources and RAM, either dedicated or shared, are expected to be managed in a manner ensuring sufficient resources are available for the nodes' proper operation.
- *Software resource management*: Software resource management includes: OS management: ensuring the node is using a specified version of the operating system and all required kernel extensions and security updates/patches; application management: ensuring the node is running a specified version of the PDL application. Upgrading the version if needed; development management: ensuring the development of software is carried out with efficiency (opensource – interaction, co-development, access to code; and international standards – applying common adopted industry standards and methods); security management – ensuring proper risk assessment and mitigation model is applied.

- *Storage resource management*: Storage resources are required for a node to store its local copy of the PDL data. Such resources are expected to be managed in a manner ensuring: sufficient storage space is available for the expected volume of data; data integrity is maintained (through, e.g., replication, RAID, backups); data is secured against unauthorized access and manipulation; Storage resources should comply with relevant integrity and confidentiality regulations and recommendations; in the event of network storage, not directly attached to the node, sufficient connectivity should be available to support the volumes and flows of data.
- *Node-level governance management*: Governance management on a node level (there are PDL-level and application-level governance aspects too, which are out of context of this book) should define the following aspects as a minimum: i) node lifecycle: depending on role of node (e.g., validator, regular) the addition or removal of a node to/from a PDL may vary both in process and in authority; ii) resource policies: define node-specific rules that provide probabilistic finality (e.g., always maintain sufficient resources for a specific functionality to be implementable); iii) software policies: maintain access control to the node; iv) communication policies: define rules that specify communication and messaging methods and process with other nodes under specific circumstances; and v) connectivity policies: define rules that specify connectivity methods with other nodes under specific circumstances.

Network resource management: Important to the well-being of PDLs, the following ought to be considered:

- *Bandwidth management*: Bandwidth and throughput of segments of the network should be configured to be able to contain the load of traffic at peak utilization. Network upgrades should be planned and performed in advance to avoid congestion.
- *Performance management*: Network performance is managed through adherence to SLA performance metrics. Such metrics include attributes such as availability, packet loss, jitter, and latency. Different applications and stakeholders may have different SLA requirements and the network should be capable of maintaining the SLA of the most stringent application (PDL or other) deployed thereon. Resiliency, in the sense of failover/backup resources, may be required for certain applications.
- *Governance*: Network governance refers to the ability to monitor traffic on the network, allow or forbid certain traffic flows based on policy

or regulations, ensure traffic is routed on permitted routes, and ensure traffic is secured based on policies of regulations.Network resource governance also refers to the ability to ensure the network is deployed using permitted network gear and technologies. Such permissions are based on policies and regulations and may vary depending on geography.

- *Inter-node network management*: Network resource management applies to the following scenarios:Ledger to storage: The network resources that connect a PDL node to its respective data storage. This could be an internal hard drive (implemented through the internal bus), a directly attached NAS (typically implemented using a dedicated copper or optical connector), or a remote NAS (typically using the public internet or a data-center Ethernet fabric).Ledger to ledger: The network resources that connect PDL nodes to each other. This would typically by the public internet, but a PDL network can also be deployed over a private network using other technologies such as Ethernet, Layer-1 or others.
- *Inter-node network and security management*: Network resource security is in a subsequent section.

Identity management: Identity verification and management is an integral part of PDL, as well as many other aspects of our day-to-day lives. Compared to permissionless ledgers, where the identity of the participant is not known and none of the interest to other users, in a PDL, which is based on allowing only permitted users to transact (and thus possibly use less stringent consensus mechanisms) knowing certain facts about the identity of the participants and ensuring they are not using a false/fake identity is paramount to its proper function.

There are three scenarios pertaining to sharing of participant data between nodes and participants:

- *All details*: In this scenario all information is visible and shared with all other participants.
- *Partial details*: In this scenario certain information is shared with others and certain information is withheld according to applicable policies and regulations. For instance, when signing up to an online petition, sharing of first and last name but withholding the email address.
- "*KYC-due-diligence-passed*": In this scenario the participant will be identified by a key indicating it has passed KYC due-diligence (meaning its identity had been validated and is not fake/false), but the identity itself is withheld from other participants.

The choice of identity information to be shared depends on the application and the applicable policies and regulations. There are multiple methods to ascertain an identity. The methods can be divided into electronic (with near real-time verification) and manual (which may require time to complete).

Electronic methods include:

- KYC processes vary by jurisdiction but serve as sufficient proof, according to that jurisdiction, that the identity of an entity (e.g., human, company, machine, etc.) is indeed what it claims to be.
- Digital records that can be attested as belonging to the person through biometric means (e.g., facial recognition compared to a photo-ID).
- Mobile-phone SMS return message.
- Code-generator.
- Two-step verification.

Manual methods include:

- Trusted-fellow referral.
- Company referral.
- Registration documents presented in-person.
- Postal verification.

Some of the above methods can be both electronic and manual.

Inter-ledger management: Inter-ledger operations can be performed in at least two ways as depicted in Figure 11.8.

1. Through an application at the application layer. Similar to the "API Gateway" and "Oracle" approaches defined in the World Economic Forum (WEF) document "A Framework for Blockchain Interoperability" [7].
2. Through the PDL management functionality within the PDL layer. This requires that the PDL management functionality being capable of managing multiple and different PDLs simultaneously. This is similar to the "cross-authentication" approach defined in that same document [8].

Inter-ledger management can be performed through the governance functionality and implemented using smart contracts versioned for the different PDL types. Information exchange across PDL types may be recorded on a third, neutral, PDL for census and validation. Inter-ledger interoperability is discussed in more detail in a subsequent chapter of this book.

Inter-layer management: Inter-layer communications will typically be implemented through an API that serves as an abstraction between the two layers. Thus, the management of inter-layer functionality is highly dependent

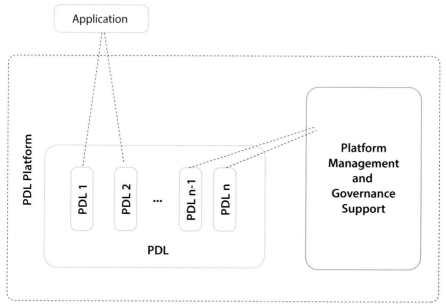

Figure 11.8 Inter-ledger management.

on the design and implementation of such API, the data models applied on both layers toward such API and the process/program implemented on both sides of the API as a result of information exchange though such API. When both layers are developed in a coordinated manner the processes and data models will likely match by design. However, when each layer is developed independently, possibly by different and uncoordinated teams, there may be a need for a standard or and intermediator that ensures proper flow between layers.

11.4 PDL Middleware and APIs

11.4.1 Introduction

Any application would typically include at least one component of the three infrastructure elements listed in the previous section, and often an application will include a mix of all three. An example would be an application such as Dropbox^{TM} that offers storage, but in order to provide such storage it must also include certain connectivity elements to move the data back and forth, and computational capabilities to identify users, calculate usage, perform billing and so forth. Another example would be a vehicle collision prevention application that uses computation to calculate its location and trajectory, and uses connectivity and storage to compare it with the location and trajectory of other vehicles in the vicinity.

Applications may be offered to individual users and enterprises, and can also be consumed or integrated by other stakeholders to generate other applications. As an example, a GPS positioning application may be used to indicate the geographical coordinates of an item. A mapping platform may be used to display a map of a certain place. Both can be integrated into a navigation platform that shows the location of an item on a map, as well as propose a route from that location to another.

11.4.2 Templates

Template considerations: Templates may be used throughout the architectural stack and may include one or more of the below items and functionalities. When designing a PDL one may use such templates to simplify design and re-use features and functionalities previously developed for similar purposes.

Applications: Applications may be re-used for multiple implementations. For instance, an application allowing SWIFT transactions through a bank can be used by multiple implementations that require such function. Applications should be open sourced in order to provide transparency to the development community and the specific platform developer.

APIs: APIs and API gateways serve as a bridge between entities exchanging data and functionality. Their aim is to provide consistency across platforms and implementations. This includes a common, agreed-upon/standard-based structure and a model-based data format. API security compliance provides end to end security and prevention of fraudulent or malicious activity.

Common functions: Common functions are reusable snippets of code, functions, smart contracts, libraries or even applications. Those functions should be available as templates for the benefit and re-use of developers and users of PDLs. Similar to applications – common functions should be open sourced.

PDL implementations: There is no "one-size-fits-all" PDL type for digital services. Multiple PDL types exist for a reason and the developer should have a choice to fit the purpose. A library of PDL templates allows choice and, in certain cases, also allows experimentation that leads to selection of the best fit.

Platform management and governance: There may be different approaches to platform management in the form of governance, membership management, node privileges, fees, incentive plans, regulation conformance, and consensus mechanism (to the extent possible within specific PDL implementations). Templates for same offer a menu of options for a developer to choose from and generate a best fit for purpose.

Infrastructure: Infrastructure recommendations should be available as templates that will allow the developer to ensure that the computation, storage, and connectivity infrastructure can support the software components and expected workloads.

11.4.3 PDL middleware

PDL-application abstraction: As illustrated in Figure 11.5, depending on the PDL implementation, there may be a separation between the application and the PDL layer on which it operates.

In the event that the application is developed for a specific PDL implementation where the user or application interacts with the PDL layer directly, it may be very difficult to abstract the application from the PDL. In the event that the application needs to be ported to a different PDL type, it has to be reprogramed almost in its entirety.

On the other hand, if the application operates independently from the PDL and interfaces with the PDL through an abstraction layer (e.g., API gateway) all southbound functionalities will use a unified method to access to the PDL, agnostic to the choice of underlying PDL type. Such abstraction layer could be implemented though an API-gateway other types of middleware. The benefit of such abstraction is that it allows separation of application from the underlying PDL so that an application developed by a certain vendor can be easily implemented on different PDL types.

Notwithstanding the above, PDL abstraction does not imply that all applications will or should be able to operate on all PDL types. For reasons of performance or features or regulation, certain applications may not be able to operate on specific PDL types. For instance, a specific PDL type may not support the TPS rate that an application requires. Also, the use a specific PDL type may be banned in a specific jurisdiction for regulatory concerns.

Applications should specify the features and attributes required from the PDL layer. This allows the platform developer to choose an appropriate PDL type that supports such features. The PDL abstraction layer may have the ability and logic to identify the available PDL types and use the appropriate southbound (PDL facing) APIs accordingly.

Application-application abstraction: The functionality of certain applications can be implemented by multiple developers, each developing their own version of such functionality. In order for those applications to interface with one another, they are expected to be fully interoperable. Such interoperability may be obtained through a combination of three elements:

- Clear and unified application definitions, i.e., each developer may add unique features that may prompt a customer to use their solution rather than the competitors' but the basic application functionality (often referred to as MVP – minimum viable product) will then be expected to be identical and fully interoperable.
- Unified and standardized interface reference points through which such applications exchange information with one another or other parts of the architecture. For instance, the eastbound interface between one application and another, or northbound interface between the application and the user.
- Unified information models that define the abstract processes and data models of the touch point between such processes at different entities across the interface points referenced above. When new products or services or applications (e.g., KYC) are introduced, the information model should be updated to include the required features so that an enhanced standardized data model can be derived in order to enable exchange of the required information. The development of such standardized processes and information models is performed in standard bodies (e.g., ETSI, TM-Forum, ISO) or through industry collaborations that generate de-facto implementation agreements (e.g., open source initiatives).

Application developers are expected to abide by regulations and ensure that applications do not breach such regulations (e.g., GDPR). The application abstraction layer may thus be configured to restrict exchange of such information. Such regulations may vary from time to time and the information models, processes and abstraction layers should be modified accordingly to support such change.

An example that may illustrate this point would be vehicle tires: When one arrives to a garage to replace tires, there is a choice of tires from multiple manufacturers that meet the MVP (in this case the MVP is the circumference and width requirements of the tire/wheel) and the consumer may choose the tire that offers a price and quality that meets certain budget or road-surface requirements.

The abstraction layer may also be used to implement security features such as access control, authentication, authorization or identity though such features may also be implemented on the application level.

PDL-PDL abstraction: Inter-PDL functions vary depending on the parity of the PDLs:

1. Both PDLs are of the same PDL type.
2. The PDLs are of different PDL types.

In the event of a pair of PDLs of the same type the inter-PDL functions are straight forward and may be implemented either directly on the PDL layer or indirectly through a management layer.

In the event of a pair of PDLs each of which of a different type, inter-PDL functions may need to be implemented through a management layer as it may be impossible to implement such management on the PDL layer itself.

The management layer interfaces with each PDL-type through an API. Such API, while likely being unique for each PDL type, will provide the full PDL functionality such as governance, access control and security, and data read/write.

An additional aspect of PDL-PDL abstraction is ownership of the PDL Platform. When two PDLs are each operated by a different organization/entity/consortium they may be subject to different jurisdictions and regulations and thus may use a different vocabulary to read/write and store data. An API gateway may need to be deployed to make the necessary translations from one vocabulary to another.

11.4.4 Platform APIs

Platform APIs are internal to the PDL platform. They convey information between the functional elements of a PDL platform. Those include:

- APIs between the PDL management functions and the PDL (or PDLs).
- APIs between the PDL (or PDLs) and the underlying compute and storage platforms.
- APIs between the PDL management functions and the compute and storage platforms.

Some APIs may be considered partly internal because they represent interactions with elements of the architecture that may, in certain cases, be internal, and in other – external. Those include:

- APIs between the application and the PDL/PDLs (optionally, in absence of a PDL-application abstraction layer).
- APIs between the PDL platform and the templates. The templates may be integral to the platform management functionality or be external.

11.5 Service and ecosystem APIs

Service and ecosystem APIs allow a PDL to interface with external entities and functionalities such as other PDL nodes, application users (through, e.g., a GUI), other applications (e.g., a digital wallet) and sometimes even the applications themselves (depending on availability of a PDL-application abstraction layer). They can be grouped as follows:

- Inter-application: APIs for the exchange of information between applications. For instance, an API used for money transfer between digital wallets.
- User-application: APIs used to exchange information between the users of the application and the application. For instance, an API used to display the balance of a digital wallet.
- User-PDL: APIs used to exchange information between the user and the PDL. It will be implemented in the event that the application is embedded into the PDL. For instance, an API used to display the balance of tokens in a PDL.
- PDL-PDL: APIs used for exchange of information between PDLs. For instance, an API used for performing a consensus protocol between nodes.

Service and ecosystem APIs can also be used for audit purposes in order to ensure the platform meets regulatory requirements.

This concludes this chapter where we have provided ETSI PDL's view on PDL and application governance. This allows us to define ETSI's PDL reference architecture, as discussed in the next chapter.

References

[1] https://www.etsi.org/committee/pdl
[2] https://www.etsi.org/deliver/etsi_gr/PDL/001_099/003/01.01.01_60/gr_PDL003v010101p.pdf
[3] https://www.etsi.org/deliver/etsi_gr/PDL/001_099/003/01.01.01_60/gr_PDL003v010101p.pdf

[4] https://jfin-swufe.springeropen.com/track/pdf/10.1186/s40854-016-004
    6-5

[5] https://eprint.iacr.org/2019/775.pdf

[6] https://www.etsi.org/deliver/etsi_gr/PDL/001_099/003/01.01.01_60/gr
    _PDL003v010101p.pdf

[7] https://www.weforum.org/whitepapers/inclusive-deployment-of-blockc
    hain-for-supply-chains-part-6-a-framework-for-blockchain-interoperab
    ility

[8] https://www.weforum.org/whitepapers/inclusive-deployment-of-blockc
    hain-for-supply-chains-part-6-a-framework-for-blockchain-interoperab
    ility

12

Reference Architecture

In this chapter, we detail the ETSI PDL reference architecture. It was developed based on the governance issues identified in the previous chapter as well as wider industry and standards interoperability requirements.

12.1 Overview of the PDL Reference Architecture

12.1.1 Definition of functional blocks

ETSI PDL stimulated the use of a functional block architecture to define the PDL software reference architecture.

A functional block is an abstract concept that defines a "black box" structural representation of the functionality (i.e., capabilities, behavior, and relationships) of a component, module, or system. A software reference model is an abstract definition of a set of architectural patterns and other supporting artifacts that presents a set of unifying terminology, concepts, axioms, and functional blocks within a particular problem domain.

A set of functional blocks interact using a set of internal and external interface reference points (IRPs) that standardize communication, and collectively define the functionality provided independent of specific technologies, implementations, or other concrete details. A software reference architecture provides a template for defining interoperable solutions to a particular problem domain (e.g., an interoperable settlement platform) in accordance with applicable business rules, regulations, and other constraints.

Thus, a software reference architecture specifies the salient characteristics and behavior of a platform. This takes the form of a set of functions and services that can be used to build more complex and detailed functions and services.

129

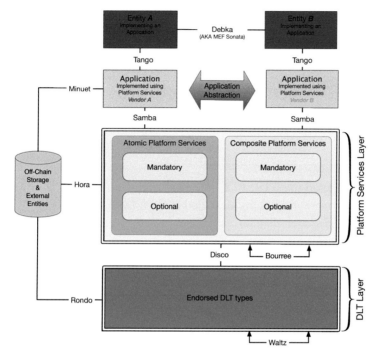

Figure 12.1   Main components of the ETSI PDL reference architecture.

12.1.2 Reference architecture

The ETSI PDL reference architecture (RA) is depicted in Figure 12.1. It is a modular architecture, and reuses individual functional blocks to compose new, more powerful, functional blocks. Accordingly:

1. *PDL applications*, which are applications using PDL technology.
2. *Application abstraction layer*, which are data model brokers/gateways enabling applications that use different data models to communicate with ETSI PDL compliant platforms. This layer is implemented through the "Samba" IRP and the data-model broker platform service where necessary.
3. *PDL platform services layer*, which may support various types of applications. In general, a good architecture design would have a PDL service layer providing useful services for applications. As a result, an application could simply leverage services from the PDL service layer, which will reduce the application's complexity, accelerate application development and deployment and increase interoperability. For

Table 12.1 Service types.

	Mandatory	**Optional**
Atomic	Mandatory atomic PDL platform services	Optional atomic PDL platform services
Composite	Mandatory composite PDL platform services	Optional composite PDL platform services

example, the PDL service layer could have transaction management service to facilitate an application to easily create transactions without knowing details of a specific PDL type (i.e., a specific deployed PDL network). In essence, this transaction management service can perform transaction transformation/adaptation between applications running on different PDL types to facilitate application operations in a complex environment. For abstraction purposes the service layer is divided to sub-groups according to the matrix defined in Table 12.1. Applications' access to services is independent of service classification and is subject to governance, identity, and security considerations.

a) *PDL mandatory platform services* are services which a PDL platform has to include in order to be considered ETSI PDL compliant.
b) *PDL optional platform services* are services a PDL platform does not need to include in order to be considered ETSI PDL compliant. Such services should be included if required by the applications running on such platform.
c) *PDL atomic platform services*, which are services and functionalities provided by the PDL platform that are independent of any other PDL platform service. Such services may use external resources which are not a PDL platform service offered by said PDL platform (e.g., a location service may use a GPS receiver, and an identity service may use a certification authority).
d) *PDL composite platform services*, which are services and functionality provided by the PDL platform that are dependent on other PDL platform services offered by said PDL platform (e.g., security service is dependent on identity service).
   In addition to the above matrix there is an additional category of PDL platform services:
e) *Application specific platform services*, which are used by specific applications and are not needed or cannot be made useful for other applications (e.g., measurement of precipitation is useful for agriculture and weather applications but has no use for data

storage applications). Such services will typically be integrated into the specific application that requires them, but the developer and platform governance may reach an agreement to include such service as part of the PDL platform in order to make it useful for other applications or in order to make use of the distributed nature of the PDL.

4. *DLT abstraction*, which consists of a data model broker/gateway enabling common and platform services to communicate with ETSI PDL compliant PDL types regardless of the specific type of that underlying PDL. An additional functionality of such abstraction layer is to allow interoperability between different DLT types, which may differ not only in data model structure but also on consensus mechanism and smart-contract functionality. Such abstraction layer hides the differences between PDL types and provides a unified service-facing interface on the services side and a PDL specific interface on the PDL side. This layer is implemented through the "Disco" IRP and the data-model broker platform service where applicable.

5. *DLT*, which is an implementation of a PDL using a specific DLT type.

6. *IRPs*, which define communication channels through which the functional blocks defined above, communicate with each other. The IRPs are given names for reference purposes (e.g., Debka, Tango, etc.).

12.1.3 Gateway and interfaces

A *PDL data model broker/gateway* allows different clients (applications, external systems/entities) that use proprietary data models to interact and communicate with the PDL platform using APIs or other communication methods. The data-model broker/gateway service together with the respective external IRPs ("Samba," "Disco," "Rondo," "Hora," and "Minuet") are used to allow such communications. ETSI PDL stimulates:

- An ETSI-PDL-compliant PDL platform shall include all mandatory services.
- An ETSI-PDL-compliant PDL platform shall include all optional services required by applications using such platform.
- An ETSI-PDL-compliant PDL platform may include application specific services.

An *IRP* is a logical point of interaction. ETSI PDL defines two types of IRPs: 1) A PDL *External IRP* is an IRP that is used to communicate between a PDL functional block and an external system; 2) A PDL *Internal IRP* is used to communicate between two or more PDL functional blocks; this communication stays within the PDL system and is not seen by systems that are external to the PDL. Based on Figure 12.1, the following IRPs are external: Minuet, Hora, Rondo, and Tango; and the following IRPs are Internal: Samba, Bouree, and Waltz.

A software or hardware *interface* describes the public characteristics and behavior that specify a software contract for performing a service specific action that is implemented through an IRP. There may be multiple interfaces implemented on an IRP. ETSI PDL will define software and application programming interfaces (APIs), and optionally, hardware interfaces. A PDL External IRP defines a *message channel*, which is a dedicated communications path connecting two endpoints that has specific associated semantics.

There are two types of ETSI PDL interfaces:

- A *PDL software interface* defines a point through which communication with a set of resources (e.g., memory or CPU) of a set of objects is performed. This decouples the implementation of a software function from the rest of the system. It consists of tools, object methods, and other elements of a model and/or code. A commonly used software interface is an API that is a set of communication mechanisms through which a developer constructs a computer program. APIs simplify producing programs, since they abstract the underlying implementation and only expose the objects, and the characteristics and behavior of those objects that are needed. Other software interfaces may include protocols, domain-specific language (DSL) and more.
- A *PDL hardware interface* is a point across which electrical, mechanical, and/or optical signals are conveyed from a sender to one or more receivers using one or more protocols. A hardware interface decouples the hardware implementation from other functional blocks in a system. Examples may include a sensor (e.g., thermometer) connected by wire to a node, an Ethernet cable connected to a node, a fiber-channel connection between a node and directly attached storage.

The ETSI PDL platform shall use external reference points to communicate to external systems, should be DLT-independent and may be DLT-specific.

12.2 Development Guiding Principles

12.2.1 Platform development guiding principles

Platform categories: ETSI PDL platforms fall into four major categories:

- Platforms that are designed, developed, delivered, and integrated to all users of said platform by a single vendor using a single DLT technology. Such platforms are labeled as *"Category Alpha Platforms."*
- Platforms that are designed, developed, delivered, and integrated to all users of said platform by a single vendor, but can operate using two or more underlying DLT technologies. Such platforms are labeled as *"Category Bravo Platforms."*
- Platforms that can operate using two or more underlying DLT technologies and are designed and developed toward a specification of an application abstraction layer so that any application that supports such an abstraction layer can interface with said platform. Such platforms are labeled as *"Category Charlie Platforms."*
- Platforms using a single DLT technology that are designed and developed toward a specification of an application abstraction layer so that any application that supports such an abstraction layer can interface with said platform. Such platforms are labeled as *"Category Delta Platforms."*

Category Alpha platform: A category "Alpha" platform is designed, developed, delivered, and integrated to all users of said platform by a single vendor using a single DLT technology. This is illustrated in Figure 12.2.

The "Alpha" category is broken down into two options: Category Alpha-1 platform, i.e., the DLT and some or all the platform services are proprietary to the vendor; and category Alpha-2 platform, i.e., the DLT and all the platform services are open-sourced.

Category Bravo platform: A category "Bravo" platform is designed, developed, delivered, and integrated to all users of said platform by a single vendor, but can operate using two or more underlying DLT technologies. This is illustrated in Figure 12.3.

A category "Bravo" platform includes an abstraction layer between the DLT layer and the platform services layer that offers a unified northbound interface between the abstraction layer and the services layer, and a unique, per DLT type, interface between the abstraction layer and the specific DLT types. This abstraction layer is labeled as the *"DLT Abstraction Layer."*

The "Bravo" category is broken down into two options: category Bravo-1 platform, i.e., one or more of the underlying DLT types and some or all the

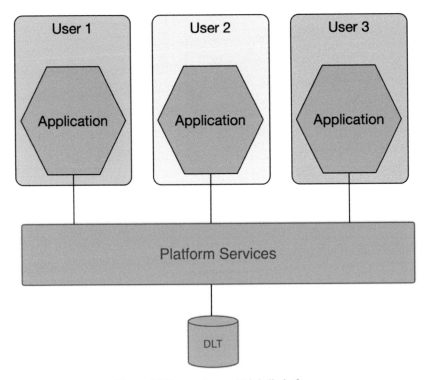

Figure 12.2 A category "Alpha" platform.

platform services are proprietary to a vendor; and category Bravo-2 platform, i.e., the DLTs and all the platform services are open-sourced.

Category "Charlie" platform: A category "Charlie" platform is designed and developed toward a specification of an application abstraction layer so that any application that supports such an abstraction layer can interface with said platform. This is illustrated in Figure 12.4.

This abstraction layer is labeled as the *"Application Abstraction Layer."* The application abstraction layer implements a unified northbound interface between the abstraction layer and the applications using the platform, and a per-platform-specific-service interface between the abstraction layer and the underlying services implemented in the platform services layer.

The "Charlie" category is broken down into four options:

- *Category Charlie-1 platform*: The platform is being developed and integrated by a single vendor who may integrate third party elements into the platform and may include proprietary elements in the platform.

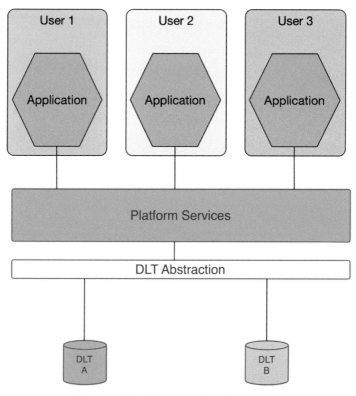

Figure 12.3   Category "Bravo" platform.

- *Category Charlie-2 platform*: The platform is being developed and integrated by a single vendor who may integrate third party elements into the platform and all elements, including the third-party elements, are open-sourced.
- *Category Charlie-3 platform*: The platform consists of a collection of interoperable modules, each offering one or more of the platform services. Such modules may be developed by different vendors toward service specifications defined or endorsed by ETSI PDL. Integration of such modules into an operational platform may be performed by any entity as long as the resulting platform complies with certification tests performed by ETSI PDL or a certification entity endorsed by ETSI PDL. Some or all of the modules may be proprietary.
- *Category Charlie-4 platform*: Like category Charlie-3 platform but all modules have to be open-sourced.

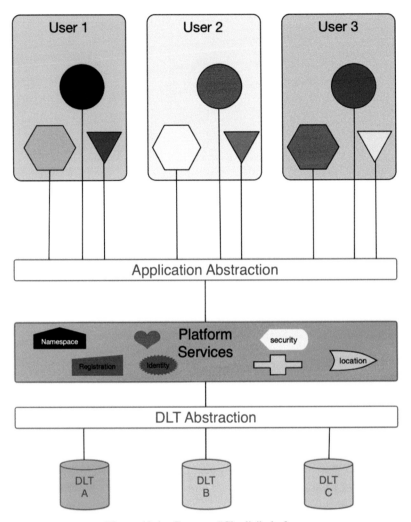

Figure 12.4 Category "Charlie" platform.

Category Delta platform: A category "Delta" platform is the same as category Charlie with the exception that it uses a single DLT, thus eliminating the need for the DLT abstraction layer. This is illustrated in Figure 12.5.

The "Delta" category is broken down into four options:

- *Category Delta-1 platform*: The platform is being developed and integrated by a single vendor who may integrate third party elements into the platform and may include proprietary elements in the platform.

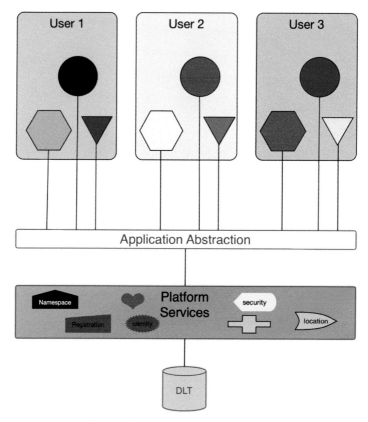

Figure 12.5   Category "Delta" platform.

- *Category Delta-2 platform*: The platform is being developed and integrated by a single vendor who may integrate third party elements into the platform and all elements, including the third-party elements, are open-sourced.
- *Category Delta-3 platform*: The platform consists of a collection of interoperable modules, each offering one or more of the platform services. Such modules may be developed by different vendors toward service specifications defined or endorsed by ETSI PDL. Integration of such modules into an operational platform may be performed by any entity as long as the resulting platform complies with certification tests performed by ETSI PDL or a certification entity endorsed by ETSI PDL. Some or all of the modules may be proprietary.

- *Category Delta-4 platform*: Like Category Delta-3 platform but all modules have to be open-sourced.

12.2.2 Application development guiding principles

The guiding principles of application development follow similar logic and categorization of platform development principles:

- Applications that are developed and delivered to all users of said application by a single vendor using a category Alpha platform developed by that same vendor and thus can only use a prescribed DLT type. Such applications labeled as *"Category Alpha Applications."*
- Applications that are developed and delivered to all users of said application by a single vendor using a category Bravo platform developed by that same vendor. Such applications are labeled as *"Category Bravo Applications."* Category Bravo applications are not limited to a prescribed DLT type and can be implemented using any DLT type supported by the Category Bravo platform.
- Applications that are developed toward a specification of an application so that any user of an application supporting such specifications can fully interoperate with other users of other applications built toward the same application specifications. Such applications are labeled as *"Category Charlie Applications."*

Note that *Category Delta Applications*, if such category was defined, would be redundant to *Category Charlie Applications* as the platform services layer hides the underlying DLT type hence there is no such category defined.

12.2.3 Platform services dependency

Due to the dependency of composite platform services on other platform services, when a composite platform service is implemented in a specific PDL platform, and that composite platform service is using an optional platform service, that optional platform service has to be implemented on that specific PDL platform.

12.2.4 Abstraction layer implementation

An abstraction layer is an abstract structure that serves as an intermediator between subsystems that may be using different vocabulary and methods that serves their respective purposes. As discussed earlier, an ETSI PDL platform

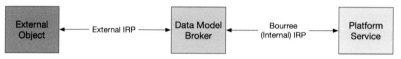

Figure 12.6   Abstraction layer implementation.

may include up to two abstraction layers: An *application abstraction layer* and a *DLT abstraction layer*. The functionality of an abstraction layer is implemented by routing all ingress and egress communications traversing through the external IRPs to the data-model broker/gateway platform service. A typical implementation is described in Figure 12.6.

The "External Objects" depicted above may be any object external to the platform services layer; for instance, an application, a DLT, external storage, an external service/platform, etc.

12.3 PDL Platform Services

12.3.1 List of important platform services

As discussed above, the ETSI PDL platform services are a set of modular functional blocks that are either PDL platform services themselves (atomic services) or are used to create PDL platform composite services. In order to maximize reusability, composite services are built using composition. This enables improved components of a composition to be used without affecting other services. Table 12.2 lists the most important ETSI PDL platform services.

12.3.2 PDL atomic platform services

Atomic services: The ETSI PDL atomic services are a set of PDL platform services that other ETSI PDL platform services may use, either directly or indirectly. Atomic platform services do not use any other PDL platform service but may use services external to the PDL platform.

There are five (5) PDL atomic platform services, four (4) of which are also mandatory platform services. They are shown in Figure 12.7.

Namespace platform service: The ETSI PDL Namespace platform service ensures that all of a given set of objects for a particular function have unique names so that they can be easily identified. This enables multiple internal and external domains to communicate and interact with each other while avoiding name collisions between multiple identifiers that share the

Table 12.2   ETSI PDL platform services.

PDL Platform Service Name	Mandatory (M) or Optional (O)	Atomic (A) or Composite (C)	Short Description
Namespace	M	A	Ensures that all of a given set of objects for a particular function have unique names.
Identity	M	A	Unambiguously identifies an instance of an entity from all other instances of this and other objects.
Location	O	A	Associates an object with a location.
Registration	O	A	List a managed object with authorities or registries.
Discovery	O	A	Discovery of services offered by the services layer and discovery of PDL networks.
Messaging	M	C	Enables communication between a group of entities.
Policy	O	C	Manage and control the changing and/or maintaining of the state of managed objects.
Security	M	C	A collection of services that assess, reduce, protect, and manage security risks.
Authentication	M	C	Verifies that a subject requesting to perform an operation on a target is who they say they are.
Authorization	O	C	Permitting or denying access to a target by a subject.
Cryptography	O	C	Managing protocols that prevent third parties from reading private communications.
Encryption	O	C	Encoding information using a key into an unintelligible form.
Identity Management	O	C	Access control based on the identity of an entity.
Key Management	O	C	Management of cryptographic keys.
Logging	O	C	Dynamic ingestion and collection of logs.
Governance	M	C	Rules and tools that control the behavior and function of a PDL.
Implementation Agreements	O	C	Rules and agreements that describe how ETSI PDL Services are implemented and control the behavior of a PDL platform.
Governing Entity	M	C	Defines the rules and implementation agreements. Ensures compliance. Resolves conflicts where needed.
Composition	O	C	Defines who can compose new services and how such new services are composed.
Access Control	M	C	Defines who can perform which operations on which set of *target* entities.

Table 12.2   Continued.

PDL Platform Service Name	Mandatory (M) or Optional (O)	Atomic (A) or Composite (C)	Short Description
Fault Tolerance	O	C	Defines how to handle faulty instructions.
Distribution Transparency	O	C	defines how to maintain transparency when distributing information to target entities.
Publish and Subscribe	O	C	Defines how entities publish services and subscribe to services.
Concurrency	O	C	Defines how entities handle concurrency.
Storage	M	C	A group of services related to storage.
In Memory Storage	M	C	Data that is stored in the RAM of a computer running an application.
File System Storage	M	C	Storage on a directly connected storage device.
On-chain Storage	M	C	Application data that is stored in blocks on all nodes using the chain.
Off-chain storage	O	C	Information in a digital, machine-readable medium that is not stored on the main chain.
Distributed Blockchain Storage	M	C	Storage on a distributed blockchain ledger.
Modeling	M	C	A group of services related to modeling.
Information Model	M	C	Presentation of concepts of interest to platform management environment in a *technology-neutral* form as *abstract* objects and relationships between objects.
Data Model	M	C	Representation of applicable concepts in a *technology-specific concrete* form.
Model Search	O	C	Enables search for specific or generic models within existing information and data models.
Model Stitching	O	C	Enables integrating multiple models or parts of models into a single model.
Topology	M	C	Allows a node to identify other nodes on the PDL and identify which nodes to communicate with when performing PDL related tasks.
Event Processing	M	C	Processes node-specific and platform-wide events as they occur.
Distributed Data Collection	O	C	Performs tasks related to collection of data.
Distributed Secret Sharing	O	C	Sharing of confidential data between nodes in a manner that maintains confidentiality of the data.

Table 12.2 Continued.

PDL Platform Service Name	Mandatory (M) or Optional (O)	Atomic (A) or Composite (C)	Short Description
Resource Management	M	C	Defines how to administer and manage resources.
Resource Discovery	O	C	Enables discovery of resources available to applications and nodes.
Resource Virtualization	O	C	Creating a virtual resource that mimics the behavior of a physical resource.
Resource Inventory Management	O	C	Management of node-specific and platform-wide Resource inventory.
Resource Admin and Management	M	C	Administration and management of node-specific and platform-wide resources.
Resource FCAPS	O	C	Resource management tasks defined by the ISO model.
Resource Composition	O	C	Management of composite resources.
Platform Services Management	M	C	Defines how to administer and manage platform services.
Platform Service Discovery	M	C	Provides means to discover services available to applications and nodes.
Platform Service Virtualization	O	C	Creating a service using virtual resources.
Platform Service Inventory Management	O	C	Keeping track of inventory and serviceability of platform services.
Platform Service Admin and Management	M	C	Administration and management of platform services through governance.
Platform Service FCAPS	O	C	Platform service management tasks defined by the ISO model.
Platform Service Composition	O	C	Management of the composition of composite platform services.
Application Management	M	C	Handles composition and orchestration of applications.

Table 12.2   Continued.

PDL Platform Service Name	Mandatory (M) or Optional (O)	Atomic (A) or Composite (C)	Short Description
Application Composition	M	C	Composing an application from two or more managed objects.
Application and Service Orchestration	O	C	Orchestrating multiple managed objects so that they are chained in the right sequence and their operation is synchronized.
Orchestration	O	C	Orchestration of objects so that they are chained in the right sequence and topology resulting in new functionality.
Platform Exploration	O123	C	Allows an application to indicate its requirements and explore whether the platform offers such service capabilities
Application Registration	O	C	Registers and lists all applications operated on a platform.
Transaction Management	O	C	Facilitates transaction related interactions between applications/services and underlying PDL networks.
Data Model Gateway/Broker	O	C	Defines tools that enable two systems with different data models to interact.
API Presentation	O	C	A specific Data Model Gateway/Broker implementation for environments that use APIs to exchange data between objects.
Application Specific Services	O	C	Serve a specific application or a group of applications but not required or used by other applications using the platform.

same name for a given object. Examples of internal domains are different administrative domains within an organization (e.g., engineering and sales), while examples of external domains include different partners (e.g., service and content providers) of an organization.

An ETSI PDL Namespace platform service shall provide a unique name that distinguishes each object instance from all other object instances (including multiple instances of the same object) that it contains.

Namespaces provide a scope for names. Namespaces are typically structured as hierarchies to allow reuse of names in different contexts. Examples include file systems and domain name system (DNS). A namespace is a *scoping container*. Examples include application container and messaging container services.

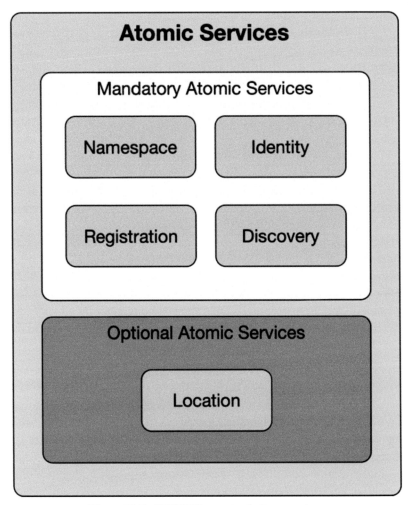

Figure 12.7 ETSI PDL atomic platform services.

An ETSI PDL Namespace platform service should support hierarchical names. Namespaces may be simplified by using consistent prefixes for each namespace. A name in an ETSI PDL Namespace should consist of a namespace identifier and a local (to that namespace) unique name.

Identity platform service: The identity of an entity is a set of context-dependent digital identifiers that unambiguously identify an instance of that entity from all other instances of this and other objects. An identity may require multiple attributes to uniquely identify it (e.g., two products with the same name have other different attributes, such as different serial numbers).

An ETSI PDL Identity shall be constructed using one or more context-dependent digital identifiers that enable an object instance to be unambiguously identified. A digital identifier is a secure object that is unique within a particular namespace. It is recommended that every digital identifier is assigned a namespace.

An ETSI PDL digital identifier should be defined within a namespace to guarantee its uniqueness. An entity may be used in different situations. Therefore, the same entity may be identified using a different set of digital identifiers for each situation. This enables the semantics of the use of an entity in each situation to be taken into account.

An ETSI PDL managed object may have multiple context-dependent digital identifiers for establishing the identity of that managed object in different situations in which it is used. An ETSI PDL identity service provides a single identity token per instance of an entity for all services so that this instance is identified unambiguously and in the same manner by all services.

An ETSI PDL identity service shall provide a single digital identity token per instance of an entity.

Location platform service: The location of an entity may or may not be relevant to the function of a PDL or a service, thus this atomic platform service is optional. In applications and scenarios where location is of essence, it may affect factors such as network latency (and the resulting transaction speeds), governing laws and regulations, costs, access restrictions and more. There are multiple methods of defining locations. There are physical addresses (e.g., GPS longitude/latitude coordinates, street addresses, postal codes, building names), relative addresses (e.g., 50 meters east of the main gate, and virtual locations [e.g., IP address, telephone number, medium access control (MAC) address]. Certain location descriptors are more accurate than others (e.g., a postal code may relate to a whole street while GPS coordinates may define a location with an accuracy of a few meters).

An ETSI PDL managed object may be associated with a location. The location of an ETSI PDL managed object associated with a location shall be represented in a method understood in the respective geography where it is located. The location of an ETSI PDL managed object associated with a location shall be defined using a location method compliant with the level of accuracy required by the respective application.

Registration platform service: Registration services provide means to list an ETSI PDL managed object with local or international authorities or registries. Such registries allow reference to such managed objects for legal, commercial and operational purposes. Registration requirements vary with geography. Certain managed objects (e.g., a PDL serving a geographically diverse application) operate in multiple geographies and may require multiple registrations.

An ETSI PDL managed object may be registered in one or more registries. A registered ETSI PDL managed object shall be registered in accordance with the regulations and rules applicable in the geographies in which it operates.

Discovery platform service: Discovery services provide means to discover ETSI PDL platform services offered by an ETSI PDL platform services layer; and/or discover a registered DLT network.

For example, an application can discover the ETSI PDL platform services available on a PDL platform. In another example, an ETSI PDL platform service can discover an underlying DLT network, which has been registered to an ETSI PDL platform services layer.

An ETSI PDL platform services layer shall have an ETSI PDL discovery service. An ETSI PDL discovery service shall support discovery of ETSI PDL platform services of an ETSI PDL platform services layer. An ETSI PDL discovery service shall support discovery of DLT networks that have been registered to an ETSI PDL service layer.

12.3.3 PDL composite services

The ETSI PDL composite platform services are a set of functional blocks that provide services that other platform services use, either directly or indirectly. They use one or more other platform service in order to fulfill their functionality. Composition allows building more complex architectural concepts and functions.

There is a total of 53 composite platform services, 16 of which are mandatory. Services are grouped into sub-groups by their function for reference purposes but are non-hierarchical. Any platform service or application may use any other platform service. Some of the composite platforms are mandatory and some are optional.

They are shown in Figure 12.8. Exposing their functionalities in detail in this book would take too much space. The reader is referred to Section 5.4.3 in [1].

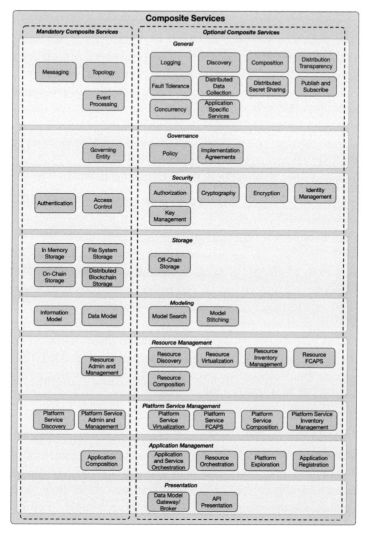

Figure 12.8   ETSI PDL composite platform services.

12.4 PDL Application Clients [PDL 12]

12.4.1 Introduction to application clients

Application clients are the user front end that allows the user to interface with an application and perform application tasks such as initiating a transaction, performing a query, participating in a consensus vote, etc.

There may be multiple application clients to the same application, which differ in terms of the hardware and software implementation of the underlying device being used for the application client.

12.4.2 PDL computer applications

Computer applications are running on a personal computer. There are multiple types of personal computers in common use today, notably the Microsoft Windows enabled PC (typically using an Intel or similar processor), the Apple Mac (which runs on both Intel and Apple processors), Linux, the Chrome devices and numerous others.

An application has to be tailored to the specific hardware and operating system that personal computer is using and offer a uniform interface to the user regardless of that operating system.

An ETSI PDL computer application should offer functionality in a manner agnostic to the underlying hardware and operating system of the computer it is implemented on. It requires specific minimum hardware and software configurations to function properly; and it may also be used as a network node.

12.4.3 PDL mobile device application

Mobile applications run on mobile devices such as smartphones and tablets. Such mobile devices may run on various hardware types and vary in terms of operating system, screen size, computation power, and internal architecture. While there is a challenge to maintain software compatibility with multiple mobile environments the benefit is the wide-spread adoption and availability of such devices that makes the application available to larger audiences. An additional benefit is the portability of mobile devices that makes a mobile device application available in locations where a personal computer cannot be operated or cannot be connected to the network.

Since mobile devices may be limited in resources, computation power, and storage space, and would typically not have directly connected storage, they would not typically be used as network nodes. Furthermore, the application interface may lack some functionality that may only be available on other application types.

An ETSI PDL mobile device application shall offer sufficient functionality as required by the PDL application to perform tasks required by its user. An ETSI PDL mobile device application may offer reduced functionality compared to other device application types.

12.4.4 PDL cloud applications

Cloud applications run on a network-based machine (typically a virtual machine) and are accessible through the public Internet, through private networks or through Intranets, depending on the network environment implementation. Such applications would typically be accessed through an HTML GUI (e.g., web browser) using HTTP or HTTPS or other mark-up languages as used by the respective developers. The GUI would typically offer access to most, or all, application features.

The GUI implementation may vary depending on the web browser used and the operating system of the device used to run such web browser.

An ETSI PDL cloud application should be compatible with all commonly used web browsers on all commonly used operating systems as prescribed by the governance. It shall use a secure connection (e.g., HTTPS) to the web client; and shall be compatible with a list of web browsers and operating system environments defined by the governance for each such application.

References

[1] https://www.etsi.org/deliver/etsi_gs/PDL/001_099/012/01.01.01_60/gs_PDL012v010101p.pdf

13

Smart Contracts

In this chapter, we focus on PDL-enabled smart contracts. We will dwell on important properties first, before exploring design requirements and architectural implementation solutions. We also touch upon the topics of governance, data, testing, and cybersecurity.

13.1 Properties of Smart Contracts

Smart contracts are executable codes which are installed on distributed ledgers – PDLs for the purpose of this book. Therefore, their characteristics are dependent on their underlying ledger technology. Some of these characteristics such as immutability and transparency are by-design properties of a PDL and hence common to all PDL types. Smart contracts inherit these properties from PDLs, which are discussed in this section.

13.1.1 Inherent properties

Immutability: Smart contracts are immutable, which means an already registered smart contract cannot be modified or deleted and cannot be tampered with. This way, the integrity of a contract is guaranteed; that is to say, a contractual agreement installed as a smart contract on a PDL becomes hardened, and none of the participants can make any changes retroactively. Immutability produces tamperproof contracts and prevents document frauds. However, immutability comes with a cost of scalability and has two significant problems:

- *Expired smart contracts*: Even a smart contract that is expired still lives on the ledger and occupies the storage. For example, if a vendor and an operator are in a contract, the contract may be valid/active for some certain duration and will expire. Such contracts if installed as smart contracts cannot be deleted from the ledger, and cause scalability problem.
- *Erroneous smart contracts*: If a smart contract has bugs or errors, it can make unwanted and unintentional, possibly harmful transactions. It is

151

to be noted here that all the transactions either wanted or unwanted are recorded in a PDL. A bug-free and corrected contract may replace the old contract, but records already stored in the PDL cannot be altered.

Transparency: In PDLs, all the ledger nodes keep an identical copy of a ledger; this means they all share the same information. As a result, all the transactions are transparent or known to all the participants of the PDL. Hence, none of them can deny the details of a transaction. In certain cases, or events, when some of the participants of a PDL want private dealings, transparency is not required and may not even defeat the purpose of privacy.

For example, a sub-group of participants in a large PDL want to do some business and install a smart contract for the contractual terms and do not want to reveal their contractual details to the rest of the PDL users. In a typical PDL, every node will have a copy of this contract but here a private smart contract is required.

A possible solution to this challenge would be private chains or private channels, such as implementation of private channels in Hyperledger Fabric. There, smart contracts can be installed on separate, private channels only visible to the sub-group involved in a contract.

Auto-executability: Smart contracts are triggered by a software condition and can even be executed without human intervention. Auto-executable smart contracts provide an automated method of contract execution in which parties can install the contracts as smart contracts which are executed by the code itself. However, this property instigates the following challenges:

- *Uncontrollable executions*: Erroneous code can trigger uncontrollable executions. As an example, unwanted automated payments may cause monetary losses or delivery of incorrect amount of goods due to uncontrollable and out-of-order delivery instruction.
- *Malicious executions*: If malicious parties create backdoors to a smart contract, they can execute smart contracts and it may be difficult to stop such executions without a hard fork to the ledger or installing a revised smart contract that blocks further execution of the malicious smart contract.

13.1.2 Interoperability/ledger dependency

Smart contracts are dynamic in nature, i.e., they take inputs, perform executions and record results to the ledger they are installed on, or may send the execution results to other ledgers or other smart contracts. Smart contracts may also take inputs from other ledgers. Below are the scenarios when a smart contract will interact with other ledgers (inter-ledger) and within the ledger it is installed on (intra-ledger):

- A smart contract's interaction with other smart contracts in the same ledger (intra-ledger): Smart contracts within the same ledger can call each other without any need of harmonization because they all use the same ledger type. The only consideration here is that if an execution of a smart contract is dependent on another smart contract, they shall be sequential such that an execution is not started until the previous execution is completed and its results are recorded. The reason for that sequence is that the results of the previous executions may later be used as inputs for the next contract in the chain.
- A smart contract's interaction with smart contracts in other ledgers (inter-ledger): A smart contract may send execution results to another ledger, but the smart contract should have correct access rights to the other ledger. Moreover, both of the ledgers may have different and incompatible data formats which should be addressed. PDL inter-ledger interoperability is discussed in a later chapter of this book.

13.1.3 Operational inefficiency

This problem is not limited to smart contracts and is applied to every aspect of PDLs. Since any data or contract loaded to PDL stays there for lifetime of the ledger, the ledger keeps growing. The ledger will eventually require compute/storage resources that will prevent scale.

For example, in the context of smart contracts, if a consortium of telecom operators runs a ledger to offer service contracts to their customers, this ledger may be running for several years and in those years millions of contracts may be issued. If old and unused contracts are not deleted and removed but can be only deactivated, the ledger will be cluttered with several unused and dormant contracts and ledger resources will be wasted.

13.1.4 Synchronization of offline smart contracts

In a typical PDL, transactions and smart contracts are installed on distributed nodes and these nodes are connected to form a ledger to take part in consensus (i.e., approve or reject transactions). In situations when some of the nodes go offline – possibly due to network outages or duty cycle – an offline operation and posterior synchronization is needed; this will be discussed in a subsequent chapter of this book. For the time being, two example challenges are highlighted here:

1. Independent smart contracts – which may depend on authenticated data from offline nodes (i.e., nodes not connected to the PDL). Such smart contracts may or may not proceed processing depending on same.
2. Chained smart contracts – when smart contract execution is dependent on other smart contract execution, then execution will not continue/commence until the required number of nodes are back online.

13.1.5 Ledger time synchronization

Like all distributed systems, PDL nodes are distributed across several time zones and do not have a common solitary clock. This may have several implications, such as local clock of the machine which may or may not be synchronized with atomic clock resulting in inconsistent timestamps. Furthermore, time zones need to be included to compare with the universal time used for governance timing.

13.2 Requirements for Designing Smart Contracts

13.2.1 Smart contract actors

All the actors within the PDL network shall be assigned unique identities and access control rights. The governance is responsible to ensure that all the actors are allocated unique access rights, and the role of governance is outside the scope of ETSI PDL.

The actors related to smart contracts are chosen by the governance and defined as follows:

- **Lifecycle management governance committee**: Lifecycle management of the PDL is performed by a governance committee or a group of participants chosen by the PDL members by mutual consensus. Typically, management decisions include access rights and protocols PDL members will be adhere to. Lifecycle management can be performed by a single party or multiple parties.
- **Owner**: The contract owner is the party who programs and installs the smart contract. In some scenarios, for example, when a smart contract is expected to be shared among several PDL participants, the governance of the PDL can be the owner of the contract.

- **Stakeholders**: All the parties involved in the smart contract executions; for example, two contractual partners. There can be different categories of stakeholders:
  - ○ Contracting parties – the parties that sign the contracts.
  - ○ Beneficiaries – the parties that affect by the contract with advantages or disadvantages.

13.2.2 Requirements during design

Smart contracts are expected to follow the complete lifecycle explained in [1]. The stepwise approach proposed therein facilitates an error-free design of smart contracts. The main advantages of adopting such approach are:

- **Access control and ownerships**: Ownership and access control strategies decided during the planning phase will prevent future disputes. This will also facilitate the developers to accurately code the assigned rights while coding the smart contracts. Access control and ownership shall be defined, discussed, and agreed between the stakeholders and the governance before smart contract coding starts. It is the governance responsibility to ensure this.
- **Reusability**: Smart contracts shall be reusable and parametrized for economical storage. During the planning phase, the stakeholders shall adopt strategies to design parameterized smart contracts to enable maximum reusability. It is the developers' responsibility to ensure a reusable contract.
- **Minimize human error**: Human errors may cause erroneous contracts and may result in a security breach of smart contracts. For example, if a developer mistakenly makes the execution function inaccessible, the contract will never be executed. A smart contract shall be tested before the deployment.
  Note that human error, such as developer mistakes, may be alleviated through methodical development practices. This occurs during two stages of the smart contract life cycle: 1) the planning phase – by carefully outlining the requirements from the smart contract; and 2) the development and testing phase – by testing the smart contract code against the requirements.
- **Pre-installation checks**: The smart contract shall be checked before the final deployment.

- **Online auditing/monitoring**: The smart contracts shall be audited during their execution.

13.2.3 Available technologies

Smart contracts are expected to be widely adopted; hence they should be cautious toward:

- **Programming languages**: The programming language for writing a smart contract is usually ledger dependent but, if possible, widely available, and widely adopted programming languages shall be used.
- **Hyperledger Fabric**: Developers have the choice between several languages (e.g., Golang, JavaScript); in such cases, widely available programming language should be adopted. This will be advantageous to the PDL consortium members in the future as well, for example, it will be easier to recruit developers.
- **Language libraries**: Programming languages often have external libraries, used for different functions such as hashing or digital signing. These external, third-party libraries may include functions which can cause dangers to a smart contracts' security. Only authorized and verified libraries shall be used.

13.2.4 Usage of auditable libraries

Developers shall use auditable libraries for smart contract programming for the purpose of verifiable smart contract program/code. Such libraries shall be testable through governance approved testing techniques (e.g., certification laboratory using an approved test suite).

The auditable libraries used in smart contract programming shall be available for free use for auditing purpose. However, users/developers may or may not pay to use them.

13.2.5 Input to smart contracts

Smart contract developers shall ensure that a smart contract only accepts inputs from authorized sources (e.g., authorized APIs). These sources shall be approved by and given access rights by the governance functions of the PDL.

13.2.6 Universal clock

PDLs lack universal clock mechanisms due to the distributed nature of the nodes. Smart contracts shall thus follow:

- Smart contracts shall use governance defined clock – the time/zone format determined by the PDL network governance.
- The clock of the node is local to the machine/hardware and thus may differ from the governance clock. In such a case, the owner of the node shall ensure the synchronize with the governance clock.
- The node shall derive the time from an atomic clock or from another node designated as a source clock (timing source). All nodes shall use the same time specified by the governance. This is to avoid time mismatch between nodes.
- The nodes have the capability to follow and note the PDL time specified by the governance, even if it deviates from the local time (geographical time). For instance, the governance clock may be at UTC time and all the nodes shall use UTC time as their time even if they are not at UTC.

13.2.7 Terminatable

Eternal contracts can cause problems such as unwanted executions and unauthorized future access. There should be a mechanism to terminate or deactivate smart contracts after a certain date/time.

If a developer does not provide a mechanism to deactivate the smart contract, then it shall be known before the deployment of the contract. Consequently, it is advised to have a management action to perform the same.

A smart contract shall be terminatable. It shall include a function that can terminate the smart contract. The owner and governance shall ensure that the parties which execute the contract should also safely terminate the smart contract.

13.3 Architectural and Functional Requirements

13.3.1 Lifecycle of a smart contract

ETSI PDL stimulates that all smart contracts shall follow the lifecycle shown in Figure 13.1. All the smart contracts will need to have terminations, with more details provided below. The owner/governance keeps the rights to destruct the smart contract.

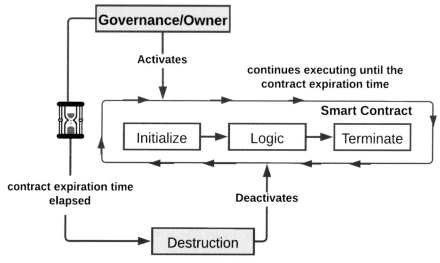

Figure 13.1   Smart contract lifecycle.

13.3.2 Template smart contracts

Smart contracts are immutable and if there is an error (e.g., due to a developer mistake), they may need to be obsolete by a newer improved smart contract. To avoid that, the following strategies can be applied to ensure safe and well-tested contracts:

- It is recommended to use template contracts that have been tested and debugged to reduce the chance of such errors.
- Template contracts are designed with more consideration and secured with several security checks.
- Templates may require specification of the throughput/bandwidth of the contract and depend on the governance, application of the contract and the stakeholders involved.

13.3.3 Time-limit, termination and destruction

Eternal smart contracts can cause unwanted executions in future. Therefore, smart contracts shall have internal and external ways to limit their lifetime.

The following are requirements in the context of *internal termination*:

- Smart contracts shall be terminable with an internal termination signal/command.

- Every smart contract should have a termination function that can disable further executions of the smart contract after a certain period or upon notice.
- If a contract is generalized enough to be shared among several users, such contract should have means of terminating/deactivating itself after an end-date or upon a specific condition.

An internal termination is facilitated by a *short-term timer*. A deactivated smart contract may be reactivated for future contract executions with different parameters upon signal or specific conditions.

Smart contracts can be assigned very sensitive tasks, so it is important to safely terminate them to avoid future attacks. The requirements for *safe termination* are as follows:

- Governance and owners of the contract shall ensure a safe termination of such order.
- Ensure that none of the terminated smart contract functions is callable or executable.
- All the access rights of the current execution for the smart contract are revoked.
- Data is archived for future reference such that data integrity should be maintained.
- When a smart contract is required to be terminated, the reason of the termination shall be sent as an argument of the contract. The reasons for the termination can be as follows:
  - Natural termination, e.g., the purpose of the smart contract is fulfilled.
  - One of the parties is pulled-off the contract or revoked the contract (interruptive termination).
  - Timeout of the contract reached.
  - Other reasons such as malicious activities or other non-contractual actions.

Finally, *destruction* occurs when the long-term timer of the smart contract is elapsed, and the contract end date/time is reached. Destruction is different from termination (both natural and interruptive) of the smart contracts because a destructed smart contract cannot be reactivated. Following are the requirements of a smart contract destruction:

- Once destroyed, the contract cannot be reinstated.
- All the functions shall be inactivated before the destruction.

- If a smart contract is required to be revised, that is, a new/revised version to be installed, it shall be classed as a termination, not as a destruction.

13.3.4 Secure access control mechanisms

In PDLs, smart contracts are accessed by the PDL participants (e.g., owners) and external sources (e.g., off-chain sources) through strict *access-control mechanisms*. The following are the requirements for accessing a smart contract:

- Smart contracts should be accessible by the owner(s) of the contract, or any other party authorized/delegated by the governance.
- The governance of the PDL shall ensure that access rights are granted to authorized members (internal and external) only.
- Smart contracts access shall be in a time-controlled manner, i.e., every access to every smart contract shall have a limited time access only.
- Stringent access control mechanism should be implemented.
- Governance shall maintain a record of access rights granted to parties/entities in an access control list (ACL).
- The fields of an ACL shall include:

  ○ Node identity (different from public key, and is assigned by the governance when the node joins a PDL)
  ○ Access start date
  ○ Access end date
  ○ Access start time
  ○ Access end time
  ○ Smart contract identity
  ○ Functions granted access to the smart contract

- The access revocation shall be automated, and software based. After the agreed condition(s) are met the access rights are revoked automatically.

In some cases, the owner of the contract or governance may temporarily use *delegates* to assign rights of a contract:

- Access delegation should be for a limited time and will be revoked when such time elapses.
- If the delegation is changed, i.e., a delegate further delegates the rights, a delegate will have most of the rights as the owner but not all. More specifically, a delegate may not be allowed to further delegate the smart contract rights to another party.

- Such delegation rights will stay exclusive to the owner and the governance of the PDL. However, an owner may allow the further delegation to the delegates with discretion in some situations.
- It is possible that some of the delegates further delegate the access rights without authorization. To handle this, the device authentication should be implemented. That is to say, the access keys assigned to the delegate shall also check for the device identification.
- If a different device is identified than the authorized one, then the access of the delegate shall be blocked, and a warning should be issued.
- The delegation rights should be the function of the governance layer. The governance of some PDLs may allow delegation of all functionalities and the governance of some PDLs may prefer to restrict delegation of some functionalities only.
- The delegate identification can be done through node identifier which is assigned by the governance to the nodes of the PDL.

13.3.5 Control instructions

Control instructions are functions which are executed in special circumstances, other than usual smart contract operations. For example, sending an interrupt instruction:

1. Blocking/unblocking instruction – if a smart contract is not performing as planned (because of reasons such as error in a contract). Such a contract should be stopped or blocked by exclusive instructions. Depending on the requirements of the contract, such instructions can be of several types.
2. Function updates – depends on the PDL type. For example, at some instance, certain functions are mandatory to update/modify.
3. Destruct instruction – as discussed above.

Note that only the values of the functions can be modified; the code of the functions is immutable.

Below are the requirements for smart contracts to include control instructions:

- Smart contract shall include instructions as functions to allow interrupt the execution.

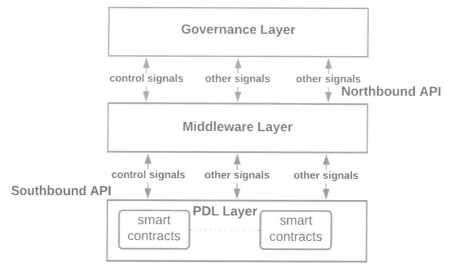

Figure 13.2 Control instruction flow between the layers.

Table 13.1 Function instructions.

Functions	Governance	Owner	Delegate
Change of owner	Yes	No	No
Interrupt	Yes	Yes	Yes
Terminate	Yes	Yes	Yes
Access duration	Lifetime of the contract	Limited	Limited
Delegation	Yes	Yes	-
End date	Yes	No	No

- The following control instructions shall be defined in smart contracts: internal termination; interrupt execution – that immediately stops the smart contract execution; destruct.
- Control instructions are of high importance and shall be accessible only by the governance and the owner of the contract with exclusive access control credentials.

Above is illustrated in Figure 13.2.

13.3.6 Archived and stale data

In some cases, users of the smart contract may wish to terminate the contract completely, e.g., using the self-destruct function in Ethereum which completely removes all the states from the ledger. In that case, the users may want to **archive data** with examples given in Table 13.2.

Table 13.2 Examples of to-be-archived data depending on the use case.

Contract Type	Data Archived
Financial contracts	Payment functions
Identity contracts	Public keys, certificates
Auction contracts	Bid values, minimum bid value
Service level agreement contracts	Contract between vendors and operators

Archiving is achieved by means of a local record of the smart contract and its data. In such cases, ensuring integrity of the data is very important. Other participants may not trust the locally stored data of the smart contract. Below are some of the storage methods owners may wish to use to store their data:

- Back up the executions and data in a cold storage with a timestamp.
- Create a sidechain, and copy the executions there.
- Hash the smart contract and the respective data and store it in a local storage.

Stale data can also occur, particularly if a smart contract is destructed or deactivated. The data generated by the smart contract will stay in the ledger for the lifetime of the ledger. Then the smart contract logic and code shall be stored in a secure way within the ledger to keep the record of the operations performed on the data in the past.

13.3.7 Mandatory and optional smart contract fields

A smart contract is initialized with some data that typically identifies the smart contract; there are two important types of fields:

- **Mandatory fields** – These fields shall be the part of a smart contract.
- **Optional fields** – Owner/governance may introduce bespoke fields to serve the purpose of a smart contract.

In terms of **mandatory fields**, every smart contract shall include two components, i.e., *fixed fields* and *parameterized fields*. Developers/testers shall ensure that all the mandatory fields listed below are included in the smart contract before deployment.

In terms of the *fixed mandatory fields*, smart contracts are required to have the following fields that are set at the time of the deployment:

- **Contract ID** – an internal identity of smart contract. This identity is allocated by the governance of the PDL. The following are fields that shall be included in the ContractID: ContractID =

LedgerID:OwnerID:ContractIdentifier, where there are three components including ledger identity (LedgerID), owner identity (OwnerID), and contract identifier. Note that the contract identifier is different than Contract ID, and the contract identifier is a unique identifier that represents the contract within a PDL.

- **Ledger ID** – Every ledger shall be identified by a unique identity; all the regulated ledgers should be assigned an ID by the relevant authorities (such as governance or the owner). The following fields may include in a Ledger ID, and the construct of the Ledger ID is out of ETSI PDL: region identity (RegionID) (e.g., GB, IT); company identity (CompanyID).
- **Owner ID** – Typically a smart contract should be owned by the governance and borrowed/leased to users of the PDL. However, it is possible that some users wish to install customized contracts for specific purposes. In both the cases, the owner ID should be the mandatory section of a smart contract.
- **Start time** (governance-defined clock) – the start time of the contract, i.e., the time when the contract is deployed in the ledger and is different from the execution/invocation time of the ledger.
- **End time** (All times will be represented according to governance-defined clock) – the end time of the contract. The self-destruct clause will execute at this time and the contract will be terminated. Users of the contract shall ensure that all the sub-contract execution time is within the end time of the contract. Depending on the scenario, it may be changeable; for example, an interrupt instruction may change this time to stop and revise the contract version.
- **Version No.** – Version number of the smart contract, if a smart contract is re-deployed after termination, same versioning sequence shall be followed.

In terms of the *parameterized mandatory fields*, the following parameters ought to be set:

- **Execution start time** – Start time of a particular smart contract execution.
- **Execution end time** – End time of a particular smart contract execution. It shall be before the contract end time.
- **Execution ID** – Identity of execution by a user of the PDL or external entity.
- **Executing party ID** – Identity of the participant executing the smart contract. This is different from the public key and is the permanent

identity assigned by the governance of the PDL. In a typical PDL, the transaction ID or public key of the executing participant is recorded in the ledger at the time of the contract execution, but it should be the part of the contract as well. Anonymization should be resolvable to ensure accountability in PDLs. Pseudo-anonymization by the PDL governance may be considered.

In terms of *optional fields*, they depend on several issues, such as purpose, usage and timing. It is up to the governance and the owners of the contract to introduce optional fields as per their requirements. These fields are out of scope of ETSI PDL; however, some examples are listed below:

- Smart contract genre description.
- Corresponding paper contract reference numbers/identifiers.
- List of middle parties involved in the contract.
- Corresponding country/region laws if applicable.

Note these fields should be clearly identified as optional fields within the contract.

13.4 Description of Required Functions

13.4.1 Initialization of the smart contract

The contract is initialized with the initialization function that is the constructor of a contract and prepares the smart contract for executions such as initialization of the variables:

- The initialization function shall include initialization of variables.
- The initialization function shall be checked explicitly, along with logic functions at the testing stage because if not present, the smart contract can become dormant.
- It may call the logic functions of a smart contract; the initialization function may also verify the login credentials.

The key elements of the initialization function a smart contract are shown in Figure 13.3.

The timer of the smart contract is initialized whenever the smart contract is executed. In some cases, the timer may be initialized with the first execution of the smart contract and keeps running (possibly pausing from time to time on certain conditions) until the contract is deactivated.

Some of the conditions for pausing/deactivating are listed below:

- Achieved the lifetime of the contract.

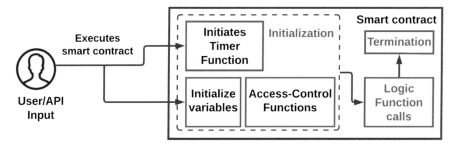

Figure 13.3   Initialization elements of a smart contract.

- Once execution is completed (but the contract can be executed in future).
- Malfunctioning of a smart contract.
- Access rights given to malicious users accidently or otherwise.

13.4.2 Access control

The access control function inside the smart contract will ensure that users who are executing the smart contract functions are authorized to access those functions:

- Access control functions shall verify if the user has sufficient rights to access a particular function.
- Access control functions shall be hardcoded and grant/block access by checking the role of the caller.
- Developers should design a smart contract to ensure that the access control function is not callable by any other function (within or outside a smart contract).

For example, in an auction contract, bidders can place a bid in the auction but may not be allowed to stop it. Therefore, they will not be allowed to access the endAuction() function of the smart contract.

13.4.3 Logic functions

Logic functions are the main tasks of a smart contract:

- Logic functions shall be accessible by strict access control mechanisms as discussed above.
- They may include several classes and functions that do the executions to serve the smart contract purpose.

13.4.4 Entry functions

Users of a smart contract shall be able to access only a certain subset of functions upon initialization, also referred to as entry functions. Any interaction between smart contract functions should be limited and controlled to prevent unauthorized access to other user data.

By default, initialization functions defined above are entry functions because they are the entry point for any outside request. However, other smart contract functions accessible by oracles/APIs shall also be classified as entry functions. Illustrated in Figure 13.4, engineers shall test and verify that no backdoor is present from entry functions to other functions.

13.4.5 Termination functions

As explained above, smart contracts shall be terminated at a certain point when certain conditions are fulfilled so as to avoid future accidental executions. A function – the termination function – that performs the termination of a smart contract shall always be present in the smart contract.

The termination function shall be accessible by the governance/delegate or the owner of the contract with appropriate access rights. In the case of interruptive terminations, for example, termination before the end of the

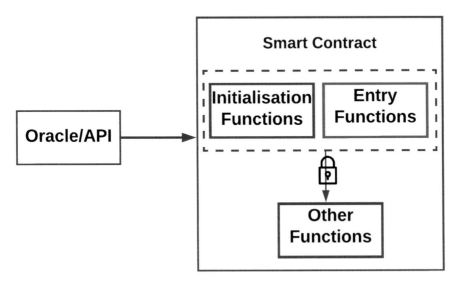

Figure 13.4   Entry functions shall not create back doors to other functions of the contract.

contract, a smart contract shall not be terminated without the agreement of all the stakeholders and the governance.

The governance of the PDL shall ensure that only valid inputs are sent to the termination functions. If any participants identified sending invalid string as argument, governance shall take necessary measures of compliance such as blacklisting of the nodes (e.g., based on node reputation).

Meaningless reasons, that is the reasons that do not clearly identify the problem of the interrupt shall be categorized as invalid reasons. All the reasons shall provide the details of the interruption. Brief reasons shall not be used, that is, few words description shall not be used, and the reasons shall provide the complete description with identifiers. The reasons shall provide complete information specific to the jurisdiction and the contract.

Some of the examples for invalid reasons are as follows:

- Invalid version – invalid version is not a valid reason, details such as why the version is invalid should be included.
- Human error – shall specify the type error for example, typo with missing information along with corrections.
- Example corrected version – should also include the date and type of error such as Person A has activated the contract with wrong parameters.
- Missing information – specify the missing fields.

Example of valid reasons:

- Smart contract completed life cycle.
- New version of the contract is required.

13.4.6 Example architecture of a smart contract

Examples of reference architectures of smart contracts with external and internal inputs are respectively shown in Figures 13.5 and 13.6.

13.5 Data Inputs and Outputs

When interacting with the environment, smart contracts may take inputs from internal and external data sources such as other smart contracts or web servers. They may also provide outputs to other sources such as local and foreign PDLs and web servers.

Several combinations of data inputs and outputs are possible. A smart contract may take inputs from:

- Other smart contracts (internal or external).
- Oracle services.
- Other sources such as web servers and databases.

And it may provide outputs to:

- Other smart contracts (internal or external).
- Oracle services.
- Other sources such as webservers and databases.

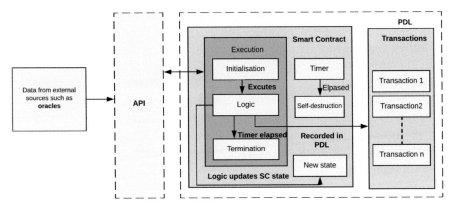

Figure 13.5 Reference architecture of smart contract with external inputs.

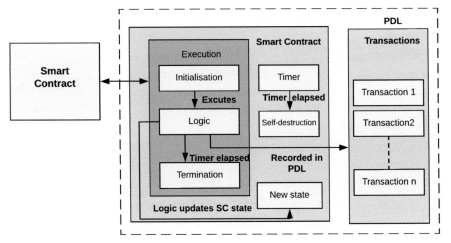

Figure 13.6 Reference architecture of smart contract with internal inputs.

13.5.1 Generalized input/output requirements

Smart contracts do not have any built-in mechanisms to verify the integrity of data. Therefore, it is important that the data input to a smart contract is trustworthy. The generalized requirements for the data inputs are:

- **Integrity**: Data shall be untampered and unaltered. It is forbidden to send altered or tampered data. Governance shall take punitive actions against entities that enter/or try to enter altered or tampered data.
- **Accuracy**: The data input shall be accurate and trustworthy.
- **Quality of the data (e.g., syntax, semantics, and context)**: A smart contract shall be given accurate inputs. Parties executing the smart contract shall ensure that they send accurate and timely inputs to the smart contract.
- **Security**: The inputs are secure from attacks such as the "Man-in-the-Middle Attack." This type of attacks can be dangerous in some use cases such as in an auction contract if a bid value is intercepted, since it can affect the validity of the auction.
- **Authenticity**: Data shall be from the authorized users with appropriate access rights only.
- **Sequencing and synchronizing inter-ledger and intra-ledger executions**: Some smart contracts are dependent on operations/inputs from other smart contracts, which may be internal or external. In such a case, it is important that the execution of the pre-requisite shall be completed before hand.

13.5.2 Internal data inputs

Internal data inputs are the inputs stemming from the same PDL network or trusted infrastructure. When all the permanent nodes belong to the same PDL network, we will refer to it as Home PDL-Network (HPN). A smart contract may take internal input from:

- HPN participants and
- HPN smart contracts.

Typically, *HPN participants* access smart contracts through a transaction request. The smart contract shall receive data from authorized participants only. The participants sending the data/parameters to smart contracts shall ensure that data is accurate. The access control mechanism shall be handled through identity and permission control services defined in PDL reference architecture (see the previous chapter).

In terms of *HPN smart contracts*, when a smart contract is dependent on the data from another smart contracts' outputs, the important challenge is the completion of the pre-requisite contract.

The pre-requisite smart contract shall be completed before sending the subsequent request. Only some fields and functions of a smart contract are accessible by other smart contracts. Developers shall ensure that there is no ambiguity in access allocation.

Execution triggered by unauthorized smart contracts shall be rejected. The unauthorized access will be granted by chain of the contracts due auto-execution property of smart contracts.

13.5.3 External data inputs

A smart contract may take input from foreign PDL networks, external participants or smart contract. In such a scenario, following requirements shall be met:

- The foreign PDL governance shall manage access of their respective PDL's smart contracts and assign access-rights accordingly.
- Appropriate access-rights shall be acquired before such access.
- External data shall be exchanged or accessed through the governance-channel only and participants from any side shall not have any direct access to the foreign PDLs.

The two possible approaches to access the data from a foreign PDL are a) a faster approach; and b) a secure approach.

In terms of the *faster approach*, when PDL participants want to access the data from a foreign PDL, they can generate a request-to-access message to their local governance which will subsequently send this request to the *gateway*.

The gateway can be maintained and administrated by both the internal and external governance and elected by mutual consensus of all participating PDL governance. All the access from a foreign PDL shall be recorded by the gateway in a separate secured storage as well for future audit.

In Figure 13.7, the possible architecture for external data access is shown. The gateway maintains an access control list, which keeps the record of the data shared between the PDLs. Note that this access control list is also maintained in a secured data structure.

This is a faster approach but has some security considerations. The major security consideration here is the single point of failure for the Gateway. This means that if the Gateway is compromised, the malicious party can take over

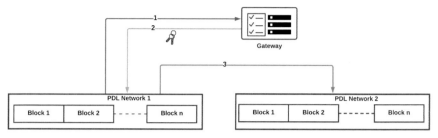

Figure 13.7   Smart contract inputs from foreign PDL/non-HPN (*faster approach*).

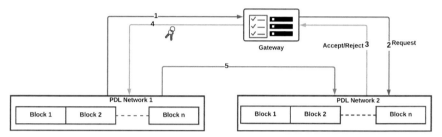

Figure 13.8   Smart contract inputs from foreign PDL/non-HPN (*faster approach*).

the system and issue the keys to themselves or possibly to other malicious parties.

To resolve such a vulnerability, a *secured approach* is proposed by ETSI PDL. Illustrated in Figure 13.8, when PDL participants generate a request-to-access message to their local PDL governance, the governance forwards this request to the Gateway. The gateway sends the access request to the governance of the foreign PDLs. Upon approval access is granted or rejected.

Note that, in this case there is no access list maintained by the gateway and decision to grant/reject access rights are made dynamically. However, the gateway does maintain a list of access granted by the PDLs for future audit.

13.5.4 Oracles

Smart contracts often interact with the outside environment, i.e., in many situations, they may take data from external sources (e.g., marketplaces and weather data). They may also send data to the outside world. A common medium to do so is often referred to as the "oracle."

Oracles extract and verify data inputs for the smart contracts and PDLs, as illustrated in Figure 13.9. They also send the data to the outside world from the PDL in the similar manner. Typically, oracles are services (e.g., WebAPIs)

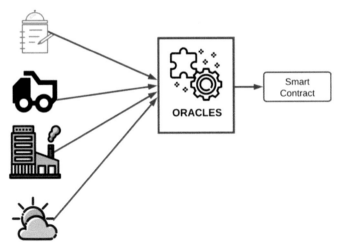

Figure 13.9 Oracles take inputs from several data sources, processes them and provides inputs to smart contracts.

which extract the data from external data sources and translates it into PDL-understandable format.

Generally, there are **hardware and software oracles**:

1. Hardware oracles: Many applications of PDLs require data inputs from hardware probes such as thermometers, pressure gauges, and distance measurement devices. Some of these hardware devices generate analogue outputs that need to be digitized using A/D convertor, where A/D convertors are known to have an intrinsic element of error.
2. Software oracles: The input sources for the oracles are software such as stock exchange data from their website/WebAPIs. This data is digital to begin with, so no conversion is needed, and the above element of error is eliminated.

In both cases the oracles should be programmed to convert the information into meaningful data format for the purpose of the PDL application.

Oracles are blockchain-agnostic and typically generalized enough to access any PDL and provide the data. The problem with oracles is that they are sometimes not trustworthy.

To avoid delay in transaction processing, the **properties of oracles** shall be:

- Availability – Governance shall implement strategies to ensure the availability of the oracles. That is, when a smart contract needs the data, it shall be pre-processed by the oracles and available for the smart contract input.

- Security – Governance shall implement strategies to ensure the source of the data is trustworthy and the channels are secured to prevent interception such as man-in-the-middle attack.
- Governance approved oracles list – In the case of external oracle services, they shall be authorized by the governance. That is, governance shall have a list of approved oracle services which may provide the data to the PDL.
- Trustworthiness – PDL governance shall ensure that the malicious oracles cannot provide data to smart contracts. Oracles may process the data from several other sources. Generally, there are several websites/APIs publishing this data. This compromises the integrity of the data. To tackle with this problem, oracle services shall only take inputs from the verified data sources.
- Performance – Oracles shall have performance matching to the PDL. For example, some PDLs have high transaction throughput. The oracles shall match the performance or throughput of the PDLs, to ensure the availability and timely data. Oracle services shall also ensure that they can cope with the demand of the PDL data, for example, some PDLs may request large amount of data. Oracle services shall ensure that they can match with the volume demand. Oracle services shall be scalable such that they can cope with inflated demand of the requests from a PDL.
- Access rights – The governance shall assign the access rights for the oracles and for the required duration only. In other words, the start and end dates should be explicitly defined in the request to access the data.

In terms of the *criteria for the oracle service approval*, the governance of the PDL will register the services of oracles through application procedures. Application procedures are up to the preferred methods of governance. For example, governance may take oracle service applications through an open call or specific invite. Yet, the approval requires mandatory requirements listed below:

- The smart contract shall have a built-in mechanism to verify the validity of oracle.
- The list of approved oracles shall be updated periodically. This is the governance discretion to set the timeline of this review, but the review period shall not be more than three calendar months.

- Governance shall define the criteria of the approval before or at the time of the PDL formation. This shall include:
  - Oracles shall be from authorized and validated sources only.
  - Time-limited approval – approve the oracles for a certain governance-defined time only. After this time, the access shall automatically be revoked and come under review.
  - Oracles services shall be using transparent and auditable software to translate the data.
  - The oracle services code and architecture shall be auditable without any additional monetary transaction.
  - The oracle services shall be transparent.
  - Oracle services shall be using government-approved software libraries only.
  - The author/source of data shall be specified by the oracles before/at the time of approval.
  - Oracles shall be using authorized sources only. That is, they shall sign IPR agreement with the data sources before making application request with PDL governance.
- Oracle sources shall provide details of their software and hardware security methods for data protection and authentication to the oracle services.
- Oracle services shall maintain an online open directory for their available oracles.
- All oracles shall be verifiable through this open directory.

13.6 Governance in Smart Contract Life

Generally, Governance of a PDL oversees the overall operations of the PDL. This includes but is not limited to access control and operational strategies. The role of governance depends on the consensus of the PDL founding participants. Governance can be automated as well, in which a software program can take the decisions based on the pre-programmed conditions.

13.6.1 Key decisions of governance

Governance of a PDL *shall* take the following decisions for smart contracts:

- Listing the approved oracles for smart contracts.
- Listing the test strategies for smart contracts.

- Identification and acceptance of new members for a smart contract.
- Updating a smart contract.
- Access to smart contracts from external sources shall be contingent on approval of both internal and external governance.

Governance of a PDL *may* take the following decisions for smart contracts:

- Transaction approval time – a time that smart contract shall wait to for its next executions.
- Installing a smart contract – a new smart contract is installed with the governance's approval.

13.6.2 Operational decisions

Operational decisions are the responsibility of governance, and the owner of the contract shall follow the governance's advice to ensure the successful operation of a smart contract. The operational decisions a *governance shall* involve in are listed below:

- Start date/time and end date/time of the contract.
- Allocate access rights to all the actors with in the PDL network.
- Updating the contract.
- Contract versioning.
- Approved software/hardware technologies.
- Access control strategies, technologies, and algorithms.
- The external participants who can access the contract – this is important because the owner shall not allow the external entities to access the contract if not allowed by the governance.
- Allocate unique identities to all the actors with in the PDL network.

The *owner shall* be responsible to decide on:

- The internal participants who can access the contract.
- Choose between governance approved technologies.
- Testing strategies listed in governance guidelines.
- Oracle's list approved in governance guidelines.

13.6.3 Termination of contract

Smart contract termination is a critical event that may affect (e.g., adversely) the behavior and content of the PDL. Following are the requirements for smart contract termination:

- Owners of the contracts shall not initiate termination without the agreement of the governance.
- All the stakeholders and the governance shall approve the termination before the termination is initiated. That is, participants of the contract shall not pull out of the contract by terminating it.
- Participants shall take the full responsibility of the smart contract and ensure the termination follows a standard procedure.
- When it is identified that a smart contract is not working as required and needs to be terminated the governance shall be informed of this problem without any delay.
- In case of malfunctioning, after the governances' consent, if the smart contract is still active it will be turned off.
- If a revised (updated) smart contract is required, it will need to be activated either before or after the termination of the previous contract as applicable.
- If it is not active and/or does not require a replacement (e.g., dormant), the governance shall terminate the contract without a revised smart contract.

13.6.4 General compliance guidelines

PDL governance may follow the following guidelines and strategies to make a smart contract secure:

- Compliance measures are dependent on the local laws. The PDL governance shall ensure that a contract follow the laws in the respective jurisdiction.
- In case of cross-border PDL, that is, a PDL network where many governance laws are involved, the governance of the PDL shall outline the strategies of laws coded in smart contracts, when initiating the PDL and as per the laws applicable for such scenarios.
- Penalties are the governance and PDL founders' decision. However, all the compensation and penalties shall be recorded in a document and signed by all the parties at the time of PDL initialization.
- The PDL participants that join the network later, shall made aware of the document and its contents and sign the document before joining the PDL.
- Any wrongdoing detected after the damage the governance may blacklist/ block the node. Penalties/compensation can be imposed on the malicious nodes.

- Step wise approach – first offence, second offence and so on. At the end node can have lifetime ban or high penalties.

13.7 Testing Smart Contracts

Testing for any software program is an essential step before its deployment. Rigorous testing can prevent errors and enable designing safe and correct smart contracts.

Smart contracts can be tested like any other software, but an additional layer of testing shall be applied. That is, to ensure a smart contract interaction within itself and external entities (inter-PDL and intra-PDL) is protected through rigorous access control mechanism at the governance and smart contract layers.

13.7.1 Testing requirements

Testing is an important indicator for the unintended smart contract behavior and shall ensure the following:

- **Modularity** – If the test fails, the smart contract shall clearly indicate which part of the test failed.
- **Well-structured** – The test codes should have clear indicators of the errors. For example, instead of generalized term such as exception, a more specific exception type (e.g., IntegerOverflow Exception) shall be used.
- **Clear and self-explanatory** – The tests shall use meaningful variable names; this will assist future debugging.
- **Parameterized** – A testing code shall be parameterized, that is, it shall allow test engineers to pass a wide range of parameters to validate and verify the smart contracts' behavior with different data types.

Typically, smart contracts shall be tested in two stages:

- **Unit tests** – Tests small units or functional blocks of a smart contract.
- **Integration test** – Compile or add all the functional blocks and test the complete end-to-end smart contract.

13.7.2 Testing strategies

The smart contract testing shall follow the security protocol listed below. To achieve this, developers can follow test strategies best suited to them.

- **Modular and reusable** – Smart contract tests are designed in a modular and reusable fashion. These modular tests are managed by the governance and can be shared among the participants of the PDL. This can be useful, as it will ensure the reusability of the tests and may save time to design specific tests.
- **Automated testing** – Some of the tests may be automated, that is, a smart contract can be verified through automated engines (for example, Remix), that may be able to verify some traits of a smart contract, for example, presence of certain required libraries.
- **Outsource testing** – In some cases, the governance of the PDL may prefer to outsource the testing procedure. In case of outsourcing testing, it is required that the testing firm meets the standards and follows the same procedures as listed herein.
- **CI/CD** – To avoid several branches and conflicts at the end, the developers may choose to use continuous integration and continuous delivery (CI/CD) technique. In this technique, a small code is written and integration to avoid the conflicts. In the situations where enhanced testing is required, the code can be integrated to test environment to measure its behavior in the production PDL.

13.7.3 Generalized testing targets

It is up to the developers to adopt the strategies to test a smart contract. However, the following generalized testing targets listed below shall be met.

- Validate expected behavior – verify the expected behavior with the achieved one.
- Improve code quality – the code shall be clearly and professionally designed.
- Design efficient smart contracts by *adopting efficient programming strategies* (e.g., some built-in language functions perform better than others).
- Using widely available libraries – that is, some libraries may be not generalized enough.
- Behavior in edge cases (e.g., Genesis block, divided-by-zero error, lack of input and memory including errors resulting from network failures).
- Sequence check – check for sequential flow of the code. That is, for example, the pre-requisites shall be executed before the follow-up.

13.7.4 Testing checklist

The desired output of a smart contract depends on its purpose. Therefore, the testing checklist varies depending on the requirement and expectation from the smart contract. The following conditions shall be checked explicitly and documented:

- Entry functions – they are secured and do not create back doors to other functions without access-control.
- Termination function – A smart contract shall have a safe and callable termination condition.
- Logic functions – Functions that perform the operations of a smart contract shall be present. Without such functions a smart contract is not usable.
- Access rights – Only authorized user(s) shall have access to the functions of a smart contract. At the testing phase, accessibility to different functions with different roles (e.g., admin and user) shall be verified and validated.

13.7.5 Offline testing

In offline testing a smart contract is tested locally, without connecting to the production PDL. Offline testing is typically being done by two means:

- Sandbox testing: This may include a standalone test node able to emulate the operational environment.
- Testbeds: This includes a larger testbed, closest to the actual operating conditions.

Typically, *sandboxes* run on a single machine with several containers acting as nodes of that PDL. Some of parameters may not be accurate with sandbox testing such as transaction latency, which will obviously be very low when all the containers are in a same machine. However, sandbox testing is still helpful for measuring and validating the behavior of certain aspects of a smart contract.

Sandboxes should emulate production environment with the exception of execution latency. Below are some requirements of the sandboxes that shall be used for smart contract testing:

- Use the same PDL type and version which the smart contract is expected to be installed to. For example, Hyperledger Fabric version 2.0 smart contract shall be tested on a Hyperledger Fabric version 2.0 sandbox.

- The sandbox shall be using/downloaded from the same source as the PDL type. For example, for Corda testbed, the ledger artifacts shall be downloaded/extracted from the verified Corda source.
- If resources are available (e.g., enough computation availability), a sandbox shall use the same/or close to the same number of nodes as the production PDL.
- Operating system of the underlying sandbox shall be the same (or as close as possible) to the production environment (e.g., Kubernetes and Docker).

If the resources allow for a fully fletched *testbed*, then it is always better to use a group of test nodes and mimic a production PDL. Smart contracts can be tested on such test-PDLs for additional parameters such as transaction throughput. Below are the requirements for testbeds:

- All nodes shall use same PDL type and version number as the production PDL.
- All the smart contracts shall be using the same programming language, libraries, and software as they are expected to be using in the production environment.
- All the PDL nodes shall be using same software configuration as the production-PDL (e.g., operating system and developers' environment).

13.7.6 Online monitoring

In online monitoring, a smart contract is installed on a production PDL and the outputs as well as interaction with other entities (e.g., other smart contracts and foreign PDLs) are monitored.

One approach is to conduct a *time-limited test*. Before the online monitoring initiates, a smart contract shall be installed on the production PDL and be tested for a limited time. All the participants of the PDL, shall be made aware of the test-status of the contract. That is, any transactions done by the test smart contract shall not be valid until the test time is elapsed. After the testing time, the governance may choose to extend the lifetime of the contract and take it to production or terminate it for improvements.

Post testing, a PDL shall be monitored for its lifetime. It is essential to monitor a smart contract continuously because – despite thorough testing – some of the cases may lead to unexpected (possibly harmful) outcomes.

A smart contract can have a programmed function which can generate periodic reports to the governance. The parameters of the reports may be specific to the purpose of the smart contract and the discretion of the PDL governance.

As such an approach will occupy bandwidth, it may be feasible to program reporting transactions to off-peak times. These reports may include the number of execution requests in a unit time; and the input and outputs. Based on these reports, the following decisions can be taken: suspension and upgrade of smart contract; adjusting/updating access control to smart contracts.

13.8 Updating Smart Contracts

It is sometimes required to update a smart contract, for example, change its end date or owner details. Yet, smart contracts on a PDL are immutable, so an installed smart contract cannot be amended. However, this can be upgraded through installing a newer version of the smart contract and deactivating the old contract.

It is up to the governance, owners and stakeholders to make the decision when updates are required. Some scenarios requiring updates are outlined below:

- New terms are identified which need to be included in future versions.
- Vulnerability found in the old contract. Notably, new vulnerability are identified in the programming language, or any library used in the code of a smart contract.
- Old contract reached its end date and stakeholders wish to continue using the contract (in this case, stakeholders may choose to change the end date of the old contract instead of installing a new version).
- Change/update in governing laws or standards.
- The smart contract is not acting as planned.

13.8.1 Updating an old version

The means to update an old smart contract version are as follows:

- **Deactivating the old contract** – the old contract shall be deactivated properly which means, ensuring the end date is the past date and all the variables are deactivated. Note that, two versions of a smart contract shall not be operational at a same time.
- **Back up data and variables** – the old version stays on the ledger even after the deactivation. However, some stakeholders may prefer to keep

a local copy due to unforeseen circumstances such as deletion of the complete chain.

When a smart contract is updated, it shall follow the version number in continuation with the old contract. For example, if the old version was xx:xxx:01 the next version shall be xx:xxx:02.

13.8.2 Updating steps

Once the governance and stakeholders agree to update a smart contract, all of the following steps shall be taken:

- Identify the changes to be made (i.e., functions or software library).
- Make the changes.
- Test the smart contract.
- Redeploy the smart contract – a new version of a smart contract shall not be deployed before it has passed the testing.

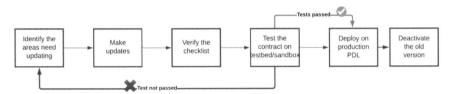

Figure 13.10   Smart contract update process.

These steps before redeployment are mandatory and similar to initial deployment of the smart contract:

- Passed the code test (test engineers or developers shall check and verify this).
- Passed the testbed/sandbox test (test engineers or developers shall check and verify this).
- If the test is carried out by test engineers, then confirmation is required from developers that the tests met the requirements.

This is illustrated in Figure 13.10.

13.8.3 Securely deactivating old contract

The old smart contract version needs also to be securely deactivated:

- The old version of the smart contract shall be terminated before or concurrently with the redeployment of a new/updated version.

- The sequence is decided on a case-by-case basis by the stakeholders and the governance.
- In either case, the agreement or the smart contract shall not be affected by this transition from the old to the new/revised contract.

 The following requirements should be fulfilled:

- The start date of the new version shall be after the termination date of the old version.
- The time between the start of new version and end of old version is up to the stakeholders and the governance but.
- In no circumstances two versions of a smart contracts shall be active at the same time.

13.9 Smart Contract Cybersecurity Threats

To use smart contracts for contractual purposes with an underpinning service level agreement (SLA), they ought to be secured and impenetrable. Threats and dangers to a smart contract are thus discussed subsequently.

13.9.1 Threats due to programming errors

Since smart contracts are immutable, any error done in programming would make a smart contract perform invalid/erroneous executions. Such an action may cause people and corporations hefty damages such as monetary losses and reputational damages. It is the contract owners' and developers' shared responsibility that the testing checklist is followed before the deployment of the contract.

Governance shall thus ensure that all the owners of the contracts are following the correct procedures for the coding and testing as specified above. A smart contract shall be tested against a pre-defined list of tests based on the requirements defined in earlier sections to ensure that it passes those tests as a pre-condition to deployment.

13.9.2 Internal threats

There are several internal threats, in addition to the fundamental threat due to programming errors. The first threat we will discuss pertains to *transaction ordering*.

Notably, smart contracts may require information resulting from previous transactions. It is then important that the following is adhered to:

- The governance shall sequence the transaction executions such that dependent smart contracts operate in a consecutive manner.
- A smart contract shall receive correct data for its execution.
- Governance of the PDL shall keep track of PDL latency.

For instance, there may be a wait time before the execution of smart contract. If a PDL has a 5 ms transaction latency, the smart contract ought to wait for this time before starting the execution to ensure a proper order of transactions.

There are also *malicious/accidental executions*. Albeit solid access control mechanisms, it is still possible that some of the users send incorrect data to the PDL. Such a behavior can be benign or intentional. The following thus ought to be ensured:

- Governance shall ensure that all the nodes (i.e., PDL participants) shall follow security protocols (i.e., SSL) to access the PDL to avoid attacks such as the man-in-the-middle attack.
- Governance shall ensure that the nodes (i.e., PDL participants), shall not send invalid/wrong transactions.
- Governance of the PDL shall introduce compliance strategies such as applying penalties (such as temporary blacklisting) to nodes that do not follow the protocol.
- Node owners should ensure that they have adequate network resources to meet smart contract execution requirements.

There is also the issue of *reporting wrong parameters*. Users may advertently and inadvertently report incorrect data, which may affect the smart contract executions and results.

For example, when a user is reporting its own device managed data (e.g., QoS parameters) and it is in their benefit to overstate their parameters. It is likely that they may send wrong/incorrect parameters to the ledger.

In some of the cases when data is at very fast speed such as routers' data, due to speed of execution, it may be difficult to identify such behavior in real time. It is not always the users who will try to send the wrong data to the ledger; other factors, such as man-in-the-middle or benign mistakes can also result in wrong data inputs.

This can be mitigated through online monitoring where the smart contract and associated data is monitored. If wrong parameters are reported following measures shall be taken:

- The node owners shall take all the necessary measures that accurate and timely parameters are passed to a smart contract.

- Governance shall observe execution activities periodically and take necessary compliance measures of potential problems identified.
- Governance observation intervals/periods is dependent on case-to-case bases and up to the discretion of the governance.

Another solution may be to adopt interrogation protocol. With such a protocol, the devices keep the local record of the data forwarded by them and only the details of the flow at the source and the destination are recorded on the ledger.

13.9.3 External threats

External threats to a smart contract emerge from external entities such as foreign PDLs or oracles. The governance shall ensure the safety and security of smart contracts and shall not allow the external entities to access the contracts without rigorous checking.

To avoid external threats following are the *requirements*:

- Too many transactions – may not be able to process by a smart contract, may cause congestion at the ledger. Governance will be responsible to keep track of this.
- Authorized access – the keys should be revoked without any delay.
- Governance shall ensure the smart contract only gets as many calls as it can handle.

The first external threat we will discuss are *malicious oracles*. They can send the wrong/delayed information to the PDL. It is required that governance of the PDL shall maintain a list of trusted oracles:

- To ensure the timely data, governance of the PDL shall define the threshold time to accept the data from oracles.
- This time would differ with the use case. For example, for weather data, hourly update would be appropriate but for stock exchange a finer interval would be required.
- Oracles may be vulnerable to attacks such as bribery; precautions ought to be taken.
- Malicious oracles cause denial of service attacks because if there is no API in the middle it can overwhelm the PDL.

There are also *malicious attacks*. Some of the below can be adopted to protect against these:

- Systems should be self-protecting, that is a smart contract shall have mechanisms to pick up erroneous and malicious calls and shall have mechanisms to report such a behavior to the governance.
- Malicious attacks should be penalized by the governance. Governance can maintain a list of entities/parties trying to behave maliciously and take necessary measures to block their future access.

There is also *denial of service attacks*. Some of the following can be adopted to protect against these:

- Governance of the PDL shall ensure all the external inputs to the PDL are through an API, i.e., shall be checked before allowed in the PDL network.
- The number of transaction requests altogether (i.e., both local requests and external requests) shall not exceed the throughput of the PDL.

References

[1] https://www.etsi.org/deliver/etsi_gr/PDL/001_099/004/01.01.01_60/gr _PDL004v010101p.pdf

14

Distributed Data Management

In this chapter, we focus on distributed data management which is one of the main use cases of PDLs. We first explore different use cases, and then introduce architecture solutions along with key challenges. The technical approach taken in this chapter is based on the governance and architecture exposure of the previous chapters.

14.1 Use Cases for Federated Data Management

14.1.1 Introduction to federated use cases

We describe here some selected federated data management use cases or scenarios, which could benefit from the use of permissioned distributed ledgers (PDLs).

As illustrated in Figure 14.1, a general data pipeline in federated data management could consist of a set of relatively sequential stages such as data collection, data storing, data computing, data sharing, and data visualization.

For each stage, multiple organizations could participate and work together. Each organization could have their own data, for example, generated from ubiquitous devices deployed for different applications such as connected vehicles.

In general, a data pipeline (e.g., data pipeline A and data pipeline B) starts with data collection from devices, but it could complete in different places in the networking system.

For example, data pipeline B in Figure 14.1 stops in edge networks leveraging edge servers for data storing, data computing and data visualization, while data pipeline A ends in the cloud.

ETSI PDL does not cover the entire data pipeline but focuses more on the stages and corresponding scenarios, which are more relevant to PDL technologies.

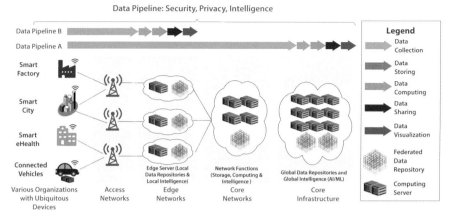

Figure 14.1   General data pipeline in federated data management.

14.1.2 Federated data collection

Our daily lives are surrounded by a variety of sensors and devices. Internet of Things (IoT) technologies enable us to leverage these sensors/devices to monitor and measure the physical world in a real-time manner. In many data-driven IoT applications, the first and most important stage is data collection.

During data collection, the system can collect data from different devices such as consumer equipment, personal devices, cameras, and wearable health devices; data can also be collected from commercial equipment including security monitoring systems, traffic monitoring equipment, production lines, logistics and supply chain systems, etc.

These devices generate different types of data and could belong to and be owned by multiple organizations; the resulted data collection that contains multiple data types and/or relies on multiple organizations is referred to as federated data collection.

Figure 14.2 shows an industrial Internet of Things (IIoT) use case, which includes a few processes such as smart manufacturing, smart logistics, and customer experience monitoring. Multiple scenarios could be involved in each process. For example, the smart manufacturing process could cover product quality control, storage management, onsite energy management, equipment maintenance, etc.

All those processes and scenarios need to be monitored in real-time to ensure overall product delivery and product quality. As a result, a large amount of production, logistics and customer experience data are generated at all times and need to be collected.

However, in a real-world production environment, manufacturing equipment and information technology (IT) systems usually involve multiple manufacturers; in the meantime, a complete manufacturing process could involve different departments or even different companies/organizations.

Similarly, during the smart logistics process, products will be transported from factories to customers through multiple intermediate transit places, where multiple organizations are involved as well. All of these facts demonstrate that data collection in IIoT is a complex system and needs multi-party collaboration, which is referred to as federated data collection.

Please note that Industrial Internet Consortium (IIC) [1] defines more IIoT use cases, which are not limited to Figure 14.1. In these use cases being considered, data security could be needed; as a result, data at rest and/or data in transit could be encrypted when there is a risk of data leakage.

Industrial Internet of Things [IIoT]

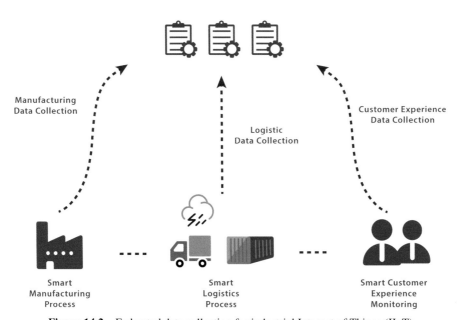

Figure 14.2 Federated data collection for industrial Internet of Things (IIoT).

14.1.3 Federated learning

Traditional machine learning (ML) is usually centralized, in the sense that:

1) training data is usually collected to be stored at a centralized location such as a centralized database; and
2) learning process is performed at a centralized location such as clouds as well. However, traditional ML could cause data leakage issues, since training data is maintained at a location, different than its original place and likely losing data privacy protection.

As a distributed ML technology and a type of federated data computing, federated learning (FL) implements a distributed ML model training process by means of multiple FL participants while still ensuring data privacy, security and legal compliance. Using FL-based mobile keyboard prediction as an example, FL usually consists of the following steps:

- Step 1: Mobile phones as FL participants participating in an FL task first download initial training model (i.e., the initial global model) from an FL Server.
- Step 2: Each mobile phone conducts the local training over its local data to train the model and generate its local model (or model update).
- Step 3: After the local model is trained, the mobile phone uploads the encrypted local model update (i.e., gradients) to the FL sever.
- Step 4: The FL server aggregates all local model updates collected from multiple mobile phones to obtain a new/updated global model. The updated global model will be then further sent to each mobile phone for the next round of training (Similar to Step 1).
- Overall, steps 1–4 will be executed for multiple rounds to improve the global model with expected quality and/or other requirements.

From the above process, it can be seen that FL can make full use of the data and computing power of the FL participants. Multiple parties (i.e., participants) can collaborate to build a more robust ML model without sharing/moving their data. This is very important for ML tasks when a strict data law/supervision is enforced.

For example, the General Data Protection Regulation (GDPR) in Europe puts forward strict requirements on the storage, use, and transfer of users' private data. Therefore, FL can be used to solve key issues such as data ownership, data privacy, and data access rights in this environment.

Consider a general use case of smart city and smart transportation as shown in Figure 14.3:

- In smart city applications, many cameras will be deployed on streets and generate continuous data or data streams. These urban camera data can be used to train an ML model for urban environmental monitoring and predicting. However, uploading all camera data to cloud could be cumbersome or unrealistic. Accordingly, FL is a more feasible and efficient method.
- Similarly, in smart transportation applications, there will be a large number of vehicles driving on the road, and each vehicle will generate massive real-time driving data. These data can be trained to generate many ML models (e.g., to predict which road sections or during which time periods vehicles are most likely to have poor driving behavior/performance). However, these data are not only large in quantity, but also contain personal privacy information; as a result, it is unwise or inefficient to upload these data to a cloud for centralized processing/training as in traditional ML. FL can be applied in this use case such that a global ML model can be jointly trained by vehicles without uploading driving data from vehicles to cloud.

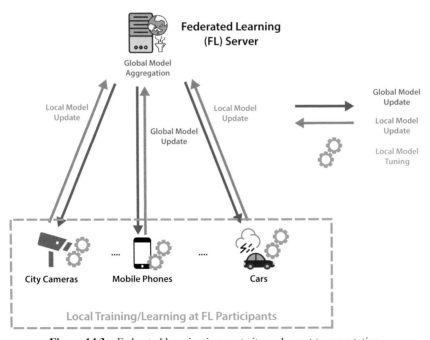

Figure 14.3   Federated learning in smart city and smart transportation.

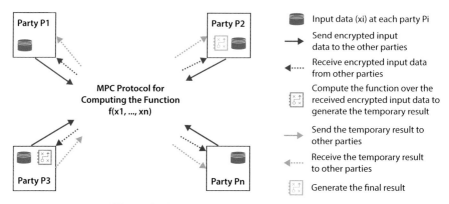

Figure 14.4   General multi-party computation.

14.1.4 Multi-party computation use case

Secure multi-party computation (MPC) was originally introduced in [2] in the form of "The Millionaire's Problem." Since then, many advances have been made in both MPC theories and practical MPC deployments [3, 4].

In a general setting of MPC, there are n parties. Each party Pi hosts its own input data xi. They want to jointly compute a function to get a result: *result = f(x1, x2, ..., xn)* with the requirement that no party can know or deduce input data hosted by other parties. In other words, all parties only know the function and the computed result. Figure 14.4 shows such a general MPC structure as an example of MPC use cases, which consists of the following procedures:

- Step 1: Parties encrypt their input data.
- Step 2: Parties exchange their encrypted input data.
- Step 3: One (or multiple) party computes the function over received encrypted input data from other parties to generate a temporary result.
- Step 4: The temporary result is sent to other parties.
- Step 5: One (or multiple) party computes the function over the temporary result to generate the final result.
- Step 6: The final result is sent to other parties.

14.1.5 Federated data discovery and sharing

As a critical stage of federated data management pipeline, federated data discovery and sharing refers to the process, where data discovery cannot be solely served by a single organization, but served by multiple organizations.

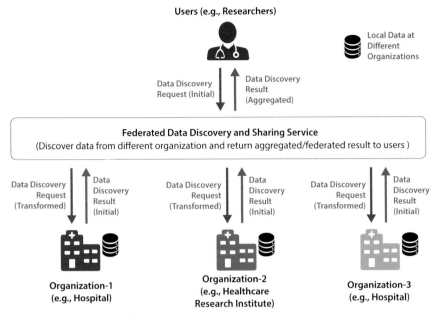

Figure 14.5 Federated data discovery.

In other words, a federated data discovery request will trigger data lookup operations on data maintained locally by different organizations, and discovery results from each organization will be combined or aggregated as the final result for the federated data discovery request.

Figure 14.5 illustrates a federated data discovery scenario, where a user (e.g., a researcher) can discover data (e.g., genomic data) from multiple organizations (e.g., hospitals). In other words, the user's data discovery request will not be served by a single organization, but served by multiple, unnecessarily trusted, organizations [5, 6]. This scenario consists of the following steps:

- Step 1: A user (e.g., a doctor or a researcher) issues an initial data discovery request to a federated data discovery and sharing service (FDDSS), which is a logical function and has access to data maintained locally at different organizations. It is assumed that the user knows the address of FDDSS (e.g., through pre-configuration or provisioning).
- Step 2: FDDSS could simply forward the initial data discovery request to organizations (e.g., Organization-1, Organization-2, and Organization-3); alternatively, it could transform the initial data discovery request to

multiple transformed data discovery requests and forward each transformed data discovery request to a different organization. Within this step, FDDSS could first authenticate and authorize if the user has the right to leverage the discovery service. Then, FDDSS could enforce certain access control rules limiting data discovery based on access criteria. As an example, access control rules could specify the list of data types or items that are not discoverable.

- Step 3: Each organization receives a separate data discovery request from FDDSS. The organization will authenticate and authorize the data discovery request, look up the data maintained locally against any discovery criteria contained in the data discovery request, and generate discovery result. If any data cannot be discovered (e.g., due to confidential or privacy considerations), the organization could reject the data discovery request and/or exclude such data from the discovery result.
- Step 4: FDDSS receives data discovery results from multiple organizations, aggregates these results, generates an aggregated result, and forwards the aggregated result to the user.

14.1.6 Possible actors in FDM systems

Dependent on the support applications (e.g., federated data collection, federated learning, federated data discovery and sharing), federated data management (FDM) systems could have various types of data and different kinds of actors (e.g., data source, data host, and data consumer):

- Data source: The entity such as end devices that generates original data.
- Data host: The entity that stores and hosts the data. A data source could send the original data to a data host; if the data source maintains the original data locally, it acts as the data host as well.
- Data consumer: The entity that requests to access the data. A data consumer requests data from a data host and/or a data source.

14.2 Key Issues with Federated Data Management

14.2.1 Key issues with federated data collection

Federated data collection is essentially a distributed system and involves multi-party collaboration, which leads to the following issues:

- The first issue is related to trust. These multiple parties or multiple organizations involved in federated data collection need to build a certain level of trust in order to jointly collect data in a trustworthy manner.

Table 14.1   Possible actors in FDM systems.

Actors		Data Source	Data Host	Data Consumer
Federated data collection		Entities (e.g., devices) that generate data	Entities (e.g., servers) that collect data	Entities (e.g., users) that use data
Federated learning	Training data	FL participants (or other entities that send training data to FL participants)	FL participants	FL participants
	Local model	FL participants	FL server and FL participants	FL server
	Global model	FL server	FL server and FL participants	FL participants and users
Multi-party computation (MPC)		MPC parties	MPC parties	MPC parties
Federated data discovery and sharing		Domain entities of an organization that generates data	Organizations that maintain data locally	Users issuing data discovery and sharing requests

- The second issue is how to guarantee the integrity of the data collected by multiple organizations. For example, in the IIoT use case, logistics data as collected from a shipping truck will probably not be tampered.
- The third issue is how to incentivize multiple organizations to participate federated data collection. For example, customer experience data in the IIoT use case can be very useful for enhancing the manufacturing process. A proper incentive mechanism is needed to encourage customers to contribute their experience data.
- The fourth issue is related to network security. For example, the IIoT use case relies on distributed IoT networks to enable federated data collection. To secure distributed IoT network is crucial.

The above issues could be solved by leveraging PDL technologies. For example, PDL technologies can be used to form a unified ledger infrastructure, which allows various companies, various equipment manufacturers and various logistic companies to achieve more trustful collaboration relationships, which will ultimately ensure the credibility, accountability, and transparency of federated data collection in the IIoT use case, and in turn improve the efficiency and reliability of next-generation smart manufacturing.

As described in federate data collection use cases, IIoT data will be transmitted and collected from various IIoT devices (e.g., factory devices, shipping vehicles) to data collection service in the cloud. This is usually done without using or interacting with PDL system. In other words, many applications currently use regular communications (i.e., off-chain communications without leveraging PDL) for normal data transmission and collection, and only leverage distributed ledgers for recording selected data collection histories (i.e., on-chain communications using PDL). This approach has two problems:

- it involves two separate processes (i.e., off-chain and on-chain communications) and is inefficient in terms of overall overhead. However, in some cases, it could be more desired to leverage PDL to support both on-chain and off-chain communication; and
- applications need to directly deal with PDL, which might not be affordable especially when applications are hosted on resource-constrained IIoT devices. As a result, new functionalities such as intermediary entities can be designed to help applications to interact with the designated PDL on behalf of applications; such intermediary entities are logical entities, which could be co-located with servers, gateways, and/or other type of network nodes.

When considering leveraging PDL systems to transmit/convey and record original application messages (or data) simultaneously, a few issues need to be considered to improve the efficiency of such concurrent data transmission and recording:

- For example, when a sender application sends an application message to a receiver application through a selected PDL chain, the selected PDL chain needs to be able to route the application message through appropriate PDL nodes and eventually arriving at the receiver application. Given the massive number of applications (e.g., hosted by IIoT devices), it is inefficient and impractical to let PDL nodes to identify application messages and their routing for these applications. In addition, an application could continuously send many application messages through a PDL chain, while another application could only send sporadic application messages through the PDL chain; different approaches will probably be designed for such applications, which have different message generation and transmission needs.
- Another consideration is how to enable that these applications can flexibly and efficiently use various PDL chains. An application could need to use different type of PDL chains but do not have adequate capability to discover any available PDL chains and maintain their information. Plus, an application could even not directly interact with any PDL nodes in order to reduce its complexity.

- In addition, how to efficiently transform and adapt application messages to the format of PDL transactions needs to be considered for several reasons:

1) it could be required that the application message content cannot be seen by all other entities but entities involved in the same application;

2) the message content also will probably be transparent to PDL nodes, but PDL nodes need to know some metadata (e.g., which messages are from which applications so that messages from different applications could be handled by PDL nodes differently based on their needs); and

3) the size of a single application message could be too small and to contain it in a PDL transaction could cause high overhead.

14.2.2 Key issues with federated learning

In smart city and smart transportation use case, FL is used to learn AI models from distributed camera data, mobile phone data and vehicle data. Although the use of FL does not need to move local data away from FL participants (e.g., cameras, mobile phones, vehicles), traditional FL still introduces a few issues:

- First, many FL participants are not from the same organization and do not trust each other, which makes effective collaboration and coordination between them difficult especially in a fully distributed scenario.

- Second, a FL participant could have useless and even malicious local data, which cannot help training a good local model.

- Third, a FL participant could inject a bad local model, which will impact the aggregated global model. The integrity of local model and global mode also needs to be guaranteed and accountable.

- Fourth, a sufficient number of FL participants are required to guarantee the quality of the global model. The issue to how to incentivize FL participants with good local data to participate FL.

- Fifth, local models generated in each FL round could provide insights on the whole FL and enable explainable AI. But it relies on how the integrity and accountability of local models can be guaranteed.

- Last but not the least, the FL aggregation server is still a single-point-of-failure. If the FL aggregation server fails, the global model will never be appropriately generated.

PDL technologies help to solve and/or mitigate the above issues. For example, local models can be stored in the ledger for future traceability and explanation purposes. Also, smart contracts can be leveraged to encourage FL participants to actively cooperate and contribute their local data and learning capabilities.

In reality, various FL tasks can be initiated and multiple FL participants in a given FL task could not be affiliated with the same organization. In other words, those FL participants could not trust or know each other, and they could join a specific FL task randomly. Those FL participants usually do not have formal business collaboration relationships with the FL task initiator and therefore the FL participants do not have obligations for contributing themselves to an FL training process. Given that, all the data related to FL training can be recorded using PDL since it can enable the traceability and accountability of the FL training process among those untrusted FL participants. For instance, when certain FL participants are malicious nodes and uploaded many bad local model updates, the FL records in the PDL can be used to identify those malicious behaviors.

In the meantime, massive data such as training data and FL models can be generated by the FL participants and the FL server during the whole FL training process:

- For example, during the FL training process, local model updates are produced by FL participants. Once the FL training process is completed, the final global model is generated by the FL server.

- Other types of data could include training progress and performance-related data/statistics (e.g., how long did an FL participant take for completing a local training during each training round? how much computing resources were allocated for the local training?).

All types of these data can be recorded in PDL chains in order to support accountability and traceability (e.g., to support rollback operations if an FL training process needs to be restarted from a certain point in order to eliminate a bad effect made by a malicious FL participant). As such, how to effectively store them in PDL remains a major design challenge, for example, based on the following design considerations:

- The type of FL-related data to be stored to PDL systems will probably be determined, for instance, based on the availability and capability of PDL systems. For a specific FL training process, it might be determined that only the final global model and/or the list of FL participants will be stored to a PDL chain to reduce overhead to PDL system.

- FL participants will probably be appropriately instructed or notified of the type of FL-related data that they need to store to PDL chains. Note that the entity that creates/initiates a specific FL training process could now know or trust involved FL participants. Note that the size of FL models (either local models or the global model) could be in tens of megabytes and even larger. An FL model could be stored with a full version or with smaller tailored versions. As such, a critical issue is how to prepare the FL model in an appropriate version based on PDL capabilities and/or constraints before storing it onto a designated PDL chain.

- An intermediary service or function can be designed to help the interaction between the FL entities and PDL systems. Otherwise, all the FL tasks/applications have to implement their own solutions for interacting with each PDL system, which increases additional development complexity and burden for FL application developers.

14.2.3 Key issues with federated data discovery and sharing

Multiple organizations and distributed data are involved in FDDSS, which leads to the following issues:

- The first issue is related to trust. A user from an organization X could issue a discovery request to a different organization Y. In the meantime, organization X could provide access to its data (including the data obtained from organization Y) to other organizations (e.g., organization Z), practically giving organization Z the access to organization Y's information. Therefore, it is critical to have a mechanism to enable and build mutual trust among these untrusted organizations.

- The second issue is how to incentivize multiple organizations to make their data discoverable and sharable to other organizations. An organization providing data could be rewarded or could collect credits, while other organizations discovering/utilizing the data could make contributions or pay credits for the data they consume.

- The third issue is guaranteeing the quality of the discovered data. Each organization could maintain and provide the same type of data or similar type of data with different quality (e.g., date can be presented in year only or in year-month-day format for higher accuracy). This can be resolved by using a tool to identify data with appropriate quality satisfying the user's discovery criteria.

- The fourth issue is related to privacy and access control. For example, the data maintained locally by an organization could only be discoverable by certain users/organizations. In another example, an organization could need to hide data source information although it is willing to make the data discoverable.

PDL technologies can be leveraged to solve or mitigate these issues. For example, any data discovery and sharing record could be recorded in PDL permanently; as such, trust relationship among all participating organizations can be automatically established. In addition, smart contracts can be used to enable incentivized interactions between organizations providing data and organizations discovering data. Furthermore, PDL governance could manage access control of federated data discovery and sharing.

14.3 Federated Data Management Architecture

14.3.1 Introduction to FDM architecture

In here we describe the PDL-based FDM architecture including primary functional components. According to key issues described earlier, the following requirements could be considered for designing the architecture for PDL-based federated data management:

- PDL can be leveraged to build trust relationships among untrusted participants/parties/organizations involved in federated data management.
- Smart contracts can be leveraged as an effective mechanism to incentivize participants/parties/organizations to participate in federated data management and to enable autonomous interactions among them.
- PDL can be leveraged not only for recording data, but also a mechanism to propagate/transmit data among participants/parties/organizations involved in federated data management.

14.3.2 Federated data management architecture

In the context of PDL-based FDM, there are two separate systems, namely PDL system and FDM applications. To leverage PDL to solve key issues as described in previous section and eventually enable PDL-based FDM, these two systems need to interact and interwork with each other.

Figure 14.6 illustrates a general proxy-based solution to interwork FDM system and PDL system, where FDM-PDL Proxy (FPP) is included as a logical entity to connect both systems. Via FPP, FDM applications (e.g.,

Figure 14.6   PDL-based federated data management via an FDM-PDL proxy.

federated data collection, federated learning, federated data discovery and sharing), which could be a data source or a data consumer, can access PDL systems, for instance, to store FDM-related data (e.g., operation records) to a PDL chain. FPP can provide the following functions:

- find appropriate PDL chains from PDL system for an FDM application based on its requirements;
- interact with PDL system on behalf of an FDM application;
- buffer and send requests (e.g., to create a transaction) from an FDM application to PDL system;
- buffer and forward notifications and/or responses from PDL system to an FDM application; and
- knows how to talk to FDM applications and how to talk to PDL systems (e.g., ledgers); and
- FPP is a logical entity, which can be deployed as a service function or as a part of PDL system in a distributed manner. For example, if FPP needs to implement PDL-related governance and intelligence, it can be implemented as a distributed function within PDL systems.

FPP can provide the following benefits:

- alleviate overheads at both FDM and PDL; and
- provide data access control and security between FDM and PDL.

14.3.3 FDM architecture scenarios

There could be multiple FPPs between FDM system and PDL system. As an example, Figure 14.7 shows an extended solution, where FDM Entity-1 and FDM Entity-2 interact with PDL system through multiple and different FPP (i.e., via FPP-1 and FPP-2, respectively). The following scenarios and operations can be supported via FPP-1 and FPP-2.

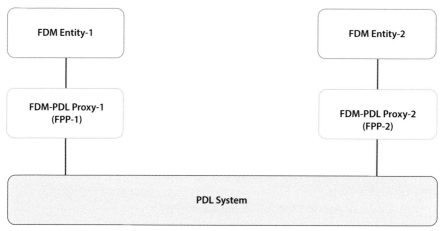

Figure 14.7   PDL-based federated data management with multiple FDM-PDL proxies.

Scenario 1: FDM Entity-1 (e.g., an FL participant) needs to record an FDM message (e.g., a local model update) to PDL system. After it is done, FDM-Entity-2 (e.g., the FL server) expects to receive a notification from PDL system:

- FDM Entity-1 creates an FDM message MSG1 and sends it to FPP-1.
- FPP-1 transforms the FDM message MSG1 to a PDL transaction TXN1. FPP-1 sends the PDL transaction TXN1 to PDL system.
- The PDL transaction TXN1 will be propagated through the PDL system, so that all PDL nodes will receive it and eventually the PDL transaction TXN1 will be included and stored in the ledger.
- After the PDL transaction TXN1 is stored in the ledger, PDL system could send a notification to FPP-2 to indicate the successful inclusion of TXN1; FPP-2 could forward the notification to FDM Entity-2.

Scenario 2: FDM Entity-1 (e.g., an IIoT device) leverages PDL system to transmit an FDM message (e.g., IIoT sensory reading) to FDM Entity-2 (e.g., IIoT data collection server), while storing this transmission record to ledgers:

- FDM Entity-1 creates an FDM message MSG1 and sends it to FPP-1.
- FPP-1 transforms the FDM message MSG1 to a PDL transaction TXN1. FPP-1 sends the PDL transaction TXN1 to PDL system.
- The PDL transaction TXN1 will be propagated through the PDL system, so that all PDL nodes will receive it.
- A PDL node forwards the PDL transaction TXN1 to FPP-2 and stores a record of this event to ledgers.

- FPP-2 receives the PDL transaction TXN1 and recovers the contained message MSG1.
- FPP-2 forwards the message MSG1 to FDM Entity-2.

14.4 Implementations of Federated PDLs

14.4.1 Solutions for PDL-based federated learning

To solve PDL-based federated learning issues, FL entities (i.e., FL task initiators, FL participants and FL servers) generally need to interact with PDL systems, for example, to store FL-related data onto PDL chains.

To make this process more efficient and alleviate extra burden to FL entities, a logical entity, referred to as ledger storage service (LSS), is proposed as a part of FDM-PDL Proxy (FPP). In fact, LSS is a value-added service to assist FL entities in leveraging PDL with minimum effort.

Basically, an FL entity acting as a LSS client just needs to specify high-layer requirements to LSS regarding how an FL task intends to leverage PDL systems such as:

1) what kinds of information will be stored onto PDL chains; and
2) whether the full version and/or tailored versions of FL model updates will probably be stored onto PDL chains.

Once those high-level requirements are conveyed to LSS, LSS needs to handle all the low-layer details in order to interact with PDL systems such as:

1) to decide which data is to be stored in which specific PDL chain; and
2) to determine whether a new PDL chain needs to be created. In other words, the application developers of FL applications need to focus on their business logic and all the interactions with PDL systems will be offloaded to and assisted by LSS.

In addition, LSS needs to figure out which FL participants are involved, and then contact each of FL participants on behalf of LSS clients, in order to convey corresponding instructions to those FL participants (e.g., what information needs to be put inside a PDL transaction, in what PDL transaction format, and stored in which specific PDL chain, etc.).

Also, LSS needs to make sure those FL participants have the appropriate privileges to manipulate the desired PDL chain (e.g., adding new blocks to a specific PDL chain). Accordingly, FL participants only need minimum effort to leverage PDL. In addition, in the case where a tailored version of FL model needs to be produced and stored in PDL, LSS needs to advise FL participants about what type of desired tailored operations will probably be conducted by the FL participants or if the tailoring operation needs to be done by LSS on behalf of FL participants.

14.4.2 Solutions for PDL-based federated data discovery and sharing

In the federated data discovery scenario, data could be stored in different locations and belong to different organizations. A given application or a User-1 issues a discovery request for discovering desired data, which could be owned and located in different organizations. In order to process or serve the discovery request from User-1, a federated discovery processing is needed, i.e., the data discovery needs to be conducted in multiple organizations.

In order to do so, third-party entities acting as discoverers can contribute to serving this discovery request but each of the entities could only have the capability for accessing or conducting discovery in one or more organizations; in other words, a single discoverer could not have the full capability for identifying the needed data among all the potential organizations.

For example, a Discoverer-1 could belong to an Organization-1 so that Discoverer-1 could have the discovery privilege in Organization-1. Alternatively, a Discoverer-2 could not belong to Organization-1, but Discoverer-2 is a domain administrator such that Organization-1 could also grant discover privilege to Discoverer-2. In addition, different discoverers could not know and trust each other at all.

Figure 14.8 illustrates a collaborative federated data discovery process, where a smart contract is leveraged to build trust between different untrusted discoverers/organizations in order to make them work collaboratively. In particular, the smart contract has the following usage:

- The user-1 could pay a service fee for its discovery request and such a service fee could be deposited in the smart contract. With this service fee, the discoverers (e.g., Discoverer-1 and Discoverer-2) could have the incentive to contribute to the discovery processing and they do not have to worry that the User-1 can refuse to pay the service fee after the User-1 obtains the discovery result (yielded by discoverers).

- In the meantime, the smart contract could also specify how the service fee will be allocated among multiple discoverers. For example, the discoverer producing high-quality discovery results or making more discovery processing effort could get a higher portion of service fee as rewards.

Pre-condition: A federated discovery service (FDS) is available in the system for supporting federated discovery requests. The FDS can interact with a PDL system for creating a smart contract; alternatively, the FDS can be a part of the PDL system. There are multiple third-party entities (e.g., Discoverer-1 and Discoverer-2) that are willing to act as discoverers and participate in

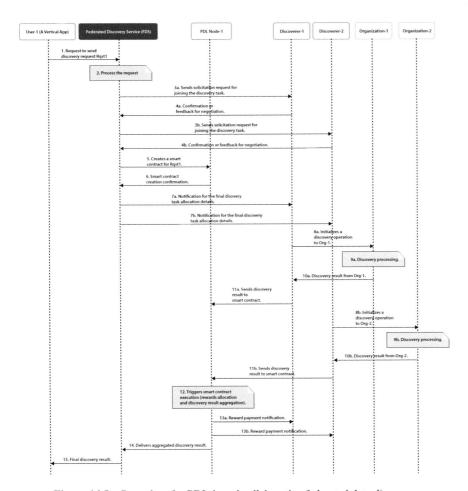

Figure 14.8 Procedure for PDL-based collaborative federated data discovery.

federated discovery processing. In particular, Discoverer-1 only has the discovery and access privilege for conducting discovery within Organization-1 while Discoverer-2 only has the discovery privilege for conducting discovery within Organization-2.

Step 1: User-1 has a certain application need and intends to identify some interesting data. User-1 intends to leverage the FDS since the desired data could reside in different organizations and be stored in different locations/nodes. User-1 sends a request (Rqst1) to the FDS to indicate desired data types and the service fee it is willing to pay.

Step 2: The FDS receives the request sent from User-1. The FDS first decides whether User-1 has the right for asking the FDS to conduct data discovery. Then, the FDS will use its own knowledge to identify which discoverers (e.g., Discoverer-1 and Discoverer-2) will probably be leveraged for serving this federated discovery request.

Step 3a: The FDS sends out a solicitation request including a data discovery proposal (e.g., desired data types and potential rewards to earn) to Discoverer-1 to ask it whether it is willing to help in processing the discovery request from the User-1. If the Discoverer-1 agrees to their received data discovery proposal, it will accept the task. Otherwise, it can also send back its suggestion for negotiating with the FDS.

Step 4a: The FDS receives the acknowledgment and feedback from the Discoverer-1.

Steps 3b and 4b are the same as Steps 3a and 4a, respectively.

Step 5: The FDS sends a transaction to PDL Node-1 (or other PDL nodes) in order to create a smart contract, which contains the agreed data discovery proposals of the involved discoverers.

Step 6: PDL Node-1 (or other PDL nodes) confirms the creation of the smart contract.

Steps 7a and 7b: For each involved discoverer (e.g., Discoverer-1 and Dsicoverer-2), the FDS sends a notification to each of them respectively for informing them of the created smart contract as well as the agreed/final discovery task.

Step 8a: For Discoverer-1, it initiates a discovery request and sends this request to Organization-1. For example, the request could indicate which types of data are to be discovered.

Step 9a: Organization-1 first needs to make sure Discoverer-1 has the right privilege to conduct data discovery within Organization-1. If so, it will accept the request and start to conduct discovery processing.

Step 10a: Organization-1 returns the discovery result to Discoverer-1. Depending on the format requirement of the smart contract inputs, Discoverer-1 could further transform or reformat the discovery result.

Step 11a: Discoverer-1 sends the discovery result to the smart contract as a smart contract trigger.

Steps 8b–11b are similar to Steps 8a–11a.

Step 12: After the smart contract receives the discovery results from all the involved discoverers, it will evaluate the quality of the discovery result. Based on that, the smart contract will automatically decide how to allocate the rewards among those different discoverers. In addition, the smart contract will also aggregate all the received discovery results in order to produce the final discovery result for the federated discovery request.

Steps 13a and 13b: The smart contract completes the rewards allocations and sends notifications to the involved discoverers (e.g., Discoverer-1 and Discoverer-2) regarding the reward payments respectively.

Step 14: The smart contract delivers the final aggregated discovery result to the FDS.

Step 15: The FDS returns the aggregated discovery result to User-1, which is the final discovery result for Rqst1.

References

[1] https://www.iiconsortium.org/pdf/IIRA-v1.9.pdf

[2] A. C. Yao: "Protocols for Secure Computations," 23rd Annual Symposium on Foundations of Computer Science (sfcs 1982), Chicago, IL, USA, 1982, Pages 160-164.

[3] D. W. Archer, D. Bogdanov, Y. Lindell, L. Kamm, K. Nielsen, J. I. Pagter, N. P. Smart and R. N. Wright: "From Keys to Databases – Real-World Applications of Secure Multi-Party Computation," The Computer Journal, Volume 61, Issue 12, December 2018, Pages 1749-1771.

[4] C. Zhao, S. Zhao, M. Zhao, Z. Chen, C.-Z. Gao, H. Li and Y. Tan: "Secure Multi-Party Computation: Theory, practice and applications," Information Sciences, Volume 476, 2019, Pages 357-372.

[5] World Economic Forum White Paper: "Federated Data Systems: Balancing Innovation and Trust in the Use of Sensitive Data," July 2019.

[6] World Economic Forum, Insight Report: "Sharing Sensitive Health Data in a Federated Data Consortium Model – An Eight-Step Guide," July 2020.

15

Offline Operations

In this chapter, we focus on offline operations of permissioned distributed ledgers (PDLs), which occur when nodes get disconnected from the main PDL. We will give an introduction to the offline mode and then discuss different offline scenarios. We then dwell on the various technical issues arising from the offline mode, followed by possible technical solutions. Finally, we reconcile all findings into an offline PDL architecture proposition.

15.1 Introduction to PDL Offline Mode

15.1.1 Reasons for PDL going offline

The underpinning technology elements of a distributed ledger may occasionally go offline. This could happen for the following reasons:

- **By design**:
  - **Maintenance**: Part of the ledger may require maintenance, such as hardware, networking or software maintenance. Whilst maintenance occurs, the normal operations of the ledger might be impacted which leads to vulnerabilities that need to be dealt with.
  - **Duty cycle**: To minimize energy consumption of the entire ledger, some of its elements might be duty cycled as per a given and prior agreed schedule. Whilst nodes are offline, possible operational issues as well as vulnerabilities may occur which ought to be dealt with.
- **By circumstance**:
  - **Temporary unavailability**: Elements of the ledger may unexpectedly become temporarily unavailable. This could be, for instance, due to an end point using wireless communications moving away from a base station and temporarily losing access to the ledger.

211

Another example occurs in very remote locations where the ledger might be connected via intermittent fixed-line or satellite network.

– **Congested network**: In the case of bandwidth-limited or highly congested networks, intra and inter ledger data may not be delivered in time (or delivered at all) and thus compromise the integrity of the ledger operations. That is, all elements are in principle connected but data is not distributed properly. The communication or PDL protocols may have mechanisms in place to resend missing data but that may not happen within the timeframe requirements by the PDL.

• **By incident**:

– **Disaster and natural phenomena**: Certain elements of the ledger might be powered by power sources which go out of operations, e.g., due to unforeseeable natural phenomena, such as a lightning strike. The loss of power can cause serious issues to the proper operations of the ledger.

– **Attack**: In the case of malicious attacks, elements of the ledger can be compromised and rendered intact or offline; in the worst case, the majority quorum capabilities are compromised. This poses serious threats to the integrity and operations of the ledger.

15.1.2 Offline challenges

In the case that a PDL or some nodes of a PDL or certain functionality of a PDL are rendered offline, a series of challenges arise which are not normally encountered in fully operational PDLs. These are summarized below and form the rational for the technical approach outlined in the later part of this chapter.

From a high level technical and operational point of view, the offline challenges can be categorized as follows:

1. **Security**: In terms of security of the PDL, the following issues arise:

   a) **Consensus capabilities**, i.e., the consensus approach underpinning the very essence of the PDL may get compromised.

   b) **Weakening security**, i.e., cryptographic primitives may become unavailable and thus certain processes become unverifiable.

2. **Availability**: In the most general terms, availability is impacted as follows:

a) **Reconciliation time**, i.e., when nodes come back online after being offline, it may take some time for them to catch up with the PDL. In the case of nodes suffering intermittent connectivity, it may be possible that by the time they reconcile, the service is interrupted again and they go offline again.

b) **Side-chains and chain merging**, i.e., the offline mode may trigger the emergence of side-chains which has an impact on integrity and availability; and certainly, will influence the approach to chain merging. The latter is typically a rare event but may happen very frequently in the discussed scenarios of offline operations.

c) **Stale transactions**, i.e., if chain merging is not successful, some transactions may become stale which ought to be dealt with by the offline ledger design.

3. **Integrity**: Important issues arise in the context of data integrity:

a) **Control data**, i.e., data a previously offline node needs to have in order to be accepted back into the PDL network. This typically pertains to authentication data, cryptographical keys, connectivity data, etc. The data related with the content of the ledger itself is out of scope here.

b) **Software code**, i.e., before being accepted back into the PDL network, checks will need to be performed to ensure that the software/program running on it have not been compromised.

15.2 PDL Offline Scenarios

This section discusses possible scenarios resulting from ledgers going offline. To aid technical understanding, a high-level technical reference architecture is introduced. Thereupon, the role of the different types of nodes is discussed. It is then possible to construct and discuss the different PDL offline scenarios. Last, temporal and spatial characteristics emerging from the different offline scenarios which are unique to a permissioned ledger having offline constituents are discussed.

15.2.1 High-level node reference architecture

The application example given above can be abstracted to a high-level reference ledger node architecture as illustrated in Figure 15.1.

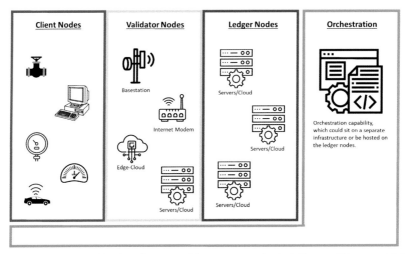

Figure 15.1 High-level node reference architecture comprised of client, validator, and ledger nodes; the system is overseen by orchestration capabilities.

Notably, a set of client nodes collects data which needs to be written onto the PDL. The data from the client nodes is transmitted via a fixed or wireless network to the validator nodes.

The validator nodes prepare the data for the specific ledger, i.e., sort the data, cast it into a specific format, check for initial consistency, etc. They then perform the PDL-specific consensus protocol to validate the content of the information provided by the client nodes.

Once validated, the content is written onto the ledger nodes which store the content for perpetuity. Ledger and validator nodes belong to several parties.

The end-to-end ledger is configured and maintained by means of PDL-orchestration. Said orchestrator may be implemented on one or several ledger nodes or on special-purpose orchestration nodes.

The links between the client and validator nodes and between validator and ledger nodes might be volatile due to intermittent connectivity or congested networks.

15.2.2 Type of nodes

As discussed above, there can be several reasons for a node to go offline, such as an engineered duty cycle or an unexpected outage of the wireless network.

In this section, the role of each node type is explained and the likelihood of them going offline estimated.

- **Client nodes**: These are nodes which belong to a client collecting, storing and/or transmitting data. From the ledger's perspective, these are temporary and transient nodes: temporary because a specific client node may lose connection with the ledger (e.g., a vehicle is going through a patch of poor connectivity) and transient because clients may sign onto the specific PDL service and after a few months/years sign off. Since their presence cannot be guaranteed, they do not take part in the consensus process nor do they form part of the storage ledger. They typically only update their state by sending transactions to validator nodes.

- **Validator nodes**: These nodes accept transactions from the client nodes, check the validity, and send them to ledger nodes. Whilst validator nodes are typically hosted in operationally reliable locations, they can go offline when, e.g., there is a network congestion or poor mid/backhaul. For that reason, a strong governance model is required which ensures the viability of the consensus approach when some of the validator nodes are OFF. For example, a requirement could be that consensus can only be reached if two-thirds of the validator nodes are online.

- **Ledger nodes**: Ledger nodes are permanent nodes of the ledger. This means that all of the nodes are generally available and online, unless of course in the case of force majeure or a cybersecurity attack. Depending on the design requirements these nodes can or cannot be validator node. Some architecture models allow ledger nodes to also serve as validator nodes and vice versa. The state of the ledger nodes is being updated by the validator nodes.

- **PDL-governance/orchestration**: Governance is important as it ensures the proper monitoring and execution of the PDL. It is particularly important in the offline scenario as the orchestration capabilities will have to maintain viability of the consensus protocol and ledger operations, among others. It may include roles like the verification of certificates or the revocation of access rights.

Each of these nodes requires trusted digital identities and trusted certificates. Operationally, they can be hosted on bare-metal servers, virtual machines (VMs) or containers. Depending on policy and regulation they may be required to be hosted on-premises of the node operator or may be hosted on a public or private cloud.

15.2.3 Offline scenarios

The possible scenarios arising due a subset of certain node types becoming unavailable are summarized in Table 15.1. Note that when nodes are offline, they may or may not be functional. If they are functional, then they can continue executing tasks locally. Note further that OFF refers to at least one of the node types not being reachable, and not necessarily all of them. The table is sorted from the most likely scenario to the least likely one:

- **Scenario #1**: Is the reference scenario where all nodes are functional and reachable. This should be the modus operandi of the PDL.
- **Scenario #2**: Occasionally, one, several or a cluster of the client nodes may go offline due to reasons discussed in previous sections. When this occurs, in most cases the nodes will remain functional, but unable to communicate with other PDL nodes. Situations where the nodes have been rendered dysfunctional or where an entire cluster of nodes has gone offline should also be catered for. It is important to note that when a node goes OFF the reason and functionality of such node are unknown to the other nodes.
- **Scenarios #3 and #4**: Rarely, one or more validator nodes go offline for reasons discussed in previous sections. Again, one needs to cater for situations where the node has been rendered dysfunctional, and not just temporarily gone offline.
- **Scenarios #5–#8**: Extremely unlikely but plausibly, one or more ledger nodes goes offline for reasons discussed in previous sections.

The likelihood of any of the scenarios to occur depends on the spatial distribution of the nodes as well as on redundancy/diversity of power and communication utilities, which also impacts the temporal behavior of the system. Unlike always-on PDLs, offline PDLs thus suffer from breaks in chain causality. This, in turn, jeopardizes the very essence of distributed ledgers and thus warrants appropriate design attention.

15.2.4 Operational characteristics

The likelihood of a node or set of nodes going offline depends on spatial and operational characteristics of the system, i.e., the node location and operational provisioning.

The spatial composition of a typical PDL is likely as follows:

- **Client nodes**: These are typically lightweight nodes with an embedded operating system (OS) and limited processing power, onboard memory,

Table 15.1 Possible operating scenarios due to different node types being reachable or offline.

	Client nodes	Validation nodes	Ledger nodes	Likelihood
Scenario #1	ON	ON	ON	*very likely*
Scenario #2	OFF	ON	ON	*occasional*
Scenario #3	ON	OFF	ON	*rare*
Scenario #4	OFF	OFF	ON	*rare*
Scenario #5	ON	ON	OFF	*unlikely*
Scenario #6	OFF	ON	OFF	*unlikely*
Scenario #7	ON	OFF	OFF	*unlikely*
Scenario #8	OFF	OFF	OFF	*unlikely*
NOTE: Nodes that are offline may or may not be functional. Furthermore, OFF refers to at least one of the node types not being reachable. The table is sorted from most likely to least likely.				

and battery power. Depending on the PDL design, they could form part of the PDL or not. In any case, client nodes write data onto the ledger and may receive instructions from the ledger via smart contracts. They are located at the very edge of the network, are typically mobile and often untethered.

- **Validator nodes**: These are typically placed physically close to the client nodes but within the networking infrastructure. For instance, in a 5G system, Validator nodes could sit in the central unit (CU) of the radio access network (RAN), or any other edge-cloud location. They would typically be virtualized via VMs or containers, and have sufficient processing power. Whilst spatially placed in a managed environment, the edge is often connected via unreliable backhaul, which makes the operational viability of these nodes volatile.
- **Ledger nodes**: These are typically placed in public or private data centers. They are well powered and well networked. They have sufficient processing power and storage capacity. They are also typically virtualized via VMs or containers.

To minimize operational outage, all nodes in the system should be provisioned as follows:

- **Physical protection**: Ideally, each node ought to be physically tamper resistant, whether IoT client node or validating/ledger nodes. This will ensure that the certificates stored on the nodes cannot be compromised. Nodes that are exposed to the elements (e.g., a sensor in an agricultural field) should be tested and calibrated at specific intervals to ensure integrity of the information they produce.
- **Power provisioning**: Each node ought to have one primary and ideally a secondary backup power source so that no power outages occur during the operations of the PDL.
- **Cyber security**: Each node should be properly protected against cyber security attacks, distributed denial of service (DDoS) attacks and other means of malicious unauthorized access to the nodes.
- **Networking connection**: Each node ought to be properly networked, using reliable and uncongested networks.
- **Critical network path**: The PDL ought to be designed such that there is no single point of failure which is critical to a plurality of nodes. In other words, enough network diversity ought to be provided so that when one network path fails, another can be used to connect the node.
- **Monitoring capabilities**: The PDL ought to have network, storage and compute monitoring capabilities so that the orchestrator obtains reliable real-time information on the state of the PDL.

Above is an ideal operational scenario which largely holds true for ledger nodes; however, validator nodes which reside at the edge of the network will likely have the following differences in a real-world deployment:

- **Networking connection**: Whilst each node is connected, an edge may experience a poor backhaul network and thus be not reachable over a given period of time.
- **Critical network path**: An edge may be connected via a single network path which creates a single point of failure (e.g., a single fiber link or single satellite link) thus not providing sufficient diversity in case that link goes down.
- **Monitoring capabilities**: Whilst monitoring capabilities might be in place, above-discussed networking problems may render the monitoring, and thus orchestration, capability ineffective. Certain implementations may use out-of-band communications for management and monitoring so that such functions are implemented using different network infrastructure that may survive failure of the main network. Such out-of-band solutions are typically costly and the self-healing features of TCP/IP

networks are such that diversified connectivity will offer sufficiently high survivability for the requirements of most PDL scenarios.

Client nodes (e.g., IoT sensors or actuators) will be even less equipped to operate in ideal operating conditions:

- **Physically protection**: Client nodes in the field are often exposed and without supervision, thus making it difficult to guarantee physical protection and tamper resistance consistently. Periodical testing and calibration may be required to ensure credibility.
- **Power provisioning**: Client nodes in the field may experience power supply issues such as batteries running low, solar panels not producing enough power, etc.
- **Cyber security**: Client nodes in the field are also exposed to cyberattacks, mainly because embedded systems are not security patched at the same level as traditional IT equipment.
- **Networking connection**: For nodes in the field, networking may be volatile over a short period due to wireless network congestion or fading/shadowing blockage. The outage may also be seasonal due to vegetation growth or rain in satellite connections obstructing an already weak wireless link.
- **Critical network path**: Client nodes rarely have networking diversity, i.e., they are typically connected via one networking interface only. Therefore, if that link breaks, the node is not accessible.
- **Monitoring capabilities**: Due to the embedded nature of the devices, monitoring capabilities will be limited. Furthermore, the duty cycling of the devices and the intermittent networking conditions may disrupt real-time monitoring periodically.

15.2.5 Temporal characteristics

An important element of offline PDLs is the temporal characteristics of certain nodes, differentiated between the following levels of planned and unplanned intermittence:

- **Schedule**: When a node goes on scheduled OFF on purpose by the owner(s). This could be done in the context of duty cycling to save energy or for planned maintenance. Whilst the schedule may have a limited impact onto the node itself, it may have a strong impact on any dependent smart contract. For instance, a smart contract may only work when a certain number of nodes provides information within a given time window which will require the schedules of the nodes to be synchronized. Clearly, there is a strong governance issue when it comes to schedules, which in the context of PDLs, goes beyond simple energy savings.

- **Graceful disappearance**: Client nodes or even validating nodes can disappear gracefully in that the connection becomes weaker and weaker over time. In the case of a validating node, this could be because the network has peaks of congestion which increase response times until the outage occurs. Equally, client nodes may suffer from network congestion or simply a weakening wireless connection as the client node moves away from the base station/access point. In principle, the PDL system could be programmed to recognize such events and initiate contingency protocols before the connection is cut off. For instance, in the case of the validating node, another or a prior-established proxy node could take over the role of a validating node. In the case of a client node, this may give an opportunity to establish a trusted local environment which is able to operate offline for a given period of time.
- **Sudden disappearance**: Nodes may of course disappear suddenly, without any prior warnings or indications. The reasons could be manifold and range from non-malicious due to power cut, equipment failure, or sudden network blockage; to malicious due to a DDoS attack or other cybersecurity breach.

In the context of temporal characteristics, it is important to pay attention to the *causality of the events*. For instance, the order in which some client nodes or validating nodes become unavailable is important to the proper functioning of the PDL and smart contracts. It will impact recovery/auto-recovery protocols, the way majority quorum is determined, the way governance is being executed, among others.

15.3 Challenges Arising from Offline Mode

In this section we discuss the technical issues which arise from elements of the PDL going offline. Discussed here are technical issues arising from the points of view of a client, validator, and ledger node. Furthermore, specific issues arising in the context of smart contracts are discussed, as well as governance and cybersecurity approaches.

15.3.1 Offline client node(s)

In the context of client nodes, technical issues arise in the following situations:

- **Client data**: A major concern is securing and ensuring a trusted environment for a client node when OFF.
- **Ledger data**: Client nodes may need access to data residing on the PDL which is not possible when OFF. Such clients may only have access to data stored locally (if any).
- **Smart contracts**: Smart contracts need to remain operational in the event that client nodes are OFF.
- **Chain reconciliation**: A major challenge is to enable the reconciliation with the main chain, once the OFF node gets connected again.

These issues are now discussed in greater detail in subsequent sections.

Securing the offline data: Securing the content and fidelity of inferred data in a client node, e.g., a remote IoT node, is a challenge whether the node is online or offline. However, the online mode allows for regular monitoring and reporting which is not possible in the offline mode. The data in the client node can be compromised through the following (non-exhaustive list of) mechanisms:

- **Challenge #1 – Deteriorating calibration**: The data collected and processed in client nodes is typically calibrated, or requires artificial intelligence (AI)/machine learning (ML) inference models. These are rarely static and more often than not require constant updating. Given the technical constraints of the client nodes, the algorithmic updates of the calibration and inference algorithms is done centrally or close to the edge. In either case, it remains inaccessible to the client node. As a result, the fidelity and accuracy of the inferred data deteriorates and thus becomes of little use to the overall PDL operations. Therefore, an important technical challenge is to find mechanisms which prevent or minimize the impact of such deteriorating calibration.
- **Challenge #2 – Cybersecurity breach**: Being out of reach of the PDL, regular monitoring is not feasible anymore. For instance, the validity of certificates installed on the client node cannot be verified through advanced hashing (e.g., SHA-256) and a secure communications tunnel [e.g., virtual private network (VPN)]. This, in turn, lowers the defenses and allows malicious hackers to gain access to the client nodes by gaining access to the last mile network and/or be in proximity to exploit

the wireless network to which the node is connected. Therefore, an important technical challenge is to ensure that access to the client node is sufficiently secure to prevent malicious network attacks.

- **Challenge #3 – Physical tampering**: In offline mode, physical access to nodes can go unnoticed. A malicious adversary may physically access the node by opening the enclosure, reading data from the node's memory, changing or reprogramming the logic on the chips, etc. When the node then re-joins the PDL, it may gain access to the overall PDL with potentially serious implications. Therefore, an important technical challenge is to create sufficiently secure trusted environments which eliminate or minimize such risk.

Enable access to ledger data: Client nodes may need access to data which resides on the PDL or which is managed through the PDL. The following technical challenges thus arise:

- **Challenge #4 – Access to ledger data**: For instance, a client node may need historical data which resides on the PDL. When the node is OFF (disconnected from the PDL) such data is not accessible. A technical challenge is therefore to cater for mechanisms which avoid or minimize the impact of such a scenario.
- **Challenge #5 – Access to third-party database data**: Idem to challenge #4 but related to accessing data from a third-party database with credentials administered through the PDL. There is a need to cater for mechanisms which avoid or minimize the impact of such a scenario.

Enable smart contract operations: Smart contracts may require data from client nodes when writing data to the PDL or may need to instruct client nodes based upon information read from the PDL. In the context of offline operations, the following technical challenges thus arise:

- **Challenge #6 – Read data from client nodes (upstream)**: A smart contract may require data from nodes for a certain logic or conditions to be triggered. That data ingest may happen regularly or when needed. In offline mode, an important technical challenge is to address the impact absence or late arrival of data from client nodes has on the viability of the smart contract.
- **Challenge #7 – Instruct client nodes (downstream)**: Likewise, the smart contract may trigger instructions to a client node. That trigger may happen regularly or be triggered through smart contract logic. In offline mode, an important technical challenge is to address the impact the absence or late arrival of the control data to the client nodes.

Enable data reconciliation: Once the client nodes return to normal online operations, the data between the client nodes and the PDL needs to be reconciled. To this end, the following challenges arise:

- **Challenge #8 – Data validation**: Any data inferred or generated in the client node whilst offline needs to be validated by the PDL system before being added to the main PDL. A technical challenge is thus to enable data validation so that only trust-worthy data is added.
- **Challenge #9 – Data reconciliation**: Once validated, said data needs to be added to the PDL. A technical challenge is thus to enable a post-event reconciliation of data generated earlier than the current PDL time stamp.

15.3.2 Offline validator node(s)

As per above, it is unlikely that validator nodes go offline but it may still occasionally happen. PDL needs to be prepared for such an occasion. To this end, the technical issues arising can be summarized as follows:

- **Control-plane data**: Whilst offline, a major concern is how to ensure that the PDL orchestrator is able to deliver/update information important to the operational part of the validator nodes, i.e., new validation approach, security certificates, access instructions to third-party databases, etc.
- **Proxy validator nodes**: The controlled nature of the validator nodes allows the establishment of proxy validator nodes which become operational once a given validator node goes offline.
- **Consensus violation**: A major challenge is to ensure that consensus majority rules are not violated with a given set of validator nodes going offline.

These issues are now discussed in greater detail in subsequently.

Control-plane data: The operational health of the validator nodes is crucial to the operations of the PDL. Validator nodes typically receive control data from the PDL and/or its orchestration framework. Not having access to this control-plane data because the validator node has gone offline poses a series of technical challenges which are summarized below:

- **Challenge #10 – PDL control plane**: The PDL validator nodes receive important control data from the PDL or orchestration frameworks. Examples of this are security certificates of the validating PDL nodes, security certificates of specific client nodes; specific algorithmic validation frameworks; timing and synchronization data; security credentials to third-party ledgers or data and networking infrastructure, etc. An important technical challenge is therefore to ensure that the overall operations of the PDL are not jeopardized when said control-plane data cannot be delivered to some of the validator nodes. This has two aspects:

a) Ensuring that an OFF node, if still functional (meaning it is powered on and can communicate with some client nodes but is isolated from the rest of the PDL and specifically the orchestration functionality) is pre-programmed to limit its functionality to specific pre-defined autonomous actions (e.g., in an agricultural plant it can still collect data from client nodes but it cannot send new irrigation instructions; or, in the case of autonomous vehicles, it can bring the vehicle to a safe halt but it cannot restart the autonomous drive afterwards until communications has resumed).

b) Ensuring the rest of the PDL can continue operation in absence of the isolated/offline nodes and ensuring the PDL does not resume operations if certain criteria are not met (e.g., allow continued operation as long as enough validator nodes are still on-line, but halt operations if an insufficient number of validator nodes is on-line or other functionalities, such as orchestration, are below certain performance criteria).

• **Challenge #11 – Third-party data access**: Similarly, to challenge #10, some validator nodes may require access to third-party databases which may not be accessible when the validator node is OFF. There are two scenarios to consider:

a) The validator node does not have connectivity to the third-party database, in which case it cannot access such data.

b) The validator node has connectivity to the third-party database but is isolated from the PDL and cannot obtain credentials or certificates in order to access that database.

In both cases, the validator node will not have access to the third-party database and should be pre-programmed (if OFF) or instructed by the orchestrator (if on-line) to take appropriate actions. Such actions need to be defined when designing the PDL.

Proxy validator nodes: Depending on PDL type, the number of validator nodes may be limited either by design or by technical/performance limitations. A Validator node going offline may thus pose a serious operational risk. A proxy validator node can take over the validation functionality of an OFF validator node. The technical challenges related to this can be summarized as follows:

- **Challenge #12 – Proxy node**: The role of the proxy node is to take over the validation work once the main validation node goes offline. The controlled nature of the PDL environment allows for the establishment of proxy validator nodes. These become operational once the main validator node(s) disappear or suffer from a graceful but measurable performance/connection degradation. An important technical challenge is to ensure the control data (certificates, validation protocols, etc.) is synchronized between validators and their respective proxy nodes. Furthermore, the proxy node election process needs to be provided, along with the monitoring and decision frameworks (e.g., pre-assignment of proxy to each validator node, pre-assignment of a pool of proxies and the selection process of a specific proxy from within that pool which could be random or round-robin or topology-based, etc.). Also, a framework needs to be provided which establishes the process once the original validator node comes back online (e.g., restore its status as a validator node, or put it in the pool of proxies in standby).
- **Challenge #13 – Disrupting ongoing validation session**: When a proxy validator node becomes active, the validation process that was performed by the now OFF primary validation node might have been interrupted. A technical challenge is thus to ensure that an ongoing validation operation can either be seamlessly handed over to a proxy node or restarted by the proxy node.

Consensus violation: As discussed above, the number of validator nodes in PDL may be limited. A simple outage or cyberattack might reduce the number of operational validator nodes thus hamper the validation consensus mechanisms in a manner that exposes the PDL to attacks. The technical challenge related to this can be summarized as follows:

- **Challenge #14 – Consensus violation**: An important technical challenge is to ensure that the majority consensus validation rules remain intact and are not prone to possible cyberattacks on the PDL. The mechanisms should cater for proxy nodes too. A practical example may be that a 2/3 majority is required for a specific consensus mechanism. If the number of validators drops down to three, and one of the three is hacked the consensus process is flawed. Thus, a possible solution may be to declare a minimum number of active validators (the exact number may depend on security levels and other risk mitigation factors) and define a situation where the number of validators drops below that minima as "consensus violation." The actions that the PDL takes when consensus violation occurs need to be properly designed (e.g., halt operations of the PDL until the number of validators meets the minimum requirements and notify the users/administrators).

15.3.3 Offline ledger node(s)

As per above, it is extremely unlikely that PDL nodes go offline. Furthermore, the PDL protocol should be able to cope with the outage of any number of ledger nodes as they are generally only used to enable the distributed nature of the PDL.

Therefore, no further technical challenges are discussed here.

15.3.4 Offline smart contract

A smart contract would typically reside on the PDL. This section summarizes specific technical challenges arising from smart contracts going OFF:

- **Challenge #15 – Synchronize data causality**: Challenges #6 and #7 arise when there is a linear relationship between client nodes and smart contracts. However, the situation can be significantly more complex. For instance, the smart contract may require input from several client nodes and send instructions back to several (possibly other) client nodes. These client nodes may go offline in a non-predictable pattern, thus interfering the causal logic of the smart contract. To support complex internal smart contract logic or a virtualized peer-to-peer network between nodes (via the smart contract of the PDL), an important technical challenge is thus to minimize the impact of breaking the data causality due to client nodes going offline and coming back online in an unpredictable manner.

- **Challenge #16 – Offline smart contract operations**: A possible solution to mitigating issues arising under challenge #15 is to permit the duplication of smart contracts into an offline environment. This, however, triggers an avalanche of technical challenges, such as the provisioning of a trusted execution environment for the duplicated smart contract; the ability to reconcile the generated data with the main ledger, access rights management, among others.

15.3.5 End-to-end cybersecurity and privacy

Given the non-causal nature of a PDL with offline nodes, end-to-end security needs to be managed more carefully. Following are some important challenges:

- **Challenge #17 – Consistent end-to-end security provisioning**: A major technical challenge is to ensure that the security of the ledger and its constituents is not jeopardized under any possible operating condition. This pertains to the validity and provenance of security certificates, encryption keys and protocols, hash functions, majority consensus algorithms, among others.
- **Challenge #18 – Ensure PDL member privacy**: Whilst the privacy of the data collected, inferred and processed by the client nodes is out of scope, the privacy requirements of the members being part of the PDL may be subject to regulations or laws (e.g., GDPR) or company policy. For instance, some consortium members may not want other members to know about specific operating conditions or decision logic. An important technical challenge is thus to guarantee (to the extent possible) the privacy of the consortium members by implementing best practice algorithmic frameworks which guarantee the privacy whilst not jeopardizing the operations of the ledger.

15.3.6 Monitoring and Orchestration Capabilities

Last but not least, the ledger orchestration and monitoring capabilities are discussed in this section. The technical challenges can be summarized as follows:

- **Challenge #19 – Monitoring capabilities**: The ability to observe the sudden or graceful deterioration of networking links or processing capabilities of client and validator nodes very much depends on the monitoring capabilities of the PDL. A technical challenge is thus to enable such monitoring capabilities across compute, storage and networking resources; whilst not creating a large operational overhead. The monitoring and probing should extend to virtualized environments, such as VMs or containers. Furthermore, alerting capabilities should be set up and triggered when monitoring identifies certain conditions.
- **Challenge #20 – Orchestration capabilities**: An important technical challenge is to enable PDL-wide orchestration capabilities which ensure a proper deployment, operations and decommission of the PDL. For

example, the orchestrator, among other, should be able to synchronize duty cycle schedules of client nodes such that smart contract operations are not jeopardized.

15.4 Technical Solutions for Offline Mode

In this section, we introduce a set of (non-exhaustive) technical approaches which address the technical challenges outlined above.

15.4.1 Summary of Challenges and Solutions

Table 15.2 summarizes how the technical solutions identified in the previous section address the challenges. The technical solutions are discussed in subsequent sections in more detail.

15.4.2 Trusted execution environments

A prerequisite for viable operations of a PDL with offline nodes is to create trusted execution environments (TEEs) which can hold the certificates, data, execution instructions and algorithmic frameworks. The TEEs ensure that data and algorithms cannot be tampered with, and thus ensure the required integrity and confidentiality. There are many ways to providing TEEs, with a non-exhaustive list provided below:

- **Hardware TEE**: The original approach to TEE is to establish a secure execution area in the main underlying processor. That ensures that code and data are protected through an isolated execution environment. Important features, such as isolated execution, integrity of applications executing with the TEE, confidentiality of data assets, and more, are therefore provided.
- **Virtualized TEE**: To aid developers and scale secure code production, an emerging trend is to virtualize the TEEs through specialized software development kits (SDKs). Said approach is similar to VMs/containers with hardware pinning, and provides the best of both hardware and software worlds.
- **Local side-chain PDL**: Another approach proposed here is to establish a local PDL, either hardware or virtualized, and thus create a TEE through the same mechanisms as the overarching governing PDL.
- **Trusted third-party side-chain**: The immutability of public blockchains or mutually independent PDLs may yield the required level of trust.

Table 15.2   Summary of technical challenges and how they can be addressed.

	Trusted Environments	Offline Operations	Proxy Mechanisms	Ledger Reconciliation	Monitoring & Orchestration
Challenge #1 – Deteriorating calibration		■			
Challenge #2 – Cybersecurity breach	■	■			
Challenge #3 – Physical tampering	■	■			
Challenge #4 – Access to ledger data	■	■			
Challenge #5 – Access to third-party database data	■	■			
Challenge #6 – Read data from client nodes (upstream)	■				
Challenge #7 – Instruct client nodes (downstream)	■				
Challenge #8 – Data validation	■				
Challenge #9 – Data reconciliation	■				
Challenge #10 – PDL control plane	■		■		
Challenge #11 – third-party data access	■				
Challenge #12 – Proxy node			■		■
Challenge #13 – Disrupting ongoing validation session			■		
Challenge #14 – Consensus violation			■		
Challenge #15 – Synchronize data causality	■			■	
Challenge #16 – Offline smart contract operations				■	
Challenge #17 – Consistent end-to-end security provisioning	■				■
Challenge #18 – Ensure PDL member privacy					■
Challenge #19 – Monitoring capabilities					■
Challenge #20 – Orchestration capabilities					■

These approaches underpin challenges #2–#18 and are now discussed in greater detail in subsequent sections.

Hardware TEE: The traditional approach in providing TEEs is in hardware. As illustrated in Figure 15.2, the TEE model follows the hardware-middleware-software layering of traditional compute environments but focuses on ensuring integrity of each component and layer.

Notably, the hardware layer of the device will have to have a secured area which ring-fences hardware resources, such as hardware security keys, hardware storage, hardware secure elements, etc.

The middleware, i.e., the operating system, is exclusively built from trusted components, such as a trusted core framework, trusted drivers and a trusted agent which is able to communicate with the less secure operating system.

The software layer hosts the trusted apps. They need to be security-vetted and the trusted operating system ensures that the integrity of the apps is maintained. Examples of such trusted apps are payment apps, trusted corporate applications or, indeed, PDL applications.

The trusted operating system with trusted apps can be built from a trusted and protected hardware area as follows: The hardware area stores the root certificates, root hashes and root keys. These are then used to sign and cryptographically link all software elements of the operating system and applications. In fact, the cryptographic linkage is very similar to the one of blockchains.

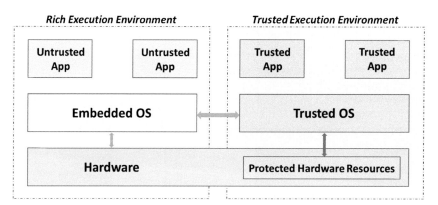

Figure 15.2 Traditional rich execution environment versus the provisioning of a trusted execution environment by means of protected hardware resources which host, e.g., root key hashes.

The described hardware TEE is able to host PDL data, applications and decision logic in a secure manner which cannot be tampered with. This ensures the required level of integrity in case a node goes offline and then reappears online again.

Virtualized TEE: A virtualized TEE still requires a secure area within the operating environment. Typically, this is done through hardware just as with above hardware TEEs. However, the operating system and apps are implemented through a virtualization approach which is typically enabled through SDKs.

The first approach is to put a VM environment on the operating system or replace the operating system with a VM environment, with each VM having its own operating system (on "bare metal"). Then, several secure VMs can host one or several securely compartmentalized apps. This further increases the security and integrity of the system.

Another approach is containerizing the system and host secure containers with their orchestration framework on the secure operating system or the secure bare metal. It caters for lighter deployments with smaller memory and compute footprints.

An emerging hybrid hardware-software TEE worth mentioning is being developed in Cambridge, UK. The TEE is referred to as CHERI, i.e., capability hardware enhanced RISC instructions. It enables memory protection, scalable compartmentalization, fine-grained decomposition of the operating system and apps. As per [1], *"CHERI is a hybrid capability architecture in that it is able to blend architectural capabilities with conventional MMU-based architectures and microarchitectures, and with conventional software stacks based on virtual memory and C/C++."*

Local side-chain PDL: Leveraging on the hardware, virtualized and hybrid TEEs, another approach of providing a trusted environment is to locally deploy a side-chain of the PDL. This could be the same as the overarching system PDL or a lightweight version specifically adapted to the embedded nature of the device or set of devices it is deployed on.

In essence, the local PDL would merge the design principles of the overarching PDL; that is, the cryptographic principles of the PDL are used to verify the system components and thus provide the required level of integrity.

The specific deployment embodiment could in principle be on a single node or a distributed but connected set of nodes:

- **Single node deployment**: If enough independent TEEs can be provided through virtualization or containerization, the PDL could be deployed within the same node with some of the containers taking the role of validator nodes and the remaining nodes the role of ledger nodes. This of course requires the client node to have sufficient compute and storage capacity.

- **Multi-node deployment**: Assume the scenario of an island of client nodes going offline from the main PDL; however, the client nodes are still connected to each other locally and each client node is able to cater for a TEE. In that case, a local PDL can be deployed using the set of available nodes. That network, if properly deployed, provides a sufficiently trusted environment.

Trusted third-party side-chain: Using a third-party external ledger could improve the security of any PDL by providing additional immutable storage and execution capabilities. Two alternatives can be envisaged:

- **Trusted third-party PDL**: The approach here would be to provide an addition trusted storage and execution environment by using independent PDLs to which the nodes of the original PDL have access.

- **Public blockchain**: Idem, public chains could be used which yield a high degree of persistence, in addition to immutability.

In both scenarios, security could be reinforced by providing a point of recovery for the original PDL. The basic procedure could be based on taking snapshots of the blockchain to be protected and storing it in the external blockchain, i.e., storing hashes of the snapshot. The external blockchain could also be used as a hash repository of devices/nodes that can connect to a specific PDL that can be updated by the vendor independently. This limits the breaches of poor or untrusted data sources.

In essence, reinforcing the original PDL with a combined protection of other PDLs or incorporating the strength of public blockchains is a safeguard not only against external attacks but also safeguards against internal security breaches.

15.4.3 Offline operations

With the TEEs in place, certificates, client data and algorithmic frameworks are stored in a trusted environment providing the required local integrity and confidentiality. That enables a viable offline operation which is discussed in this section. Notably, technical approaches to the offline operations of client nodes, validator nodes, and smart contracts are discussed below.

Offline client node operations: To maintain the operations of a client node which is about to or has gone offline, a set of previously discussed challenges need to be overcome:

- **Challenge #1 – Deteriorating calibration**: As discussed above, the sensing and/or inference algorithms may need to be recalibrated. There are several ways of solving this problem:
- *Local re-calibration*: If possible, enable a local environment which is able to locally recalibrate or locally learn new coefficients for the AI/ML inference engine. That should be done in the TEE, and enough memory and processing power ought to be made available locally.
- *Timer*: If local recalibration is not possible, a timer which clocks the recalibration intervals should be used. Once the timer has expired, said inference/sensing framework should not be used anymore.
- *Data confidence*: Several timer epochs or other forms of more sophisticated models to estimate the fidelity of the gathered data and record that fidelity along the actual data can be used. When the node comes online again, any overarching data frameworks can take a more informed estimate about the validity of the provided data.
- **Challenge #2 – Cybersecurity breach**: Such breach may occur when an adversary obtains access to the last mile network. Several solutions are available:
- *"Alive-Pings"*: A cyber breach is easy to detect if a keep-alive message is implemented between the client node and, e.g., a smart contract on the main PDL. In absence of a request or response, each party becomes aware of the client node being offline. If a zero-trust policy is implemented in the client node, no network traffic is allowed except through trusted mechanisms such that the client node can be reconnected to the main PDL once networks become available again.
- *Network monitoring*: A useful mechanism is to implement local network monitoring of data traffic, such as IP addresses, sessions, etc. The data could be discarded after a pre-defined time; for example, the network data is only stored over the last 24 h. That may prove useful in the case of in situ or remote network forensics and diagnostics.
- *Trusted networks*: Network connections should be secure by default. Ideally, only the connection between the client node and the PDL should be authorized. If needed, a secure network between third‾party hosts (e.g., third-party database) can also be established. The usage of VPNs and infrequently used ports is recommended. The usage of the secure

shell protocol (SSH) on common port 22 for user data or out-of-band (OOB) control data should be avoided so as to evade port scanning software.

- **Challenge #3 – Physical tampering**: Client nodes which are easily accessible in the field risk being physically tampered with. The following approaches are possible:
- *Physical protection*: If a prior risk assessment deems physical tampering possible, then the client node ought to be moved or protect such that the risk of physical tampering is mitigated to acceptable levels (which may vary case by case).
- *Physical alert*: Embedded, and potentially hidden, sensors could be used to provide an extra layer of physical security. Notably, an embedded vibration sensor or light sensor can be added to the client node so that when unscheduled movement has been detected (because somebody took the node off its location) or light has been detected (because somebody opened the enclosure), certain emergency protocols can be triggered, such as deletion of critical/all data and frameworks from the TEE.
- *Downstream/upstream separation*: Different risk categories for upstream and downstream data can be introduced which allows different security protocols to be implemented in case of physical tampering. The former is typically data sensed/inferred by the client node and thus anyway accessible to any adversary in the physical vicinity. The latter is control data received from the PDL which requires extra protection as it may compromise critical instructions, such as opening a critical pressure valve.
- **Challenge #4 – Access to ledger data**: A node may require data which is stored on the PDL and thus becomes inaccessible in the case of going offline. The following approaches are possible:
- *Predictive content caching*: Advanced mechanisms can be used to predict what data will be needed by a client node over a given autonomous operating horizon. That data is then cached into the memory of the client node. The predictive algorithm needs to balance availability of memory, energy consumption, network usage and minimum required window of autonomous operations. For instance, if a client node needs to be operational for 24 h, then sufficient data needs to be cached on the client node to enable 24 h operations.
- *Use of edge-cloud*: The same predictive mechanism can be used to cache data in an edge-cloud which might be far from any of the PDL nodes but

close to the client node. This will not work if the client node itself goes offline but will be useful if the edge-cloud is isolated from the PDL due to backhaul faults. Another approach would be to replicate the entire PDL in the edge-cloud making it a de-facto ledger node.

- **Challenge #5 – Access to third-party database data**: Similarly, to the PDL data access, a node may need data from a third-party database. The following approaches are possible here:
- *Predictive content caching*: The same mechanisms as for above challenge #4 can be used here where data from the third-party database is cached intelligently.
- *Use of edge-cloud*: The same mechanisms as for above challenge #4 can be used here where data from the third-party database is stored in a trusted environment in an accessible edge-cloud.
- *Direct database access*: Access to a third-party database is normally managed via the PDL. If the client node still has networking access, then a direct and trusted peer-to-peer link can be established.
- **Challenge #6 – Read data from client nodes (upstream)**: Smart contract and other operations are impacted here which are discussed subsequently in more detail.
- **Challenge #7 – Instruct client nodes (downstream)**: The offline mode may become critical for the downstream data as it may contain control data. There are several methods to deal with that issue:
- *Schedule or predictive analytics*: If control instructions can be scheduled or have a predictable pattern, then such schedule can be implemented at the client side and operate autonomously even when OFF.
- *Available third⁻party proxy*: A client node may lose connection to the PDL but may still have networking connection which would enable the use of a proxy node. That proxy node is different from the PDL-proxies introduced earlier in that it may not belong to the PDL. Specific security measures thus need to be put in place to ensure end-to-end security.
- **Challenge #8 – Data validation**: Upon rejoining the PDL, the client node will need to transfer data to the PDL. Before doing so, data validation is required. To this end, the PDL needs to verify that a TEE was established and operational, and is trusted; furthermore, it needs to verify that all protocols and contingency plans have been followed to ensure integrity of data.
- **Challenge #9 – Data reconciliation**: The methods proposed to ensure a proper reconciliation with the main ledger are discussed in a subsequent section.

Offline validator node operations: To maintain the operations of a validator node, a set of previously discussed challenges need to be overcome:

- **Challenge #10 – PDL control plane**: The validator node is receiving regular control data updates pertaining, e.g., to updated security certificates or updated validation protocols. With the validator node going offline, the following methods can be implemented to ensure continuing operability:
- *Freeze control plane updates*: Put control plane updates on a regular schedule which is known to both ledger and validator nodes. That can be achieved with a timer and regular coarse synchronization of clocks. In that case, when an update notification is not received by the validator node, it will stop the validation process.
- *Pre-emptive update delivery*: Another method is to send updates a certain time window before they are due to become effective. For instance, the ledger can update control information 24 h before they are becoming effective which prevents validator outages with short offline periods.
- *Proxy node(s)*: Coupled into above methods, a proxy node can be activated when the PDL does not receive a response from the validator node. The proxy approach is discussed in greater detail in a subsequent section.
- **Challenge #11 – third-party data access**: Similar to the client node data access, a validator node may need data from a third-party database which become inaccessible once the node goes offline. The following approaches are possible here:
- *Predictive content caching*: As already discussed in the context of client nodes, data from a third-party database can be cached intelligently in the TEE of the validator node.
- *Direct database access*: Access to a third-party database is normally managed via the PDL. If the validator node still has networking access, then a direct and trusted peer-to-peer link can be established between the validator node and said third-party database.
- **Challenge #12 – Proxy node**: The proxy mechanisms for the validator node are discussed below.
- **Challenge #13 – Disrupting ongoing validation session**: The integrity and trustworthiness of the data put onto the ledger should be of highest priority in any PDL deployment. Therefore, any validation session which is disrupted ought to be discarded and proper mechanism at

the PDL governance level ought to be implemented to handle such a situation.

- **Challenge #14 – Consensus violation**: Similarly, consensus violations ought to be handled at the governance level through proper monitoring and orchestration. An individual validator node cannot efficiently handle such a situation.

Offline smart contract execution: The smart contract resides in the PDL and is unlikely to go offline. However, client and validator nodes may go offline and thus jeopardize the operations of the smart contract. The following challenges need to be addressed:

- **Challenge #15 – Synchronize data causality**: With client and validator nodes going offline, the operations of smart contracts could jeopardize. Whilst the complexity of this problem ought to be dealt with at orchestration level, some approaches are possible to aid the smart contracts operations:
- *Client node diversity*: The most likely cause of a smart contract failure is due to one or more client nodes going offline, the data of which is required for the smart contract logic. Mission critical contracts may thus rely on secondary and tertiary data from diverse client nodes. For instance, rather than just deploying one IoT node in the field, two or three are deployed and connected via independent networks.
- *Predictive capabilities*: If predictive algorithms work within the error margins of client node data acquisition, then this could also be used to feed client data into the smart contract logic. For instance, assume that an IoT node has a 20% measurement error due to imperfect sensors; then, any predictive algorithms which are able to predict that IoT data flow within a 20% error margin could be deployed.
- **Challenge #16 – Offline smart contract operations**: The following approaches are possible here:
- *Create side-chain PDL*: A suitable approach here is to create an operational offline copy of the smart contract through a local PDL, which in essence is a side-chain and should be referred to as sPDL. That can only be done if the Smart contract relies exclusively on data which is generated and consumed locally.
- *Predictive capabilities*: As already discussed above, predictive algorithms can be used to provide for the missing data within the measurement errors.

15.4.4　Proxy mechanisms

The availability of validator nodes is utmost important to the well-being of the PDL. However, validator nodes may go offline. To ensure the operability of the ledger with validator nodes going offline, the notion of proxy nodes had been introduced. This section describes the election and operational approach to proxy nodes in greater detail.

What is a proxy node: A proxy node is in essence a dormant or idle stand-by validator node. It is not operational, i.e., does not perform any validation, until triggered to do so. The proxy node becomes operational when another validator node experiences operational or networking difficulties.

A proxy node is typically attached to one or several operational validator nodes so that when they fail, the proxy node can continue the required validation process.

A proxy node should be part of the PDL, i.e., belong to the trusted infrastructure which constitutes the PDL. It would typically reside in trusted VMs belonging to the PDL consortium.

It should be noted that, whilst proxy nodes improve the viability of the PDL ledger, introducing them yields an operational overhead in terms of communication bandwidth, compute and storage overheads.

When to elect a proxy node: A proper election of the proxy node addresses challenge #12, and should determine the trigger upon which a proxy node is being elected. Similar to routing protocols, the election of proxy nodes can be reactive or proactive:

- **Reactive establishment of a proxy node**: A proxy node is established once a given validator node goes offline. The establishment of the proxy node takes time, and therefore, a reactive approach yields some operational delays. The advantage, however, is that no operational resources are wasted in the case the set of validator nodes works reliably.
- **Proactive establishment of a proxy node**: The governance framework may associate a proxy node to one or several operational validating nodes prior to any incidence. That allows for a quicker handover in case of failure of validating nodes; however, it creates a management overhead compared to the reactive approach.
- **Hybrid approach**: Yet another approach might be to proactively establish a pool of trusted proxy nodes in zones of high volatility, whilst in stable zones a reactive approach is taken. These zones could be updated dynamically to ensure the most efficient trade-off between operability and overheads.

How to elect proxy nodes: Addressing challenges #12 and #14, the actual election process would typically be administered by the governance layer. Notably, the following is important to note:

- **Ensure validity of consensus**: The governance methods should ensure that proxy nodes are elected such that, once they become operational, consensus fairness cannot be jeopardized. If not done properly, a malicious member of the PDL consortium could attack network segments and operational validator nodes such that the thus-triggered proxy nodes give that member consensus majority.

- **1-2-1 vs. 1-2-Many**: Another important decision point is if to associate a proxy node to one operational validator node or to a set of validator nodes. Whilst a 1-2-Many association is more efficient in terms of control overheads, a new proxy selection may need to be triggered once a given proxy node from the pool has become operational so as to ensure that the remaining validating nodes still have a proxy node backup.

Operations of proxy node: Addressing challenges #12, #13, and #14, the operations of a proxy node should address the following:

- **Cold vs. idle vs. fully operational proxy node**: Depending on the operational state of the proxy node, it could be cold, idle or fully operational. A cold proxy node needs to be activated and configured; an idle proxy node needs only to be activated as it has been configured already; and a fully operational proxy node is both configured and ready to take over at any instance. The three modes trade managerial overhead and energy consumption with the latency experienced during handover from the main node.

- **Inform client nodes**: Once a proxy node or a set of proxy nodes has been established by the PDL, the associated client nodes should be notified, and possibly reconfigured, so they perform further communications with the proxy node rather than attempt communicating with the defunct validator node.

- **Synch with PDL**: The PDL will push regular control data updates to the validator nodes. To minimize delays during validation hand-offs, the PDL should push the same control data updates to the proxy nodes. That requires both proxy nodes and the PDL to stay synchronized and is only applicable for the proactive and hybrid approaches where the proxy node is already operational and is part of the PDL and does not require powering up and configuring.

- **Synch with operational validator node(s)**: Idem, it is recommended that the proxy node synchronizes with the attached operational validation nodes. That allows exchange of important data, such as the set of trusted client nodes, timers, etc.

15.4.5 PDL reconciliation

We introduce the possibility of the establishment of an offline side-chain (sPDL). It is, in essence, an operational copy of the main PDL and proactively/reactively helps in the event that client nodes go offline. One of the biggest challenges is to reconcile the main PDL and the side-chain sPDL, which is the focus of this section and is illustrated in Figure 15.3.

Ledger reconciliation: Addressing challenges #8 and #9, the following is important to note in the context of PDL reconciliation:

- **Hindsight consensus**: This approach would require a re-run of the consensus mechanisms in the main PDL as the sPDL comes online again. Assuming that correct timing information is recorded, the hindsight consensus mechanism should be able to order the data correctly and therefore run any cryptographic consensus mechanisms again.

For occasional outages, that approach would work but for frequent outages this can cause an avalanche of parallel hindsight consensus runs making universal consensus impossible. This is because it would create many forks in the ledger and ultimately disrupt the deterministic execution of transactions. Hindsight consensus would also increase the computational resources (and the associated energy and time) consumed during the consensus process.

Shown in Figure 15.4, an approach to accomplish this is to have the reconciled blocks recorded as new blocks in-between the last block when both ledgers were separate and the new block where all nodes are back online.

- **Zipper consensus**: To avoid hindsight consensus, another approach is to cryptographically link the PDL and sPDL blocks through a separate

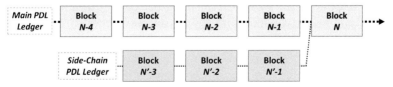

Figure 15.3 Illustration of the main PDL (green blocks) and the side-chain sPDL (yellow blocks), causally ordered in blocks.

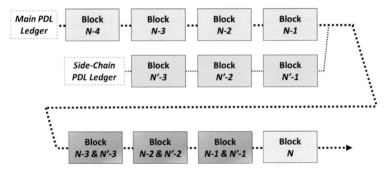

Figure 15.4 Hindsight ledger reconciliation approach where the reconciled blocks are recorded as new blocks in-between the last block when both ledgers were separate and the new block where all nodes are back online..

validation method. It would, for example, create a linking hash between blocks at the same or approximately same (within a pre-defined margin) timestamp. As illustrated in Figure 15.5, this allows a very light yet secure validation process combining two or more chains.

There are two mechanisms which help enormously with above approaches:

- **Low-bandwidth OOB control**: To aid the reconciliation, an out of band control channel can be very helpful. It can transmit control data from either validation process which could be embedded into the PDL and

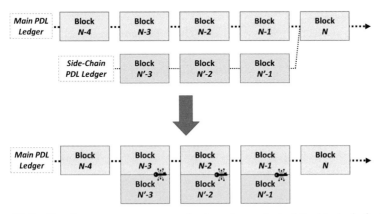

Figure 15.5 The zipper consensus approach where the content of the blocks is first time-aligned and then cryptographically linked through a separate validation procedure.

sPDL validation process, and thus provide an extra layer of trust once both ledgers are reconciled.

- **Placeholder blocks on main PDL**: It may also prove useful that the main PDL reserves placeholder blocks once it detects that certain nodes have gone offline and thus are likely to run a sidechain sPDL. Such placeholders could simplify the cryptographic procedures needed for the reconciliation process.

Smart contract reconciliation: Once committed to the main PDL, smart contracts (in the form of execution logic) cannot be modified. The creation of new smart contracts should only be permissible on the main PDL. Therefore, even if a local copy of a smart contract is created, it cannot be modified and therefore no smart contract reconciliation is required.

15.4.6 Monitoring and orchestration

The end-to-end well-being of PDLs is enabled through proper security and privacy provisioning, which in turn is enabled through monitoring and orchestration. These issues are discussed in this section.

End-to-end security: Securing the data and contracts, as well as links, instances and nodes of the PDL is enabled through certificates and cryptographic means.

Addressing challenge #17, a system-wide end-to-end security view is required to ensure that the PDL is truly secure over its lifetime. To this end, the following is recommended:

- **Risk assessment**: As with any cyber physical infrastructure, it is recommended to perform risk assessment which pertains to the infrastructure (client/validator/ledger nodes), protocols and certificates, ledger and smart contract, and participating consortium members. Such a risk assessment allows weaknesses to be identified and mitigated.

- **Consolidating physical and cyber**: Whilst focus in PDL is on the protocol and smart contract side, one should not forget that PDLs are a vulnerable mix of physical and digital entities. A consolidated security approach should be taken when designing the PDL. For instance, it is futile to implement strong physical protection, if the security certificates are outdated or no TEE provided.

- **Zero-trust policy**: By default, a zero-trust policy ought to be enforced which prohibits any form of PDL operation for a node with weak, expired or absent security credentials.

- **Security orchestration**: Since security is an important yet always-evolving element of the PDL design, a proper orchestration framework ought to be implemented which enables security with an evolving cyber physical security landscape. The orchestration framework should ideally be placed on the ledger through smart contracts, but could be run from an all-trusted node in the network. It has to be understood however that such a node becomes a liability in the end-to-end security design.

Privacy: Between PDL consortium members, privacy of data and execution logic should be guaranteed considering that the prime reason for introducing a PDL into a consortium is the *a priori* non-trusted relationship between participating members.
Addressing challenge #18, ensuring privacy preserving mechanisms is thus important and the following mechanisms could be applied:

- **Data encryption**: Data is encrypted at rest and in transit; and only decrypted when needed for algorithmic reasons. These algorithms should be executed in a TEE without external access. Smart contracts could be encrypted in their entirety or parts thereof, to hide decision/execution logic.
- **Anonymization techniques**: Advanced anonymization techniques can be applied to the data processing, such as K-anonymity, L-diversity, T-closeness, or randomization.
- **Homomorphic approaches**: Homomorphic data processing techniques could be applied which allow executing an algorithmic framework without decrypting the data at all.

Monitoring: Addressing challenge #19, a reliable monitoring of the PDL is vital. Said monitoring can be implemented in different ways, as discussed below. Furthermore, the monitored PDL node status (e.g., online or offline) can be maintained at the orchestration level and can be used to determine a proxy node for a particular PDL node when the PDL node goes offline. Some example approaches for monitoring PDL node status are described below:

- **Peer-to-peer monitoring**: PDL nodes can mutually check each other's status. For instance, a PDL node A can actively send a request to its neighboring PDL nodes (e.g., B and C) to check their status. After that, the PDL node A can report the status of itself and its neighboring PDL nodes to the orchestration node.
- **Reactive self-monitoring**: A PDL node A itself may observe the gradually degraded quality of its communication links to other PDL nodes. As a result, PDL node A may actively send a status report message

to the orchestration node and/or its neighboring nodes, before it loses connectivity.

- **Proactive monitoring**: The orchestration node may directly solicit the status report from a PDL node at given intervals, which then sends a status report message to the orchestration node.
- **Networked monitoring**: A PDL node A may continuously and indirectly monitor the status of its neighboring PDL nodes (e.g., B and C), for example, by measuring the number of transactions from neighboring PDL nodes or by measuring the round-trip time (RTT) between itself and neighboring nodes. As an example, if the PDL node A suddenly stops receiving transaction from PDL node B but there are still some transactions coming from PDL node C, PDL node A can assume PDL node B's current status as offline. Then, PDL node A can report PDL node B's status (or assumed status) to the orchestration node and/or other PDL nodes that may, on their end, perform further tests or reconcile information from additional sources to determine the status of PDL node B.

Orchestration: Addressing challenge #20, orchestration capabilities are required to ensure proper function of the PDL in offline mode. The exact functionality of each orchestration entity is not specified here; however, important operating guidelines are outlined which underpin the difference between a single trusted entity (where an orchestrator, such as ETSI MANO, would typically reside) versus PDL being a distributed consortium of non-trusted entities:

- **Single point of failure**: The orchestration entity, which could be a virtual machine or a physical node, should not become a single point of failure. Whilst one can imagine running an orchestrator from a single entity, backup entities need to be always available. The ownership structure of the running orchestration entity and the backup entities should reflect the ownership structure of the PDL or be implemented through trusted third-party escrows. Situations where a minority of PDL consortium members could bring down the orchestration entity should be avoided.

- **Orchestration decision logic**: Similar to the hosting of the orchestration entity, the logic behind orchestration should also not depend on a minority of PDL consortium members. Non-distributed but trusted decision instances are possible if trust is established through offline contracts; this, however, is not ideal since it counteracts the very nature of PDL.

- **Distributed orchestration operation**: Ideally, the orchestration framework should be implemented through smart contracts residing on the same PDL or an associated orchestration PDL. That ensures that the security, privacy, and transparency gains made with the introduction of the PDL are not lost with a poorly designed orchestration framework.

15.5 Offline PDL Architecture and Procedures

This section introduces possible architecture embodiments containing the technical solutions discussed in the previous section. Associated operational procedures are also outlined and discussed.

15.5.1 PDL architecture embodiments

Logical architecture elements: The canonical elements of a PDL are discussed in here. The client node, depicted in Figure 15.6, has internal capabilities (TEE, storage, algorithms, etc.), external interfaces (sensory data, control data, wired/wireless networking, etc.) as well as monitoring and orchestration interfaces. The validator node, depicted in Figure 15.7, has similar interfaces as the client node with the main difference that it only interfaces with client nodes, ledger nodes, and peer validator nodes, and lacks the sensory and control data interfaces. The ledger node, depicted in Figure 15.8, has the same interfaces as the validator node with the exception that it lacks an interface with client nodes.

High-level architecture: A high-level PDL architecture with offline capabilities is shown in Figure 15.9, with more details provided below.

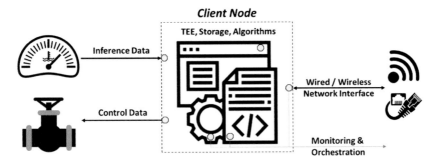

Figure 15.6 Client node with embedded TEE, secure storage and the required algorithmic frameworks which ingest inferred data and/or send control commands.

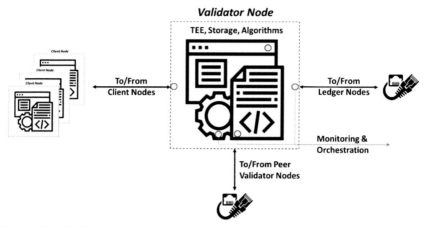

Figure 15.7   Validator node with embedded TEE, secure storage and the required algorithmic frameworks to handle the validation process.

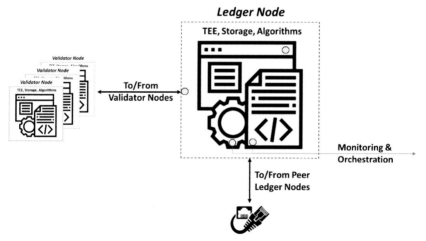

Figure 15.8   Ledger node with embedded TEE, secure storage and the required algorithmic frameworks which enable the operations of the PDL.

Notably, the client nodes are connected to the validator nodes. There are also proxy nodes that the client nodes are connected to, even though the connection is only activated when the associated validator node goes offline.

The validator nodes are connected to the ledger nodes. These nodes store the data and host as well as execute the smart contracts. The ledger nodes may also host monitoring as well as orchestration capabilities.

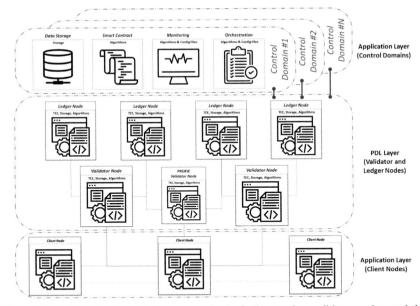

Figure 15.9 High-level architecture comprised of client nodes, validator nodes, and their proxies as well as ledger nodes, and several control domains.

Note that there are different control domains for certain components, controlled by a different set of PDL participants.

3GPP-aligned architecture: A PDL function (PDLF) can be created in the control plane (CP) of 3GPP systems, containing the operational elements shown in Figure 15.9.

The advantage of hosting the PDLF as part of the 3GPP stack is that many issues related to security and authentication are easily provided within the secure envelope of 3GPP systems.

A new network function interface would need to be created too, referred to here as *Npdlf*. It would use HTTP or JSON to communicate with the CP message bus via the service-based interface (SBI) as defined in 3GPP.

This has been illustrated in Figure 15.10. Note that PDLF would only be the control function. The physical elements of the PDL could be distributed in the mobile telecommunications system.

15.5.2 MANO-aligned orchestration framework

ETSI MANO has been introduced as a standardized orchestration framework in networking and telecommunications systems; see [2].

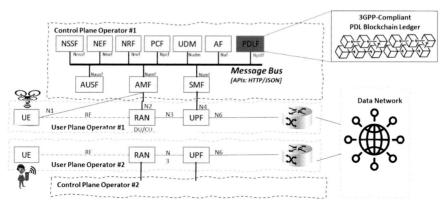

Figure 15.10   3GPP architecture and the new network function PDLF.

The orchestration of all functionalities not related and not impacting the PDL can be done in a traditional centralized way as there is no apparent benefit to distribution in a MANO framework from a centralized orchestration perspective.

However, orchestration of the PDL should follow stringent design guidelines in order not to break the paradigm of distributed ledgers. The implication is that an ETSI MANO orchestration, when applied to a PDL, may remain centralized in context but implemented in a distributed manner.

As shown in Figure 15.11, it is suggested to host the orchestration capabilities on the same or a separate PDL. If that is not possible, then a trusted escrow is also an option as it ensures the impartial execution of the orchestration tasks. The standardized management and orchestration ETSI MANO framework can be adapted to PDL by ensuring that the orchestrator is implemented through a PDL (option 1) or escrow (option 2).

15.5.3 Deployment and operational procedures

This section introduces deployment and operational procedures related to the technical solutions and architectures introduced in previous sections. Notably, the procedures related to the client node preparations as well as the offline operations of client and validator nodes are discussed herewith.

Offline client node preparations: Figure 15.12 illustrates the procedure for preparing the client node for a potential offline operation.

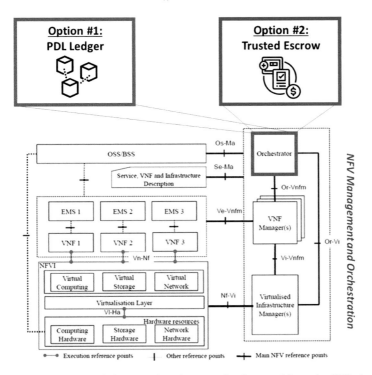

Figure 15.11 ETSI MANO framework orchestrator implementedthrough a PDL (option 1) or escrow (option 2).

First, the client node is switched on. The client node then commences the PDL discovery process using static or dynamic discovery mechanisms.

Once discovered, it connects to the ledger. The ledger validates the TEE and authenticity of the client node. Once verified, it requests orchestration information which, together with the operational information, is passed on to the client node.

The client node verifies the received information and provisions accordingly. Said information will include details on how to operate under the different offline scenarios discussed above. It will also include information about validator nodes and their proxies.

Offline client node operations: Figure 15.13 illustrates the procedures occurring when a client node is rendered offline. Notably, upon going offline, the connection between the client and validator nodes is lost both ways.

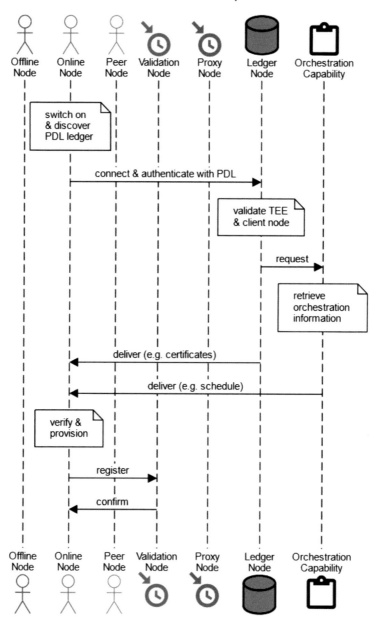

Figure 15.12 Procedure to prepare a client node for a possible offline mode.

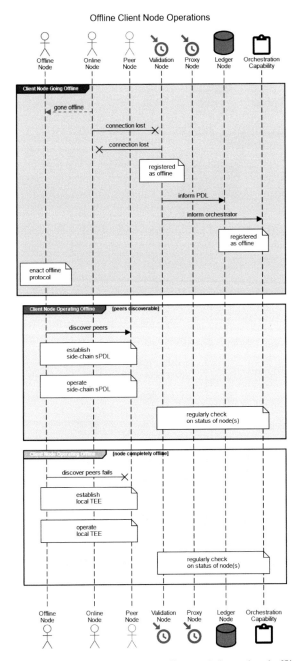

Figure 15.13 Procedure in case a client node is rendered offline.

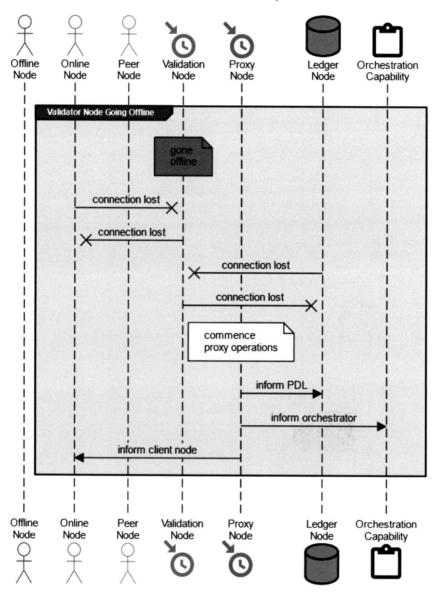

Figure 15.14   Procedure in case a validator node is rendered offline.

The validator node then registers the node as offline and informs the ledger nodes as well as the monitoring and orchestration framework.

The client node, in the meantime, enacts the offline operational protocol. If no such offline operational protocol had been defined or provisioned, the client node will stop data collection from the sensory interface and distribution of control data through the control interface, and will wait for the connection with the validator/proxy node to resume operations.

The first approach is for the client node to establish a networking connection with peer client nodes. If successful, it could establish an operational side-chain ledger sPDL.

A second approach, if no peers are discoverable, is to handle the data and smart contract operations locally using the prior-provisioned TEE.

Offline validation node operations: Figure 15.14 shows the procedures occurring when a validator node is rendered offline. In that case, the connection from both the client node(s) as well as ledger node(s) is lost.

The proxy node is then replacing the validator node which has gone offline. The choice of the proxy node will have been communicated via the orchestrator.

If no proxy node is available (either by design or due to absence of sufficient resources), then the validation procedures should be stopped or paused until a proxy node emerges.

References

[1] https://www.cl.cam.ac.uk/research/security/ctsrd/cheri
[2] ETSI GS NFV-MAN 001: "Network Functions Virtualisation (NFV); Management and Orchestration."

16

Ledger Interoperability

This chapter focuses on the key elements of interoperability to exchange information between different ledgers and to mutually use the information that has been exchanged. We first discuss types of PDL interoperability, and then focus on tools and solutions to enable PDL interoperability. We conclude with a set of ETSI PDL best practices.

16.1 Types of Interoperability

16.1.1 Why interoperability between PDLs

Combining two or more distributed ledger technologies (DLTs) using interledger mechanisms allows a different tradeoff in terms of trust and cost, allows different levels of privacy, and can increase the overall scalability and functionality.

A higher- or wider-scale trust requires a larger network with more nodes and/or a more demanding consensus model. This is the case of public ledgers, which results in a higher computation cost, hence monetary transaction cost, and higher transaction delay compared to permissioned DLTs.

Hence, transactions requiring a higher level of trust can be recorded on a public blockchain, whereas transactions which occur frequently but for which a lower level of trust is sufficient can be recorded on a permissioned DLT. Utilizing permissioned DLTs can support higher privacy, since all transactions on a public blockchain are public.

Hence, data can be stored in permissioned DLTs for privacy, whereas hashes of the data stored on permissioned DLTs can be periodically stored on public blockchains to ensure immutability of the data. Finally, multiple permissioned DLTs can be combined with a public blockchain to exploit transaction locality, hence achieving scalability, while also allowing the permissioned DLTs to support different consensus models and programming functionality.

255

The present chapter envisions the scenarios for multiple ledgers and distinguishing from the present chapter considerations intra-chain or inside the same PDL which allows interoperability between applications but do not communicate with other PDL. Although it is a very important dimension of the interoperability which is part of the intrinsic mechanism of the PDL, in this section it is an introduction for a cross-chain or inter-ledger interoperability scenario.

16.1.2 What is not interoperability between PDLs

As per Figure 16.1, if there is just one ledger, then in this scenario it is a type of interoperability that is out of the scope of ETSI PDL. Serving as an illustration, functional components, sometimes security functional components or minimal functional components or simply optional functional components, are able to provide intra-chain interoperability.

16.1.3 Unidirectional PDL interoperability

A PDL receives information from other blockchains (PDLs or not) to update their status (i.e., an oracle blockchain pushing information to a PDL). A PDL sends information to other blockchains (PDLs or not) (i.e., a PDL updates the status of a delivery to vendor/procurement PDLs).

In this basic scenario there are two ledgers that interoperate. One PDL is exchanging information with other PDL to mutually use such information in a perfected and common interest. As per Figure 16.2, the two ledgers represent two different PDLs which enable an interoperability approach via Gateway or API.

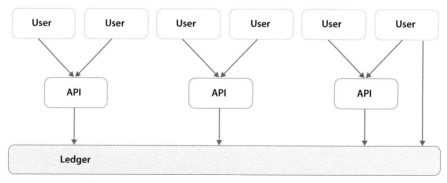

Figure 16.1 Example of non-inter-ledger interoperability.

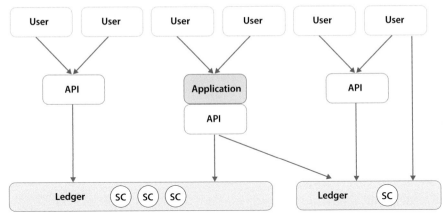

Figure 16.2 Example of ensuring unidirectional inter-ledger interoperability via API-enabled communications between ledgers.

When one PDL takes information from another PDL or an external data source the following considerations are recommended:

1) Data integrity: data to the ledger needs to be authenticated; a guarantee from the source may be attached to prove the integrity of the data.
2) Data security: ensure the prevention of attacks such as eavesdropping and man-in-the-middle attack.
3) Data format: ensure the data is in the format compatible to the PDL.

In terms of *data integrity*, when data is fed to the PDL, it is written to the PDL for eternity. Hence its integrity and authenticity are of prime importance. Moreover, if this data is required to execute further smart contracts and invoke other chained transactions, it may result in wrong executions.

For example, if a smart contract is programmed to pay to some customers, and the wrong recipient information is fed to the contract, it will cause the payment to the wrong recipient.

In terms of *data security*, the data entered in a PDL needs to be secured from cyberattacks such as man-in-the-middle attack and eavesdropping. For example, if a bid is placed by a PDL to another PDL, it is essential to secure such information exchange.

In terms of the *data format*, two ledgers need to understand each other, that is to say, that data exchange between a PDL and another PDL or storage follow a compatible format. Following mutually agreed schemas, the PDL may also function with automated chained executions of the contracts where several smart contracts are involved in a chained execution process.

In terms of the *standard fields for PDL interoperability*, when interoperating between a PDL and another PDL (unidirectionally), the following fields may be considered as essential:

1) **PDL identifier**: Every PDL should have an identifier − this will help in recording the identity of the ledger in the Gateway.
2) **Node identifier**: A unique node identifier corresponding to their PDL. For example, a PDL identifier XY can have a node with identifier XY123.
3) **Shareable data fields**: Every PDL, when they want to share their data in the future should specify the fields to the Gateway and the fields.

In terms of the *referenced architecture* for unidirectional PDL access:

1) The PDL intending to access data from the other PDL/storage makes a request to the Gateway. This Gateway is trusted by both PDLs and includes its own storage with smart contracts. This Gateway maintains all the records of shareable data between the PDLs. For example, some PDLs may not prefer to share certain details, and will thus not reveal those fields to the Gateway. Smart contracts stored by the Gateway may be maintained in another PDL.

2) The PDL requesting data may include the following details in the request:

   a) Its own (PDL) Identity; may be public key
   b) PDL Identity they are requesting data from
   c) Data fields they require
   d) Duration for which needs access

3) The Gateway checks the requesting PDL credentials in their own records and verifies the access rights; if all matches provide the keys and grants the access. A smart contract is executed at this stage and records the details of requesting data and the requester.

4) Using the keys PDL1 can access record from PDL2.

In terms of *security considerations*, the major security consideration here is the single point of failure for a Gateway. This means that if the Gateway is compromised, the malicious party can take over the system and issue the keys to themselves or possibly to other malicious parties.

The solution − shown in Figure 16.4 – can be used instead of saving all the information such as readable data fields. The PDL2 decides after running consensus and sends the accept/reject signal to the Gateway by executing a

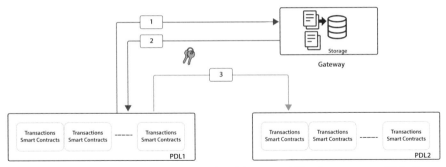

Figure 16.3 Example with simple scenario of interoperability between two PDL (faster procedure).

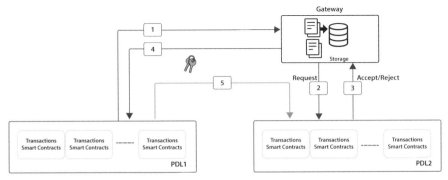

Figure 16.4 Example secured interoperability between two PDLs (live verification).

smart contract in the Gateway ledger which subsequently issues keys to PDL1 (i.e., the requesting ledger).

In this scenario there are three ledgers that consolidate a common ledger as part of one PDL. Hence inter-ledger interoperability can occur between ledgers within a same PDL or between various PDL.

The architectural model may vary from the scenario but there are three common facets for the inter-ledger interoperability which are unidirectional in the schema of Figure 16.5:

a) Immutable ledger: It represents the transactions distributed ledger whereby the replication is unstoppable between all the nodes and consolidates the validation and represents the source of truth for the PDL.

b) Services and application ledger: It represents the utilities and facilities that provide interoperability within the PDL between the different ledgers and it is normally composed of minimal functional components

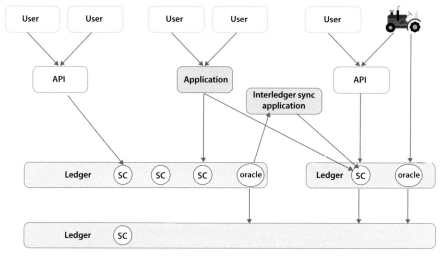

Figure 16.5   Example two of inter-ledger interoperability.

such as smart contracts and APIs that interact, usually, with a Gateway between ledgers in accordance with the particular performance.

c) User's access management: It represents the accessibility to consumers and users, and may vary between different architectural models whereby could be from different perspectives such as observing and reading the immutable ledger and/or using the services and application ledger.

In this scenario there are a variety of entities which require a minimal identification and authentication to produce effects within the PDL. This scenario usually provides oracles which are able to enhance the ledgers and contribute the performance between the services and application ledger with the immutability ledger for processes of verification and/or fraud detection by increasing the ability to be obliterated.

16.1.4 Bidirectional PDL interoperability

The main challenge of bidirectional interoperability is the synchronization of all ledgers involved; the essential scenario represents the interoperability between distributed ledgers whereby the administrative domain is decentralized.

A simple ledger can relay in a variety of layers and a variety of PDLs can coexist for the same industry whereby PDLs consolidate their flow and registries in an immutable ledger that reflects the validity of both PDLs.

Directionality is independent of direct or indirect techniques, which means that unidirectional approaches can be direct or indirect techniques and at the same time a variety of techniques can be applicable for direct or indirect considerations of bidirectional interoperability.

Let us take the following example: A is a PDL looking for interoperability, B is another PDL looking for interoperability or an application (API, Gateway API, etc.) looking for interoperability, and C is yet another PDL which is requested for interoperability or is looking for interoperability with PDL A. Possible approaches are illustrated in Figures 16.6 and 16.7.

16.2 PDL Interoperability Tools

16.2.1 Interoperability design guidelines

The European Interoperability Reference Architecture (EIRA) was created and is being maintained in the context of the New European Interoperability Framework and National Interoperability Framework Observatory ISA2 program as part of the European Interoperability Strategy (EIS).

With these key instruments, the European Interoperability Framework (EIF) is endorsed by the European Commission and composed of an Interoperability Governance Framework with four layers.

The interoperability requirements solutions compose an approach via DL SAT (Detailed-Level Interoperability Requirements Solution Architecture Template) which – through design guidelines – offers specifications extending to the EIRA. It provides solution architects with a specific solution domain in the form of a template that can be used to design related solutions. Any solution architecture template (SAT) in EIRA contains:

- Principles and requirements.
- Goal and description of supported functionalities.
- A sub-set of the EIRA core architecture building blocks (ABBs) covering the four EIF layers.
- A set of specific ABBs extending EIRA's views enabling specific functionalities to be provided by implementations derived from SAT.
- The interoperability specifications of selected ABBs.

The lifecycle model of this solutions-based architecture in the European framework is named SAT: plan, build, deliver, and run. This model reconciles the semantic and technical views with the legal and public policy views where different domain specific application services and components as well as the PDL can create top-down blueprints.

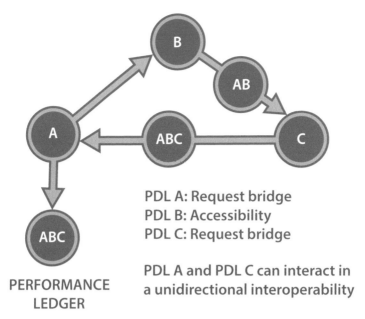

PDL A: Request bridge
PDL B: Accessibility
PDL C: Request bridge

PDL A and PDL C can interact in
a unidirectional interoperability

PERFORMANCE
LEDGER

Figure 16.6 One PDL can change the status of some registries of another PDL and vice versa.

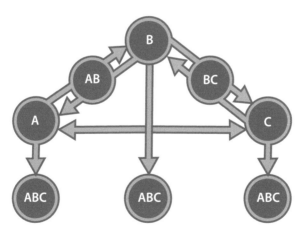

PDL A: Request interoperability Access/challenge/Secrecy
PDL B: Confirm request.
PDL C: Resolve interoperability Access/challenge/Secrecy

PDL A and PDL C can interact in bidirectional interoperability

Figure 16.7 Two PDLs share the value/status of one or more registries.

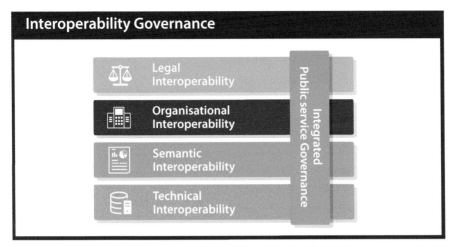

Figure 16.8   Interoperability governance in PDL.

Figure 16.9 illustrates an example of a resource description framework implementing semantic interoperability specifications grounded in the EIRA DL SAT.

The complete toolkit and libraries are released with the components as part of the EIRA Library of Interoperability Specifications (ELIS), containing: architecture building blocks, specification name, domain and URLs of the interoperability specification.

The National Interoperability Framework Observatory (NIFO) is one of the mechanisms put in place by the European Commission, to monitor the implementation of the revised version of the EIF and help to foster the capacity building policy and modernization of public administrations. By doing so, it aims at becoming an online community of practice and the prime source of information regarding digital public administration and interoperability matters within Europe.

NIFO is centering its functionalities as information observatory, assistance and support, and community practice. Through this mechanism, 36 countries are getting through interoperability matters.

16.2.2 Atomic swaps

Atomic swaps based on hashed time-lock contracts (HTLCs) are typically used in atomic cross-chain transactions for direct trading between two peers, in transactions-across-a-network (also referred to as payment networks), inter-ledger protocols (ILPs), and other bridging solutions.

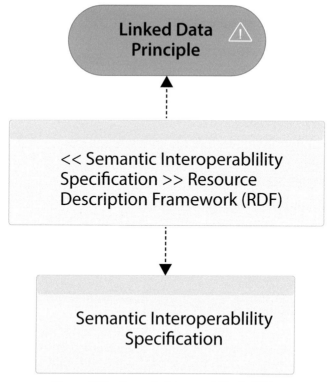

Figure 16.9   Semantic interoperability in PDL.

Atomic cross-chain transactions target peer-to-peer trading between two parties that seek to exchange value. Transactions-across-a-network solutions and ILPs generalize peer-to-peer transactions to payment networks, where payments are routed along paths that are comprised of off-chain payment channels.

Bridging approaches enable cross-chain transactions between existing ledgers. Sidechain approaches assume the existence of a main chain and support the transfer of value between the main chain and side chains, which are regarded as subordinate to the main chain.

Ledger-of-ledgers approaches introduce a new super-ledger with the goal of having multiple sidechain-like ledgers, which can also support the interconnection to existing ledgers, such as Ethereum and Bitcoin.

The various approaches differ in terms of reliability in performing inter-ledger operations. Specifically, if atomic cross-chain transactions are performed by a single entity, then this entity can be a single point of failure.

On the other hand, bridging approaches, side chains, and ledger-of-ledger approaches involve multiple nodes that implement the inter-ledger operations. Their decentralized operations thus result in high reliability.

A final note: the reliability of approaches involving transactions-across-a-network W3C ILP depend on the existence of redundant paths between the end nodes that wish to transact.

16.2.3 Sidechains

Off-chain protocols like side chains or rollups implement alternative scaling approaching. The term of sidechain initially was used to validate data between two blockchains as a solution to interoperate for such verification. It was an interoperability solution to enable two blockchains to verify information about each other's progress via light-weight proofs. The intention was to allow Bitcoins to be locked in Bitcoin and to be released in the other network (and vice versa) without trusting any intermediary with the funds.

Nowadays, the term sidechain is used to imply that an independent network in a PDL has a relationship with another network in another PDL and it is implemented with a bridge contract that allows digital assets to be moved from one PDL to another PDL.

Normally, three types of bridge contracts are used:

- Single organizational: single party has the custody.
- Multi-organizational: fixed set of independent parties have the custody.
- Crypto-economic: a dynamic set of parties determined by their weight in assets have the custody.

The bridge contract for side chains does not verify the integrity of the other network and instead relies on a set of parties to attest the validation. The term rollup originated from the work by barrywhiteHat's rollup [1]; there, a sidechain is an independent PDL network but the parties (sequencers) are responsible for providing evidence about the state of the other network to bridge the contract.

Rollup networks can retain the security of the main chain but also consume more resources from the main chain which decreases the financial sustainability to transact on a rollup in comparison with a sidechain.

From the user perspective, it is recommended to check the security of the other network and costs before transacting in a public blockchain. However, a given PDL ought to have mechanisms to unidirectionally or bidirectionally interoperate with another PDL.

16.2.4 Apps for interoperability

An application of ledger interoperability is shown in Figure 16.10, where an end-device (e.g., user equipment) can have service subscription with a network (i.e., home service provider) and the home service provider can have roaming service level agreement (SLA) with the visited network to serve the devices based on subscription (i.e., subscribed services which includes subscribed network slice) during roaming.

If the visited network rejects any service request from the device which is part of subscribed services, then the service failure related to a subscribed service can be notified by the device and serving network node(s) in a trustworthy manner (i.e., the service failure report can be sent as a transaction to the preconfigured/designated application/API) to allow the home network node or any stakeholder to access the respective ledger and resolve the settlement and/or disputes if any should arise related to the roaming SLA. The steps shown in Figure 16.10 are described as follows:

Precondition: A device requests services based on subscribed services and the serving node in the visited network rejects the requested service and provides a reference identifier which can be used for the service rejection reporting.

Step 1. The device generates a service failure report which can include the reference ID, the sender information (i.e., device ID), service provider information (i.e., serving node and network ID), service type information, failure cause, time stamp and any other required information.

Similarly, the serving node which rejected the subscribed service request can generate a service failure report which can include the reference ID, the sender information (i.e., serving node and network ID), service receiver

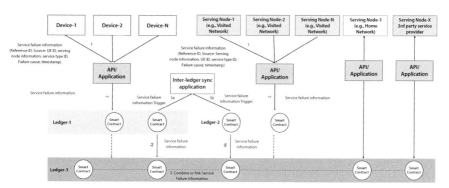

Figure 16.10   Trusted service failure reporting and handling using PDL with ledger interoperability.

information (i.e., device ID), service type information, failure cause, time stamp and any other required information. The device and the serving node can send the service failure report using any application/API by initiating a transaction to the reporting destination address locally configured.

The service type information can be specific to the type of subscribed service requested by the device and rejected by the serving node.

Step 2. The service failure report transaction from the device and the serving node can be broadcast to all validator nodes and after consensus can be added to Ledger 1 (i.e., for device reporting) and Ledger 2 (i.e., for serving network node reporting) respectively.

Steps 3a−b. A designated smart contract for Ledger 1 can send a trigger (either directly or via another smart contract responsible for ledger interoperability) related to the service failure information report to the configured inter-ledger sync application. The inter-ledger sync application can send the trigger to smart contract responsible for Ledger 2. The trigger can include the reference ID, sender information, serving node information and timestamp can be included.

Steps 4a−b. The smart contract responsible for Ledger 1 can send the service failure report as a transaction to another destination address configured in the smart contract which may broadcast transaction to a set of validator nodes responsible for reaching a common consensus across all the involved stakeholders. Stakeholder examples are the home network, a visited network your third-party service providers. After a successful consensus the service rejection report related to the device is added as a block to another common consensus ledger (i.e., Ledger 3 shown in Figure 16.10).

Similarly, the smart contract responsible for Ledger 2, on receiving the trigger (as mentioned in Step 3b), can fetch the block with the reference ID. It then sends the service failure report information as a transaction and stores it in Ledger 3 which is built over a common consensus across all the involved stakeholders (i.e., Ledger 3 shown in Figure 16.10).

Step 5. The smart contract in Ledger 3 – on receiving the service failure report transaction related to the device from Ledger 1 (i.e., Step 4a) and the service failure report transaction related to the serving node from Ledger 2 (Step 4b) – adds as inter linked blocks using the reference ID as the relation between the blocks. The smart contract stores the reference ID, device ID and serving node information along with the block reference/identification of the Ledger 3 in an online or offline ledger or storage to resolve future conflicts and settlements related to the financial and service level agreements.

Step 6. Required actions based on the complete service failure information (i.e., service failure information from device and the serving node) can be taken during SLA evaluation or related conflict resolution. Furthermore, if a smart contract responsible for Ledger 3 is configured to report any trigger to the home serving node(s) or third-party service provider node(s), then the smart contract may trigger notifications related to the service failure information (i.e., reaching any threshold) via an API/Application.

16.2.5 Ledger-of-ledger

Two or more ledgers can be combined into a unified ledger; that is fairly rare and may not be efficient due to latency, computation, concurrency and challenges with a common consensus protocol for building blocks.

Challenges: Latency, access control, redaction (hidden data to enable privacy), algorithmic governance, permissions' strategy, node's computation power, synchronization performance time, etc.

Advantages: Discoverability, uniformed information in one place, ability to operate transportability and portability, forking, reduction of dependencies and correcting lack of democratization, increased value and trusted data, improve the credibility, etc.

16.3 Interoperability Best Practice

16.3.1 Direct interoperability OOP

The concept of the once-only principle (OOP) focuses on reducing administrative burden for individual and business. It is part of the Single Digital Gateway Regulation (EU) 2018/1724 which promotes online access to every citizen and business in EU countries.

One of the innovative solutions developed is a generic federated architecture, developed in collaboration between the different Member States. The approach to federated architecture and building blocks reuses existing building blocks and components and integrates new elements in the European and participating States' ecosystem increasing a multi-disciplinary and intersectoral character of e-Government.

Basically, every business build with the OOP resolves around re-using data held by one administration, by providing it directly to another administration. It is a bidirectional relationship as required which port the data directly between peers. The OOP is not an end in itself and it is part of a range of strategic initiatives at European level supporting cross-border digital public service provision for the digital single market.

16.3.2 Auxiliary PDL

The auxiliary PDL contains part of the information of third party PDLs for the sake of interoperability between those third party PDLs. The auxiliary PDL is the consolidation of third party PDLs.

The inter-ledger can be used in various ways. For example, agricultural supply chain use cases store the hash of private transactions to the public ledger using the inter-ledger. This is to provide immutability for private transactions and help with dispute resolutions.

In the context-aware mobile gaming use case, the private ledger is used to store in-game assets used by the gamers. These assets can be traded in a public ledger between the gamers, but only if they are not active at the same time in the private ledger. The inter-ledger is used to guarantee that the state of the asset is changed in an atomic manner between the ledgers, and the asset can be active only in one ledger at the time.

In a similar manner, inter-ledger is useful for any kind of situation where trust, transparency and automation are required between multiple parties. This includes sharing cybersecurity information or automating disclosure of software vulnerabilities.

16.3.3 Traceability and auditability

Events have to be traceable and the performance, integrity, and authenticity of the interoperability have to be auditable. Keeping records/logs of transactions will allow to roll back in case of discrepancy.

Time-stamping consideration of the perfected interest between the two PDLs for interoperability is essential to ensure proper sequence of events.

It is recommended that the sequence of events has to pre-synchronize the atomic clock and other circumstances related to the configuration to mitigate risks and/or provide alternative responsive mechanism for interoperability.

16.3.4 Future-proof

The foreseen advent of quantum computers poses a threat on current PDLs, specifically in what relates to the vulnerability of digital signatures in transactions, and of the key-exchange mechanisms used for the communications among the nodes. This obviously impacts inter-ledger activity and poses the additional risk of divergent solutions to address intra-ledger quantum vulnerability.

Table 16.1   Inspired from ISO/TS 23635:2022 [2] Guidelines for governance (ISO TC 307).

	Initialization	Operation	Termination
Protocol context	Genesis block, establishment of interoperability	Alteration rules (forks, etc.)	Execution and validation
Application context	Accessibility and accountability	Discoverability, auditability, availability, accountability, syntactic interoperability	Disposal, destruction or transfer
Data context	Establishment of data governance	Collection, storage, reporting, semantic interoperability	Disposal, archiving or destruction
Behavioral context	Organic functions and operations	Decision, distribution, dispute resolution, business interoperability	Decommissioning, disposal

The current proposals on post-quantum cryptography (PQC) and quantum key distribution (QKD) are intended to address these potential vulnerabilities, and standards solutions are being produced for their application in general signature methods and communication protocols, including the convergence of key management interfaces. ETSI, IETF, and NIST are specifically active in these fields, and it is recommended to follow their results in order to provide feedback on their applicability for intra- and inter-ledger PDL scenarios, and to incorporate and adapt these results as they become available.

16.3.5 Minimal viable governance

A PDL requires a clear definition on the lifecycle whereby the minimal viable governance guidance is going to be implemented: initialization, operation, and termination. At the same time, it is necessary to make a perimeter on the context per each phase of the lifecycle where the roles and application's policies and rules are easy to audit and provide efficacy on the accountability.

References

[1] https://github.com/barryWhiteHat/roll_up
[2] https://www.iso.org/standard/76480.html

Part IV

Blockchains in 6G

17

6G Use Cases and Technologies

Part IV of this book is dedicated to the application of blockchain technologies in emerging 6G telecommunications systems. In the first chapter, we give an introduction to 6G. In subsequent sections, we then discuss the application of blockchains to data sharing and in the support of native AI. We shall also discuss the application of ledgers to the infrastructure of future telecommunication systems. Last but not least, we will cover the emergence of the metaverse in the 6G and blockchain ecosystem.

This specific chapter is dedicated to an introduction to 6G. We then also discuss prominent use cases along with performance requirements. We will dwell on some early technology enablers and finish the chapter with remaining 6G challenges.

17.1 Introduction to 6G

17.1.1 From 2G to 5G

The evolution of mobile telecommunications systems from 2G to 5G can be divided into several key stages, each of which introduced new technologies and capabilities that improved the performance and functionality of mobile networks. This has had an incredibly positive impact on consumers, industry, government and society at large.

2G, or second-generation, mobile networks were first introduced in the early 1990s and were primarily designed for voice communications. They used digital signal processing (DSP) to improve the quality of voice calls, and also introduced the concept of text messaging (i.e., SMS – short message service) for the first time. They were a massive improvement in terms of capabilities but also interoperability over analogue 1G systems. 2G was the first truly global telecommunications system.

3G, or third-generation, mobile networks were introduced in the early 2000s and were designed to support data communications in addition to

273

voice. They used advanced modulation techniques, such as code division multiple access (CDMA) and wideband CDMA (WCDMA), to increase the capacity of mobile networks and support faster data transfer speeds. This allowed for the use of mobile internet and multimedia services like video calls and music streaming.

4G, or fourth-generation, mobile networks were introduced in around the early 2010s and were designed to support even higher data transfer speeds and increased capacity. They used technologies such as long-term evolution (LTE) and later LTE-advanced (LTE-A) to achieve this. They also introduced the concept of mobile broadband, which allowed users to access the internet at speeds similar to those of fixed-line broadband connections. This allowed for new services such as high-definition (HD) video streaming, online gaming and other data-intensive applications.

5G, or fifth-generation, mobile networks are the latest generation of mobile networks that gained commercial traction around the 2020s, with roll-outs now being significantly quicker than during the equivalent 4G era. 5G is designed to support even higher data transfer speeds and increased capacity, as well as new use cases such as the Internet of Things (IoT) and mission-critical applications. They use advanced technologies such as millimeter wave (mmWave) spectrum, massive multiple input, multiple output (MIMO) and beamforming to achieve this. 5G also aims to provide more reliable and low-latency connectivity compared to previous generations.

In summary, the evolution of telecommunications systems from 2G to 5G has been driven by the increasing demand for faster data transfer speeds, increased capacity, and new use cases. Each generation has introduced new technologies and capabilities that have improved the performance and func-tionality of mobile networks, allowing for new services and applications to be developed.

17.1.2 Key trends toward 6G

The telecommunications industry has undergone significant consolidation over the past few decades, resulting in the emergence of certain key trends that have remained consistent across different generations of technology. One such trend is the "10× growth trend," which involves a roughly tenfold improvement in key performance indicators (KPIs) as we move from one generation to the next. This trend can be observed in various KPIs such as data rate, peak data rate, and latency.

For instance, during the 4G era, the average data rate experienced by consumers was around 10 Mbps. However, in the 5G era, this has improved to 100 Mbps. This trend of a tenfold improvement in data rate is expected to continue in the 6G era, where it can be expected that 6G systems will deliver an average of 1 Gbps to consumers in the future. This high data rate is expected to enable new and advanced use cases such as HD video streaming as well as virtual and augmented reality.

In addition to data rate, the uplink and downlink peak data rates are also expected to increase significantly in the 6G era. In the 5G era, these peak data rates are in the range of tens of Gbps, but it is expected that this will increase to hundreds of Gbps in 6G systems. This high peak data rate is expected to enable new use cases such as high-speed data transfer and massive machine-type communications.

The experienced latency is another KPI that is expected to significantly improve in the 6G era. In the 5G era, experienced latency is in the range of a few milliseconds. However, it is expected that this will decrease to well below one millisecond in 6G systems. This low latency is expected to enable new use cases such as ultra-reliable low-latency communications for many of the tactile internet applications envisaged so far.

While the growth trend provides insight into what characteristics we can expect from 6G systems, it does not address the questions of "why" we need such high-performing KPIs or "how" they can be achieved. The reasoning behind the need for these KPIs is often found in their use cases, which are expected to be diverse and varied. For example, the high data rate and low latency of 6G systems are expected to enable new use cases in areas such as healthcare, transportation, and manufacturing.

The methodology for achieving these KPIs will be developed by telecommunications engineers in the coming years through research and development in areas such as spectrum, modulation, and networking. It is also worth noting that while the focus on 6G is increasing today, the technological advancements are still being made and researched in 5G as well.

17.1.3 The 6G ecosystem

Telecommunications systems are so complex that only a coherent effort among industry, academia and government will ensure the successful emergence of 6G. Let us examine each group separately and then discuss how they typically interact with each other.

- **Academia**: Pockets of excellence in telecommunications research and innovation can be found all around the world. Countries, such as Australia, South Korea, Japan, China, India, most European Union countries, the UK, and the USA, have consistently been driving research in novel methods, algorithms, and architectures in telecommunications. 6G is no exception! Academic peer-reviewed publications on the topic of 6G have emerged as early as 2018.

- **Industry**: The main industry groups impacting telecoms can be summarized as:

    - *Operators*: The operators own and deploy the telco infrastructure; they acquire spectrum in government auctions; and they sell mainly telco services to consumers but also to enterprises. There are typically 3–5 tier-one operators per country or economic area: in the USA, these are Verizon, T-Mobile and AT&T; and in Europe these are Deutsche Telekom, Orange, and Telefonica.

    - *Vendors*: The vendors provide the operational telco infrastructure and associated maintenance services to the telco operators. They would acquire components from their supply chain and add their own IPR; all whilst obeying global standard requirements. There are three main vendors globally and a few smaller ones; the three main ones are Ericsson, Nokia, and Huawei.

    - *Supply chain*: The supply chain in the telco sector is gigantic! They provide any imaginable component, such as amplifiers, antenna elements, ASICs, power cables, etc. They deliver their components and solutions to one of the larger vendors.

    - *Cloud providers*: A well-established industry, however, it is fairly new to telecoms! They cater for two different compute loads: 1) the application load, i.e., they are able to host applications closer to the edge (e.g., a game rendering solution within 10 ms from the wireless user); 2) the telco load in form of core network functions (see sections below) but recently also radio access network capabilities.

- **Government**: They typically have a national and international role. Nationally, the government would appoint a regulator that is responsible for managing and procuring spectrum assets. For instance, in the UK, that is Ofcom; in the USA, for commercial spectrum, that is the FCC, and for federal spectrum, that is the NTIA. Internationally, governments are represented through various bodies, such as the International Telecommunication Union (ITU) which is the ICT agency of the United Nation (UN).

Above ecosystem is hugely competitive but agrees to work jointly across the following mechanisms:

- **Industry alliances**: Industry alliances are hugely important in that they align industry expectations before standardization. They often produce white papers which then influence subsequent standardization and technology work. Examples of important telco alliance are: GSM Association (GSMA), Next Generation Mobile Networks Alliance (NGMN), Next G Alliance (NGA), and the Alliance for Telecommunications Industry Solution (ATIS).
- **International Telecommunication Union (ITU)**: The ITU is an UN agency that acts across its 193 member states. It also enjoys a membership of over 900 companies, universities, and international and regional organizations. It is hugely influential in all matters related to spectrum, such as allocation to specific technologies and co-existence between technologies; as well as the identification of technical requirements for specific Gs.
- **Standards Development Organizations (SDOs)**: The actual technical solutions are developed as part of SDOs. The most important SDOs in the context of telecoms are 3GPP (for the overall architecture and radio technologies), ETSI (for architecture and capabilities), IETF (with specific characteristics that make it a different form of SDO) and the IEEE (for component level interactions).

17.1.4 Estimated 6G timelines

Whilst nothing is carved in stone yet at the time of writing, the industry view of the 6G timelines is shown in Figure 17.1. Based on past design approaches, it is very likely that the 3GPP will carry most if not all of the technical design duties; whilst the ITU will be responsible for frequency allocation and coexistence studies.

Also, based on past design cycles, it is likely that 6G will commence with a requirements study item (SI) in 3GPP Release 19 and then be developed through technical SI's and work items (WIs) in Releases 20−24. In subsequent chapters, we will link blockchain-related opportunities to specific SIs and WIs.

A parallel yet equally important process pertains to ensuring spectrum availability for 6G, which can be achieved in different ways; through ITU World Radiocommunication Conferences, regional decisions or decisions on a per country basis. Whichever method is pursued, harmonization of the selected frequency bands on a global (or sometimes at regional basis) is key to unlocking economies-of-scale and providing numerous benefits to consumers and enterprises across many markets.

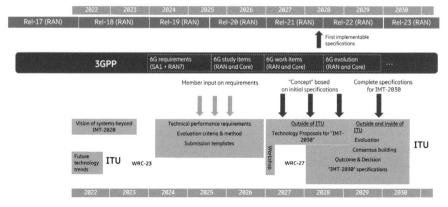

Figure 17.1   Estimated 3GPP and ITU 6G timelines.

Commercial deployments of 6G are expected toward the end of this decade, when operators are expected to upgrade their infrastructure from 5G to 6G; new devices are expected to be on the market, such as mobile AR; and immersive applications are expected to dominate the consumer market.

17.2 6G Use Cases

17.2.1 Ericsson's 6G Use Cases

As discussed in [1], Ericsson had identified several societal use cases that require 6G as an underlying connectivity solution:

- (Human-centric) **Internet of senses**: A holographic society is envisaged where people form emotional bonds over long distances through highly immersive and immediate holographic projections, which might even be augmented by touch. The expected uplink and downlink data rates, connectivity ranges and latencies cannot be offered on a wide scale by today's 5G networks. In addition, advances in security and privacy will be required from 6G.
- (Machine-centric) **Connected intelligent machines**: More and more machines are being connected through the growing IoT, a trend which will continue into the 6G era. Ericsson envisages machines not only to transmit their sensor data but to outsource their intelligent decision making, thus requiring substantially more powerful networks to cater for that exponential increase in data traffic and reduction in required and consistent latency.

- (Environment-centric) **Programmable physical worlds**: A further important paradigm shift will emerge over the years to come in that sensing and intelligent decision-making will be augmented by actuation in real-world environments. That enables reconfiguring physical environments in real time according to needs which can prove useful in industrial, enterprise and consumer industries.
- (Sustainability-centric) **Connected sustainable world**: The telco community believes that all of the above ought to be underpinned by technical and policy solutions which promote sustainability and Net Zero carbon emissions.

This is illustrated in Figure 17.2 and discussed in [2]. These use cases will likely be enabled by the following four key technology areas:

- **Limitless connectivity**: It embodies the notion of having reliable networking connectivity, catering for extreme performance and coverage when and where needed. It requires novel radio architecture approaches as well as new 6G spectrum.
- **Network compute fabric**: It pertains to the notion of "flattening" the compute fabric in that developers of the future won't need to think about where to place the applications. It is rather the digital fabric, i.e., the end-to-end architecture, which takes that decision. For instance, if an application needs extremely low latency then it will be placed closer to the edge with the digital fabric natively providing the means, i.e., compute, storage and orchestration.
- **Cognitive networks**: This capability refers to AI becoming a native ingredient in future networks. It allows networks to become automated and even autonomous, thus exhibiting cognitive properties that hide the increased network complexity from the users.
- **Trustworthy systems**: Users in the envisioned societal use cases must be able to trust the networks to perform according to expectations. This puts requirements on security, reliability, resilience, safety and privacy of the networks – thus protecting data and mitigating various kinds of attacks and disturbances, intentional or unintentional.

17.2.2 ATIS NGA 6G use cases

As per [4], the Alliance for Telecommunications Industry Solutions (ATIS) is a standards organization that develops technical and operational standards and solutions for the ICT industry. It is accredited by the American National

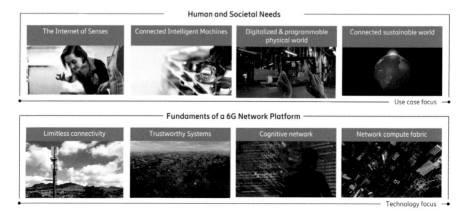

Figure 17.2   Expected use case and technology scenarios enabled by 6G [3].

Standards Institute (ANSI); and is the North American Organizational Partner for the 3rd Generation Partnership Project (3GPP); as well as a member of and major U.S. contributor to the ITU.

ATIS has 150 member companies, comprised of telecommunications service providers, vendors and equipment manufacturers. ATIS is composed of various industry committees and fora, one of which is the Next G Alliance (NGA). The focus of the NGA is to represent the USA in national and international 6G developments.

The NGA has published several influential white papers on 6G. The one discussed here is devoted to 6G use cases [5]. In there, four major use case areas have been identified:

- *"Network Enabled Robotics and Autonomous Systems"* examines the potential impact of network-connected robotics and autonomous systems on areas such as assisted living and healthcare. These systems may improve quality of life through cooperative operation among service robots and the use of robots in hazardous environments.
- *"Multi-sensory Extended Reality"* explores the potential effects of multi-sensory extended reality on immersive and interactive experiences such as online sports, remote team coordination, and interactive classrooms. Examples include highly realistic interactive sports, immersive gaming, mixed reality co-design, telepresence, immersive education, and wireless connectivity in aerial vehicles for entertainment and service.
- *"Distributed Sensing and Communications"* looks at how terrestrial and non-terrestrial connectivity services may shape the future of

connectivity in various markets such as healthcare, agriculture, environment, and public safety. This includes remote data collection, untethered wearables and implants, eliminating digital divide, public safety applications, synchronous data channels and in-body networks for healthcare.

• *"Personalized User Experiences"* examines how personalized experiences may impact the quality of living through improved user identities, preferences, and situational context. Examples include personalized leisure and travel, shopping, and learning experiences.

No quantitative analysis on 6G performance requirements was given; however, a qualitative analysis has been conducted arguing that 6G is indeed needed to drive these use case families. A preliminary set of 6G technologies needed to support these use cases was later derived in [6].

17.2.3 NICT 6G use cases

The National Institute of Information and Communications Technology (NICT) is Japan's primary national research institute for information and communications. It has released one of the impactful white papers on 6G [7].

In there, four use case scenarios were discussed in great societal and technical depth:

• **Scenario 1 – Cybernetic Avatar Society**: The following use cases were identified which relate to this first scenario:

  – *Mutual Understanding Promotion System* (across barriers of culture and values)
  – *Support Avatars for Mind and Body* (overcoming barriers of age and physical ability)
  – *Working Style Revolution with Telepresence* (transcending distance and time barriers)

• **Scenario 2 – City on the Moon**

  – *Lunar Base Connected by 6G*
  – *6G Leading up to the Moon*
  – *Avatar on the Moon/Street View in Space*
  – *Moon Travel*

• **Scenario 3 – Transcending Space and Time**

  – *Vertical Flow of People, Things, and Information*
  – *Resilient Village Forest*
  – *Omni-Cloud Gateway*

- **Scenario 4 – The Light and Shadow of the Cyber World**
  - *AI Agent*
  - *Issues of Fairness, Accountability and Transparency, Ethics and Values in AI*
  - *Avatar Identity Verification*
  - *Nudge Changing Behavior to Solve Social Issues*

The white paper has also discussed the required key technologies / architectures as well as associated technical challenges.

17.2.4 NGMN 6G use cases

As per [8], the NGMN alliance is a mobile telecommunications association of mobile operators, vendors, manufacturers and research institutes. It was founded by major mobile operators in 2006 as an open forum to evaluate candidate technologies to develop a common view of solutions for the next evolution of wireless networks. Its objective is to ensure the successful commercial launch of future mobile broadband networks through a roadmap for technology and friendly user trials.

In NGMN 6G white paper is available under [9]. It has recognized that the path toward 6G involves identifying potential use cases that anticipate major shifts in digital usage patterns. Any predictions would inform the ITU-R IMT (International Mobile Telecommunications) Vision for 2030 and beyond, which thus outlines future connectivity needs that can be used by standards to create and standardize appropriate technologies.

A similar method was employed for 5G, resulting in new capabilities that met the anticipated needs of industries and users. For example, 5G brought about improvements in both the radio access and core network. The 5G radio access network was created to be adaptable and flexible, able to support new frequency bands and a variety of new applications with more stringent KPIs. The 5G core network was designed with a service-based architecture, independent access, and a converged framework to support a wide range of services.

The advanced cloud-native design of 5G allows it to remain relevant in the coming years. Therefore, when identifying future opportunities for 6G capabilities, NGMN argued that it is important to consider the drivers and demands that will emerge in the next decade. The Alliance thus asked its members (operators, technology suppliers and academic advisors) to provide their thoughts on what demands and use cases they anticipate in the future.

The process to arrive at these use cases adopted by the Alliance comprised several stages: designing the methodology, gathering use cases, classifying them at a high level, generalizing the use cases, and analyzing them. A total of 50 use cases were submitted, which were grouped into four categories and then condensed into 14 general use cases:

- **Enhanced human communication**. It includes use cases that have the potential to enrich human communications, such as immersive experience, telepresence & multimodal interaction:

  - *XR Immersive Holographic Telepresence Communication*
  - *Multimodal Communication for Teleoperation*
  - *Intelligent Interaction & Sharing of Sensation, Skills & Thoughts*

- **Enhanced machine communication**. It reflects the growth in the use of collaborative robotics, and autonomous machines, the requirement for sensing the surrounding environment and the need for robots to communicate among themselves and with humans:

  - *Robot Network Fabric*
  - *Interacting Cobots (Collaborative Robots)*

- **Enabling services.** It includes use cases that require additional features such as high accuracy location, mapping, environmental, or body sensing data:

  - *3D Hyper-Accurate Positioning, Localization, and Tracking*
  - *Interactive Mapping*
  - *Digital Healthcare*
  - *Automatic Detection, Recognition and Inspection*
  - *Smart Industry*
  - *Trusted Composition of Services*

- **Network evolution.** It describes aspects related to the evolution of core technologies including AI as a service, energy efficiency, and delivering ubiquitous coverage:

  - *Native Trusted AI (AIaaS)*
  - *Coverage Expansion*
  - *Autonomous System for Energy Efficiency*

While various usage scenarios have been predicted for the 6G era, many can also be achieved with advanced 5G networks. As a result, the white paper made substantial efforts in differentiating between 5G and 6G.

17.2.5 6G use cases summary

With the exception of the lunar ambitions of Japan, there are a few common themes across all use-cases:

- **Extreme broadband**: Some use cases will require extreme data rates in the order of Gbps. Therefore, MBB in 5G and MBB+ in 5G-Advanced will need to be continued in 6G to "MBB++".
- **Extreme IoT**: Some use cases will require an extreme density of IoT devices. Therefore, mMTC in 5G and mMTC+ in 5G-Advanced will need to continue in 6G to "mMTC++."
- **Extreme critical communications**: Some use cases will require even more stringent capabilities when it comes to ultra-reliable and low latency communications. Therefore, URLLC in 5G and URLLC+ in 5G-Advanced will need to continue in 6G to "URLLC++."
- **Immersive communications**: Some use cases will require spatial compute and volumetric communications capabilities. This does not exist in 5G and will need to be created in 6G.
- **Native AI**: Some use cases will require the networks to be natively intelligent. This does not exist in 5G either; and thus, will need to be created in 6G.

17.3 Key Performance Indicators

At the time of writing, little is known about the final set of key performance indicators for 6G. The reason is that the ITU – who is typically chartered with providing such KPIs – has not released the exact numbers yet. We will therefore make some educated guesses about the typical KPIs used in the 4G and 5G era; and then also discuss some emerging KPIs which most likely will matter in 6G.

17.3.1 Established KPIs

The main KPIs which have driven the design of 5G were data rate (for eMBB), latency (for URLLC) and connection density (for mMTC).

In the 6G era, these will be the foundational but not the only KPIs. It is also not yet clear what their exact value will be. However, following past trends in telecommunications, we can assume that they will improve by roughly an order of magnitude, i.e., $10\times$. Summarized in Table 17.1, these key KPIs are discussed below.

Table 17.1 Comparison of established 5G KPIs with estimated 6G KPIs. Note that the 6G numbers are guesstimates only; for updates from the ITU follow [10].

Parameter	IMT-2020 (5G)	Networks-2030 (6G)
Peak data rate	DL: 20Gbps UL: 10Gbps	DL: 10x 20Gbps UL: 10x 10Gbps
User experienced data rate	100Mbps	10x 100Mbps
User Plane latency	1ms	100us
Connection density	1 000 000 devices/km^2	10x of 5G
Energy consumption	1 (normalized)	1/10x of 5G
Mobile data volume	10Tb/s/km^2	10Pb/s/km^2

This means that the **average experienced data** rate by the consumer will go from 100 Mbps in 5G to 1 Gbps in 6G. That rate will mainly be offered by mid and centimetric spectrum bands. Peak rates are also expected to increase by an order of magnitude, i.e., go from tens of Gbps in 5G to hundred(s) of Gbps in 6G. The peak rate will mainly be offered by mmWave and sub-THz spectrum bands.

In terms of *user plane latency* over the air interface, it is also expected to drop from around 1 ms in 5G to 100 μs in 6G. That can be achieved through higher sub-carrier spacings, shorter transmission time interval (TTI), etc. It is important to note that this latency is strictly one-way over the air interface only. End-to-end latencies are also expected to drop significantly but require proper core network, edge cloud and call flow designs.

Finally, the *connectivity density* of 1 m devices per square kilometer in 5G is expected to increase to 10 million devices. It is difficult to imagine 10 m devices per square kilometer. However, one can imagine drones and aerial vehicles to require such density per cubic kilometer.

A further indication that aerial communications may take center stage in 6G is the data volume. In 5G, after multiplying the respective KPIs, the mobile data volume mounted to 10 Tb/s/km^2. Following the same methodology, in 6G that will mount to 10 Pb/s/km^2. It is a spatial density which is difficult to imagine; however, a density of 10 Pb/s/km^3 might be plausible.

17.3.2 Emerging 6G KPIs

Some new KPIs are emerging in discussions on 6G. These KPIs were of course already of importance in the previous generations. However, in 6G, they will likely form a central part of the design process where they will be integrated up-front rather than added post design. These are summarized below:

A truly important design criteria is *energy efficiency*. We will see specific protocols and architectures designed such that 6G systems will be utmost energy efficient, close to theoretically possible bounds. A long-standing ambition by the community is to make devices consume zero Joules, i.e., scavenge energy from the surroundings; and have networks become carbon neutral, i.e., be able to operate from alternative energy sources. This of course, requires significant changes to protocols and architectures.

Yet another aspect gaining in importance is *trust*. It encompasses a variety of issues, such as privacy, security, reliability, etc. Whilst security is natively built into telecoms, many other issues are not. We will thus most likely see a surge of design principles natively embedding trust elements in the 6G era, and user requirements for establishing specific *levels of trust* of network services according to their intended application.

AI is now available in many production networks; however, it has not been natively embedded into telecoms yet. In 6G, we will likely see an increase of *native intelligence / AI* be embedded into algorithms, protocols and architectures. It will ensure that the networks will be able to operate efficiently and effectively, despite the exponentially increasing complexity.

Yet another trend will be for 6G to become more *platform native*, which involves cloudification and the introduction of APIs. Indeed, the first 5G Cloud RANs are emerging with the trend to continue in 6G. Furthermore, with the introduction of open RAN capabilities, future telco systems will have API access to the RAN which go beyond the traditional NEF/SCEF (network exposure function/service capability exposure function) APIs.

Last but not least, we will see a stronger drive to *beyond-ARPU business models*. Indeed, the telco business models have stalled and current income is mainly due to the number of SIMs sold. The introduction of platform and API capabilities lays the ground of micro payment approaches as well as digital payments through blockchain technologies [11].

Important to note is that above KPIs are difficult to measure and quantify. Therefore, new research will be needed which, e.g., quantifies the degree of trust.

17.4 Spectrum for 6G

17.4.1 International harmonization

A process important to the development and implementation of 6G technology is ensuring spectrum availability. This can be achieved through a variety of methods, such as the ITU World Radiocommunication Conferences (WRC), regional decisions, or decisions made on a per country basis.

However, regardless of the method chosen, harmonization of the selected frequency bands on a global or regional level is crucial in order to achieve economies-of-scale and provide numerous benefits to consumers and enterprises across a wide range of markets. This harmonization can help to ensure that the technology is widely adopted and that the necessary infrastructure is in place to support it. Additionally, harmonization can also help to reduce costs, improve network performance, and encourage innovation and research and development in the field of 6G technology.

Furthermore, it is also important to mention that harmonization of frequency bands will lead to better global coordination and cooperation between countries and regions in terms of spectrum allocation and usage, which in turn will lead to better and more efficient use of the available spectrum resources.

The most establish route to achieving this is via the ITU which oversees the WRC. WRC happens in average every four years and is attended by member nation states who send their regulatory delegates. Typically, at one WRC, the required frequency bands are identified and then – after studying them for four years – at the subsequent WRC, decisions are taken on the usage of the bands.

Specifically, WRC 2023 in Dubai examines possible new 6G spectrum bands which are then decided on at WRC 2027. Upon specific decisions at the WRC 2027, regional and national regulators will oversee implementation of the bands and procurements, if applicable.

17.4.2 Current and emerging 5G bands

As outlined in [12], regulatory agencies around the world have been releasing low-band, mid-band, and mmWave spectrum as part of the push for 5G. While progress has been uneven in some markets, by 2030, it is expected that enough spectrum in these frequency ranges will have been allocated or auctioned to fully realize the potential of 5G and 5G-Advanced:

- These frequencies will also play a role in the development of 6G, with *sub-1 GHz* spectrum, such as 600 MHz or 700 MHz, continuing to provide basic coverage and bridge the digital divide.
- *Mid-band spectrum*, such as 3.5, 4.5, and 6 GHz, will continue to support wide-area use cases that require capacity.

- *mmWave spectrum*, such as 26/28 and 40 GHz, will continue to offer high capacity in crowded areas and low latencies and high reliability for businesses.

However, new use cases and the need to improve existing ones will require even more spectrum than previous generations. An example of this is videoconferencing, where 6G is expected to deliver a full telepresence experience, building on the capabilities of 5G and 5G-Advanced.

17.4.3 Identified 6G bands

As demonstrated by the above scenarios, both existing and novel spectrum bands are imperative for the 6G era. Without the supplementary spectrum, we will fall short of fulfilling the requirements of future 6G use cases. The scientific community has identified fresh potential spectrum ranges for 6G, specifically in the centimetric range from 7-15 GHz which will be an essential range, and in the sub-THz range from 92-300 GHz which will have a supplementary role catering to specialized scenarios. The spectrum bands are illustrated in Figure 17.3.

17.4.4 Essential 6G centimetric bands

Spectrum within the 7–15 GHz range is crucial for realizing the capacity-intensive use cases in future 6G networks. The lower the frequency bands are, the more extensive the area that can be covered.

The coverage requirement that will allow for mobility and "on-the-go" applications of many 6G use cases across a broad area necessitates consideration of this range. To be more precise, what value would, for instance, the large-scale metaverse and holographic use cases add if they were only

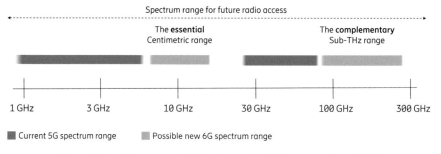

Figure 17.3   Illustration of 5G and potential 6G spectrum bands [13].

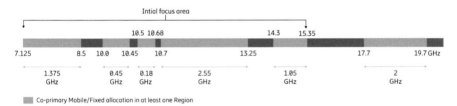

Figure 17.4 Co-primary mobile/fixed allocation example in the 7–15 GHz band [15].

enabled in a very local setting? Mobility and coverage restrictions would diminish the full potential and value of such use cases. This naturally rules out higher frequency bands and directs us toward centimetric waves where the envisioned futuristic lifestyle can be made mobile.

Ericsson has undertaken an analysis of the current usage and future trends in these bands [14] and evaluated the characteristics of the different frequency ranges to better understand their respective capabilities and limitations. These investigations have led to initially focusing on 7–15 GHz, with more details shown in Figure 17.4.

Co-primary allocations to mobile and fixed services in the 7–15 GHz range exist today in the ITU Radio Regulations, though noting that the existing use of this same spectrum by other services requires careful consideration. Hence, studying co-existence with these co-primary incumbent services will be a crucial task in the coming years.

17.4.5 Complementary sub-THz bands

The sub-THz range has the potential to offer vast regions of lightly used or even unused spectrum, which contributes to its unique yet challenging nature. It can uniquely provide the hundred(s) of Gbps or even Tbps speeds and ultra-low latencies that will be key enablers for 6G specialized use cases.

However, this benefit comes with some limitations in terms of coverage and mobility. The characteristics of this range make it complementary, and it cannot replace the need for lower frequencies (e.g., centimetric waves) to enable the coverage and mobility that will be the primary requirements for most 6G use cases.

In terms of specific frequencies, it all comes down to physics and technological development. The former drives us to prefer the lowest possible frequencies (among the very high frequencies) and their advantageous propagation characteristics and to avoid frequencies associated with atmospheric

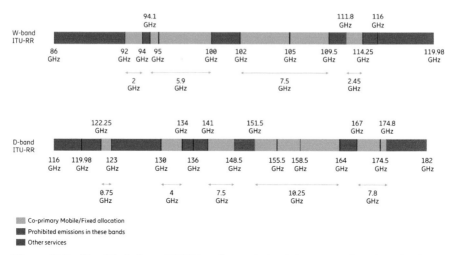

Figure 17.5   Simplified view of ITU-R radio regulations) frequency allocations for the W and D bands [16].

attenuation peaks. The attenuation factor is vital to consider in a frequency range where the size of the wavelengths is close to that of most raindrops.

The technological development and component maturity factors also indicate another advantage of the lower edge of the sub-THz range. The use of the sub-THz frequency range depends on the development of components and equipment ecosystem. This, of course, will take time to reach maturity, starting from the lowest sub-THz frequencies and slowly moving upwards in frequency.

Combining these insights, we see the emergence of two bands: the W and D bands which is illustrated in Figure 17.5. In fact, these bands are of interest for both 6G access and x-haul (e.g., fronthaul and backhaul) networks. A solution that addresses the needs of both services and guarantees an equally powerful x-haul development to support future access networks and their extreme requirements should be considered.

17.5 Overview of 6G Technologies

17.5.1 Telco architecture

We are in no position to explain specific 6G technologies as these have not been defined at the writing of this book. However, at the end of this chapter, we will explore current community approaches to the design of 6G.

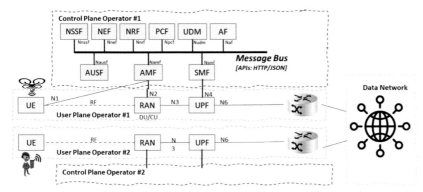

Figure 17.6   Illustration of the 5G 3GPP-compliant telecommunications architecture, where a human user communicates with a drone over the user-plane whilst being supported by the control-plane.

To start with, we shall briefly explain the current 5G 3GPP telecommunications architecture. It serves as a basis for the reader to understand subsequent chapters. The current 5G architecture is illustrated in Figure 17.6. The most important constituents in the architecture are:

- **User equipment (UE)**: It is the mobile terminal with the subscriber identity module (SIM) which communicates with the 5G infrastructure via radio frequencies.
- **Radio access network (RAN)**: It is the infrastructure between the UE and the internet. It typically consists of an antenna on, e.g., a building roof, a fiber network connecting these antennas to a very localized processing unit, and further fiber to connect the processing unit to the UPF.
- **User plane function (UPF)**: It is in essence a gatekeeping capability of the user traffic. Notably, the UPF is part of the core network and its role is to check if the user and the specific application are authorized; it ensures security is in place; among many other things.
- **Core network (CN)**: The CN is composed of many modular functions which are shown in Figure 17.6 and the details of which can be gathered from [17]. Each function executes a specialized task; for instance, the AMF is the access and mobility management function which handles access and ensures that the connection works in the case of mobility. These functions communicate with each other via a microservice

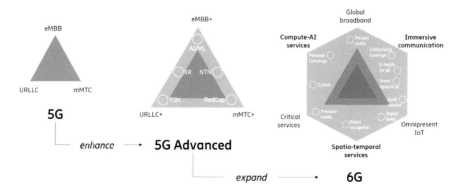

Figure 17.7   An example illustration on how the underpinning technology families will evolve from 5G to 5G advanced, and eventually 6G.

messaging bus, typically using APIs. In subsequent chapters, we will link blockchain-related opportunities to specific CN functions.

17.5.2 Technology focus

Illustrated in Figure 17.7, 5G was reliant on three underpinning technology families, i.e., eMBB (broadband), URLLC (critical communications) and mMTC (massive IoT). In 5G advanced, these capabilities will be further expanded and advanced.

In 6G, these three base capabilities will remain. However, new technology capabilities will emerge:

- **Spatio-temporal services**: The ability of 6G to not only facilitate communications but also understand the environment via joint communications and sensing.
- **Immersive communications**: Based on the volumetric and contextual understanding of the environment, 6G will be able to offer much more immersive experiences.
- **Native compute-AI services**: Intelligence will be natively built into 6G networks to ensure trustworthy execution of scalable algorithmic frameworks.

17.5.3 Example 6G radio technologies

To finalize this chapter, let us examine a few 6G candidate technologies which are being examined by the community at the time of the book writing:

- **Extreme MIMO**: MIMO in 4G has evolved to massive MIMO in 5G and is expected to evolve further in 6G to extreme MIMO. It is expected that thousands of antenna elements will be available at the base station. It does not mean, however, that all are being used at the same time. The performance gains in terms of spectral efficiency however are anticipated to be substantial.
- **Sub-THz communications**: As already discussed in this chapter, moving up into sub-THz frequency ranges offers unique opportunities to enable ultra-high data rate transmissions in both uplink and downlink. However, it comes with significant challenges, such as developing efficient power amplifiers for that spectral region; also, high resolution sampling devices will need to be developed or at least be compensated using AI.
- **Intelligent reflective surfaces**: Another interesting 6G candidate technology pertains to intelligent reflective surfaces. The idea is to deploy electromagnetic surfaces in, e.g., urban environments by embedding them into the walls of buildings, whilst being controlled such that incoming radio signals can be re-directed and/or bundled. This offers interesting opportunities to extend the range of cells, specifically into notoriously difficult indoor environments.

That concludes our chapter on the introduction to 6G. At the time of writing, many of the core technologies were not developed nor standardized. However, we hope that this chapter offered sufficient details to understand subsequent chapters.

References

[1] https://www.ericsson.com/en/blog/2022/11/why-its-time-to-talk-6g
[2] https://www.ericsson.com/en/reports-and-papers/white-papers/a-research-outlook-towards-6g
[3] https://www.ericsson.com/en/reports-and-papers/white-papers/a-research-outlook-towards-6g
[4] https://en.wikipedia.org/wiki/Alliance_for_Telecommunications_Industry_Solutions
[5] https://www.nextgalliance.org/wp-content/uploads/dlm_uploads/2022/05/Next_G_Alliance_6G_Applications_and_Use_Cases_7-1.pdf
[6] https://www.nextgalliance.org/wp-content/uploads/dlm_uploads/2022/07/TWG-report-6G-technologies.pdf

[7] https://beyond5g.nict.go.jp/images/download/NICT_B5G6G_WhitePaperEN_v2_0.pdf

[8] https://en.wikipedia.org/wiki/Next_Generation_Mobile_Networks

[9] https://www.ngmn.org/publications/6g-use-cases-and-analysis.html

[10] https://www.itu.int/en/ITU-T/focusgroups/net2030/Pages/default.aspx

[11] https://www.ericsson.com/en/blog/2022/9/metaverse-blockchain-5g

[12] https://www.ericsson.com/en/blog/2022/6/6g-spectrum-why-its-fundamental

[13] https://www.ericsson.com/en/blog/2022/11/why-its-time-to-talk-6g

[14] https://www.ericsson.com/en/blog/2022/11/why-its-time-to-talk-6g

[15] https://www.ericsson.com/en/blog/2022/11/why-its-time-to-talk-6g

[16] https://www.ericsson.com/en/blog/2022/11/why-its-time-to-talk-6g

[17] http://www.3gpp.org/

18

Blockchain for Data Collection and Sharing in 6G

In this chapter, we examine the ability of blockchains and DLTs to support a trusted data collection and sharing capability. The discussed insights are based on the technical material of the previous chapters. Notably, we first revisit current 5G best practices with respect to data collection and sharing; and then dwell on possible blockchain-based 6G implementations.

18.1 Introduction to Data Sharing

18.1.1 Rational and security considerations

Data sharing schemes are critical for various businesses, organizations, and fields, including future wireless systems, healthcare, education, the financial sector, etc. For example, data sharing in wireless communications derive valuable insights about the quality of the network, the reliability of the communication, helps in understanding more about security risks, etc. Accordingly, network providers and other third parties in wireless communications network alliances strive for actual data obtained from the network subscribers. Network subscribers' data are accessible to all 3GPP partners and their members and may be accessed by third parties with subscribers' consent during the network provisioning.

In general, data sharing models usually incorporate multiple interacting modules, including data aggregation, data control, data access management, data storage modules, etc. However, successful data sharing models usually rely on efficient and secure data control and access management schemes that consider various data-driven protection attributes to secure future data-oriented operations, including security, reliability, integrity, accessibility, portability, and scalability. Each of these attributes shapes the complexity and efficiency of the data control design. The following definitions help in better understanding the importance of each security aspect:

- *Data security* refers to the process of protecting the data control systems from unauthorized access or intentional data corruption throughout the data lifecycle. Data security usually incorporates various cryptography schemes to protect data. For example, data encryptions maintain data confidentiality; hashing provides data integrity for verification checks; data tokenization facilitates secure and authorized data accessibility.
- *Data reliability* is an assessment measure of how the data is complete and accurate. Data reliability usually indicates data levels of trust.
- *Data integrity* is another fundamental measure in any data control scheme. Data integrity usually indicates how accurate and consistent the stored data is.
- *Data access* refers to the reliable, secure, and fastest accessing or retrieving data stored within either database, cloud storage services, or other storage repositories.
- *Data portability* indicates how versatile data are during the exchange or transfer processes across different services with heterogeneous requirements without affecting the usability.
- *Scalability* refers to how possible it is to perform multiple operations on the data simultaneously without impacting the system's efficiency.
- *Data controllability* means the management oversight of the information policies by observing and reporting the processes obtained in the data.

Consequently, contemporary data control and access management schemes rely on cryptography algorithms like encryption, digital signature, and hashing scheme to ensure trust, authenticity, the confidentiality of data sharing transactions. For example, encryption and decryption processes provide data confidentiality protection. On the other hand, digital signatures and hashing schemes guarantee the integrity and verifiability of the data. Furthermore, digital signatures facilitate identifying data ownership or validate potential data accessibility.

18.1.2 Traditional data control and access management

Traditional data control and access management schemes usually rely on public key infrastructure (PKI) regulations to control, identify, and manage data accessibility. PKI provides a set of rules and policies needed to create, manage, distribute, use, store, and revoke digital certificates generated and issued by a centralized trusted authority. Each digital certificate encompasses a public/private key pair representing its holder. The private key is known and stored only with the digital certificate holder. The private key generates digital signatures that authenticate and identify its holder.

Such digital signatures are publicly verified using the corresponding public key published in the broadcasted digital certificate. From that, traditional data access models leverage digital certificates to identify data ownership and manage its accessibility. Consequently, data owners (DOs) digitally sign owned data using their PKI private keys in data control and access schemes to ensure data integrity, authenticity, and verifiability. Alternatively, data consumers (DCs) use the corresponding PKI public key published in DO's digital certificate to validate the digital signature on the provided data.

18.2 Data Collection and Sharing in 5G

18.2.1 3GPP TS 23.501

Figure 18.1 illustrates the 5G data storage architecture, which includes three data-related entities: unified data management (UDM), unified data repository (UDR), and unstructured data storage function (UDSF) as defined in 3GPP TS 23.501 [1]. Data in 3GPP is classified into unstructured data and structured data. The unstructured data could be any type of data, which structure is not defined by 3GPP. The structured data includes subscription data, policy data, structured data for exposure, and application data such as packet flow descriptions (PFDs) for application detection and AF request information for multiple UEs.

The following data storage functions are provided:

- A UDM stores subscription data to a UDR and retrieves subscription data from the UDR.
- A policy control function (PCF) stores policy data to a UDR and retrieves policy data from the UDR.
- A network exposure function (NEF) stores structured data for exposure and application data to a UDR and retrieves them from the UDR.
- A network function (NF) stores unstructured data to a UDSF and retrieves unstructured data from the UDSF.
- A UDR allows an NF consumer to retrieve, create, update, subscribe for change notifications, unsubscribe for change notifications, and delete data stored in the UDR, based on the set of data applicable to the NF consumer. A UDR can be implemented as a part of a UDM, a PCF, or an NEF or serve multiple UDMs, PCFs, and NEFs.

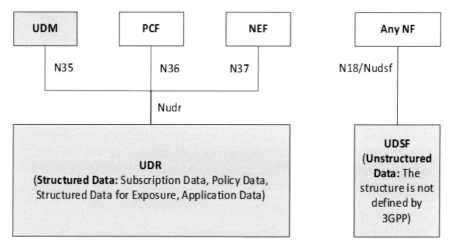

Figure 18.1   5G data storage architecture in TS 23.501.

- A UDSF allows a NF consumer to retrieve, create, update, and delete data stored in the UDSF. A UDSF can be implemented as a part of an NF or can serve multiple NFs.
- UDR and UDSF can be co-located.

18.2.2 3GPP TS 23.288

3GPP TS 23.288 [2] specifies data collection coordination and delivery especially as a part of supporting network data analytics function (NWDAF). Although data collection and delivery could happen directly between data consumers and data sources, data collection coordination function (DCCF) is defined in TS 23.288 to act as an intermediary or a proxy to make data collection and delivery between data consumers (e.g., NFs, NWDAF, etc.) and data sources (e.g., NFs, UDM, NWDAF, etc.) potentially more efficient. For example, there could be multiple data consumers to collect the same data from the same data source. Using DCCF, the data source only needs to deliver the data once to DCCF, which will propagate the data to those multiple data consumers.

DCCF basically uses a subscription mechanism to receive automatic data/event notifications and then forward them to data consumers, notification endpoints (as designated by a data consumer or by the DCCF), and/or an analytics data repository function (ADRF). Figure 18.2 illustrates the

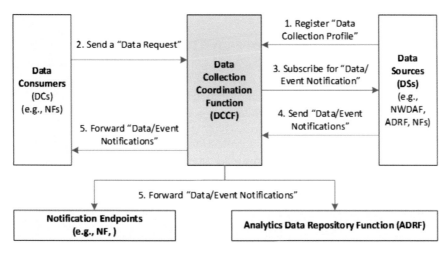

Figure 18.2 5G data collection coordination and delivery in 3GPP TS 23.288.

procedure for data collection and direct delivery via DCCF as defined in TS 23.288.

- Step 1: A data source can register one or multiple "data collection profiles" to DCCF. A "data collection profile" indicates which types of data the data source maintains and the corresponding service operations (i.e., how the data can be collected by DCCF) on each type of data.
- Step 2: A data consumer send a "data request" to DCCF requesting a specific type of data. The "data request" may also indicate data sources and/or notification endpoints. The "data request" can also contain data formatting and processing instructions, which will be used by DCCF to process collected data from data sources.
- Step 3: DCCF determines the data sources matching the "data request" and sends a subscription to each determined data source.
- Step 4: The data source sends automatic "data/event notifications" to DCCF, according to DCCF's subscription.
- Step 5: DCCF receives "data/event notifications" from the data source and forwards them to the data consumer, notification endpoints, and/or an ADRF. Optionally, DCCF may perform data formatting and processing before forwarding "data/event notifications," according to data formatting and processing instructions if any contained in the "data request."

18.2.3 3GPP TS 26.531

3GPP TS 23.288 [2] describes a need for NWDAF to collect data from UE applications. For this need, 3GPP TS 26.531 [3] specifies a generic architecture and corresponding procedures for reporting data from UE applications to NWDAF via an intermediary application function (AF), data collection AF. A simplified version this generic architecture is illustrated in Figure 18.3.

- Provisioning AF configures data collection related instructions via the R1 reference point to data reporting AF (e.g., which data to be collected from data collection clients, how the data to be processed by the data reporting AF, etc.).
- Based on the instructions from the provisioning AF, data reporting AF may need to provide data collection configurations to direction (or indirect) data collection clients via R2 (or R3) reference point. According to data collection configurations, direct (or indirect) data collection clients send data reports to data reporting AF. Direct data collection client can collect data from a UE application over R7 reference point.
- NWDAF can subscribe data reporting events from data reporting AF. As a result, when data reporting AF receives a data report from direct (or indirect) data collection client and if the data report matches NWDAF's subscription, data reporting AF will expose data reporting events to NWDAF.

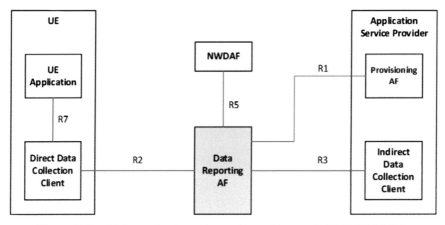

Figure 18.3   5G data collection and reporting architecture in 3GPP TS 26.531.

18.3 Data Collection and Sharing in 6G

18.3.1 Wireless data sharing

Wireless communication networks' data control and access management schemes are essential for many data-sharing-related applications, including device-to-device communication, content offloading, native artificial intelligence, network reliability statistics, emergency recording, monitoring, etc. Network providers and other third-party services strive to collect data from the subscribers and their terminal devices (i.e., user equipment – UE) for many purposes, including but not limited to, as illustrated in Figure 18.4:

- **Scenario 1) Network analysis**: To better analyze the network quality in various locations, network providers strive to gather precise service information from their subscribers better than overwhelming the deployed resources with more tasks. Such information help improving the collected network statistics, including signal strength, reliability, the quick discovery of congested areas and times, weather impact on the service quality, etc. The collected statistics help network providers to apply enhancements to the system to improve the overall quality of the service without overwhelming the deployed resources. For example, the applied

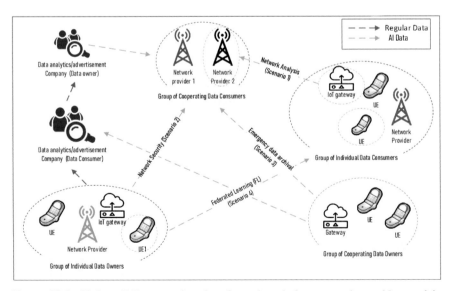

Figure 18.4 Various DCs requesting data from the wireless network providers and its subscribers.

enhancements could include but are not limited to automated network load balancing, enhanced service quality, better resource utilization to optimize investment, etc. Thus, the network provider needs to access such data after obtaining subscribers' consent to perform such analysis.

- **Scenario 2) Network security**: Network security and subscribers' privacy protection are critical aspects for any network provider. Network providers must gather enough data to assess network security, discover vulnerabilities and threat points, and train AI-based anomaly detection and prevention models. Collecting such information requires the network provider to regulate the network subscribers' activities to enable accurate time detection and prevent malicious activities. For example, the famous IMSI catcher attack invades network subscribers' privacy and broadcasts fake network information by impersonating network resources. Recently, researchers started deploying actual international mobile subscriber identity (IMSI) catching experiments to collect enough data by deploying AI models to protect UE from such a hack. However, having precise network analysis and actual data collected over time from UE during the network service provisioning would be more accurate and realistic. It would lead to discovering new hidden features about the network collected data.

- **Scenario 3) Emergency data recording/monitoring**: The network infrastructure either becomes heavy-loaded or entirely offline during catastrophic emergencies. To guarantee continuous service provisioning during such events, network providers seek all the information about the pre- and post-emergency situations to study the impact and optimize resource availability, provide alternative solutions, and guarantee continuity of the service. Thus, the network providers need to have accessibility to the collected data and events captured when service was offline. Data requested from the ad-hoc network services provided during the emergency event or actions captured by multiple witnesses during the emergency.

- **Scenario 4) Federated learning (FL)**: The next-generation wireless communication networks are contemplating the integration of machine-learning and AI-based network analysis for real-time decision-making and radio resource management. One of the most promising distributed learning algorithms is the federated learning (FL) framework considered for the future Internet of Things (IoT) systems. In FL, wireless devices can cooperatively execute a learning task by only uploading the local learning model to the base station (BS) instead of sharing their training data. The wireless devices must exchange local training results and metadata over wireless links to implement FL over wireless networks. The UE and BSs need to agree on the model parameters' accessibility and manageability methods during this process. In such a scenario, their owner should control the exchanged model parameters and training data. The data accessibility should be managed in a decentralized fashion and under its owner's control to avoid data loss, manipulation, or redundancy.

18.3.2 Data sharing in connected vehicles

Figure 18.5 illustrates a use case for connected vehicles. Each vehicle has at least a wireless connection, which connects the vehicle via a roadside unit (RSU) (or a base station) to the Internet. The RSU could have a local edge network with computing and storage resources. A vehicle could move from one RSU to another RSU. A vehicle can communicate with another vehicle, a RSU, an edge network, a core network, and/or an application server.

In this use case, Vehicle-X needs to send one-time or periodical updates (e.g., the location of Vehicle-X, events related to Vehicle-X, car conditions related to Vehicle-X) to the connected vehicle application in the cloud. In the meantime, these updates are critical for checking the history; these updates may also need to be shared with many other parties (such as the vehicle owner, the car manufacturer, the passengers, the driver, the passengers, and the owner of goods carried by the vehicle) and should be immutable.

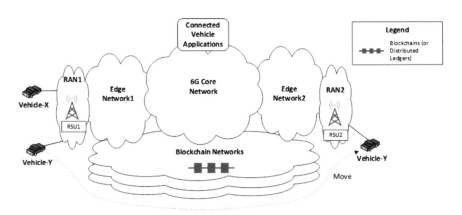

Figure 18.5 Connected vehicles.

Similarly, Vehicle-X communicates with Vehicle-Y even after Vehicle-Y moves from RSU1 to RSU2; both vehicles require their communications (e.g. event notification) to be recorded for future queries by themselves and/or other parties. Blockchain networks can be leveraged for providing shared, distributed, and immutable ledgers or blockchains to this use case.

18.3.3 Personal webcasting

Consider the example of an Olympic park, as illustrated in Figure 18.6. In the park, there are visitors/spectators from all over the world. At the same time, various sports competitions/events are being held throughout the park. As mentioned earlier, personal webcasters are very popular in the park. In this type of application, the personal network anchors broadcast live streaming (for singing, playing, selling things, etc.), and at the same time, a large number of his/her fans (as viewers) interact with network anchors.

In particular, this business model has upended the traditional media industry. For example, the providers of media data are no longer traditional TV stations or large video-on-demand websites (such as Hulu, Netflix, etc.). On the contrary, each individual can become a personal network anchor and generate income through their mobile phones. For example, a report [4] recently analyzed the market status of China's online performance (live broadcast) industry. This report data shows that the market size of China's online performance industry in 2020 reached 30 billion US dollars.

In the Olympic park, it is expected that there will also be many individual network anchors who will broadcast live events at the game sites. However, unlike traditional TV live broadcasts (which always use professorial equipment, high-speed connection, etc.), personal live broadcast in the Olympic park has the following characteristics.

- In most cases, network anchors rely on their own personal mobile phones, which are not professional equipment. The mobile phone needs to use wireless communication via a cellular access network (normally based on a personal subscription plan), especially for some mobile/outdoor sports events, such as marathons, golf, etc.
- In the Olympic park, the mobile phones/devices are so dense that the anchors' mobile phones may not be able to obtain sufficient wireless bandwidth, such that the live broadcast cannot be performed smoothly (especially if an anchor's UE does not have a VIP service subscription to the wireless operator).

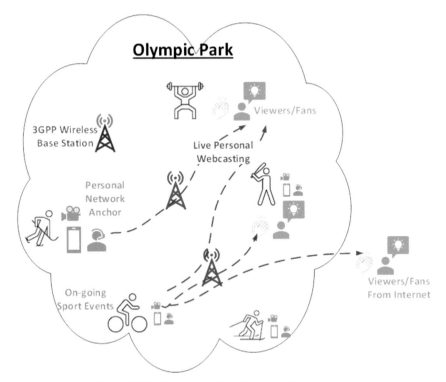

Figure 18.6 Personal webcasting in an Olympic park.

- For video viewers (i.e., the fans of those network anchors), they can be visitors who are also in the Olympic Park or can be remote video viewers accessing the content from the Internet.

In this scenario, when video viewers search for a network anchor, they not only care about the content and location of the network anchor (for example, whether an individual anchor is in the best viewing spot for a certain event), but also care about whether the anchor has good video streaming quality (especially throughout important events, such as swimming finals), which can be evaluated via certain real-time wireless context data collected from the wireless system, such as wireless signal and data rates of the network anchor, etc.

For example, a video viewer could have the following query to find qualified anchors: I want to find a network anchor who is broadcasting the final on a tennis court, very close to the player Amy's side. For the content quality and stability, I expect both high-definition (HD) video streaming and the video content that can be provided in a stable way (e.g., throughout the swimming final). Such user requirements in fact imply that the desired network anchor is expected to have continuous/excellent wireless cellular connection status and is expected to be allocated with high-speed bandwidth. It can be seen that for processing this user query, the wireless context data of the network anchor is very important for answering this query.

The data can be collected from the cellular network that the network anchor is using (as the provider of wireless data). Those wireless data can be collected and provided to the upper-layer live webcast application software (as the wireless data consumers) to support the network anchor search/filtering or other performance optimization operations.

18.4 Blockchain-Enabled Data Sharing in 6G

It is obvious that existing data collection and sharing approaches for 5G cannot meet the requirements of new data collection and sharing use cases in 6G systems, especially considering data sources and data consumers may not trust each other. Likewise, traditional centralized data collection and sharing schemes cannot satisfy 6G system.

Blockchain and distributed ledger systems offer decentralized and trustworthy approaches [5, 6] to mitigate limitation of traditional centralized data management schemes and existing data collection and sharing approaches in 5G. Some potential benefits and advantages from blockchain-enabled schemes include:

- The append-only blockchain provides a good solution for data traceability issues. The data collection and sharing process including data ownership can be easily tracked and verified anytime via the blockchain once all data transactions are added onto the blockchain.
- The immutable blockchain prevents any malicious attempt to modify data once the data is added onto the blockchain.
- The transparent blockchain could encourage data sharing between data sources and data consumers and promote a new data sharing marketplace.
- The use of blockchain removes the single-point-of-failure issue, which may be resulted from the centralized data storage server and/or the dependency on the trusted certificate authority.

This chapter describes two representative approaches for leveraging blockchains for data collection and sharing in 6G systems: 1) data collection and sharing via blockchain messaging; and 2) data collection and sharing via customized blockchains.

18.4.1 Data collection and sharing via blockchain messaging

Messaging through blockchain networks (or blockchain messaging) is proposed as a new process to optimize data collection traffic and resulted message overhead, where a sender sends messages to a target blockchain network; then, messages will be broadcasted within the target blockchain network; finally, messages will be forwarded from the sender to receivers through a target blockchain network.

As a result of this process, messages are transmitted from the sender to the receivers and also stored into the target blockchain, which means such a process, in fact, achieves two objectives at the same time, i.e., delivering messages from the sender to the receivers and recording the message exchange events in the blockchain. For example, Figure 18.7 shows two blockchain messaging scenarios.

- In **Scenario 1**, Vehicle-X sends messages to the connected vehicle application through a target blockchain network. Each message will be routed from Vehicle-X to RAN-A, Edge Network1, the Target Blockchain Network, 5G Core Network, and eventually to the connected vehicle application.
- In **Scenario 2**, Vehicle-X sends messages to Vehicle-Y through a target blockchain network. Each message will be routed from Vehicle-X to RAN-A, Edge Netwok1, the Target Blockchain Network, Edge Network2, RAN-B, and eventually to Vehicle-Y.

In both scenarios, we may need to not only support the messaging, but also need to record those messaging as system logs for future auditing or charging purpose. In particular, in those scenarios, multiple providers or stakeholders are involved, such as 5G network operator, edge network or edge service provider, connected vehicle application provider, vehicular application service provider, etc.

Therefore, it is not desired to use a centralized database of a particular stakeholder to record the messaging history due to being lack of mutual trust if those service providers do not build mutual trust agreement in advance; in fact, it is time-consuming to even build such multi-party agreements also

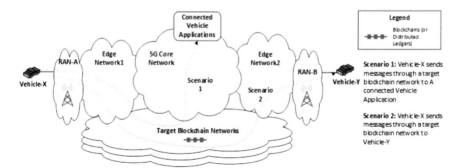

Figure 18.7 Examples of messaging through blockchain networks.

may significantly slow down the rapid deployments of new applications. Therefore, blockchain systems can be leveraged to help transmit messages and record the messaging history/log concurrently.

Various applications may need to leverage different target blockchain networks. It is inefficient to redesign functionalities for each application and each target blockchain network. A functional architecture in Figure 18.9 is proposed as a blockchain messaging enablement, which will be residing below applications but above target blockchain networks. This blockchain messaging enablement will provide various functionalities (e.g. translate application messages to blockchain transactions and recover application messages from blockchain transactions) and can be easily leveraged by various applications to leverage different target blockchain networks. The proposed blockchain messaging functional architecture in Figure 18.8 consists of the following logic entities.

- **Blockchain client application (BCA)**: A device could host multiple BCAs. A BCA could be a client-side entity for a blockchain-based vertical application, which may have one BNA as server-side entity to manage and control many BCAs belonging to the same vertical application. For example, in a blockchain-based SML application, each IoT device hosts a BCA as the client-side entity, while a BNA residing in the cloud acts as the server-side entity. A BCA (e.g. BCA1 and BCA2) is an end application, which can act as a sender to send messages to receivers (e.g. BNA) via a target blockchain network; in addition, the BCA could also receive messages from other senders (e.g. BNA) via the same or different target blockchain network. A BCA only interacts with a blockchain messaging client (BMC).

- **Blockchain messaging client (BMC)**: A BMC (e.g., BMC1 and BMC2) can serve one or multiple BCAs. On behalf of these BCAs, a BMC relays original messages or blockchain session-related requests/responses between BCAs and a blockchain messaging server (BMS). A BMC usually resides in a device or a gateway such as a 3GPP UE. A device could have one BMC only, or one BMC plus one or multiple BCAs. Optionally, a BMC could also interact with a BCN directly to relay original messages between a BCA and the BCN.
- **Blockchain messaging server (BMS)**: As for messaging functionality, a BMS (e.g., BMS1 and BMS2) is responsible for receiving original messages from a BMC or a BNA, transforming the message to blockchain transactions, and transmitting blockchain transactions to a blockchain node (BCN). On the other hand, a BMS is also responsible for receiving blockchain transactions from a BCN, transforming transactions to original messages, and transmitting original messages to a BMC or a BNA. A BMS can be implemented as a network function such as a 3GPP control plane NF.
- **Blockchain node (BCN)**: A BCN (e.g., BCN1 and BCN2) receives transactions from a BMS and sends them to a target blockchain network; on the other hand, a BCN also receives transactions from a target blockchain network and forwards them to a BMS. A BCN may also

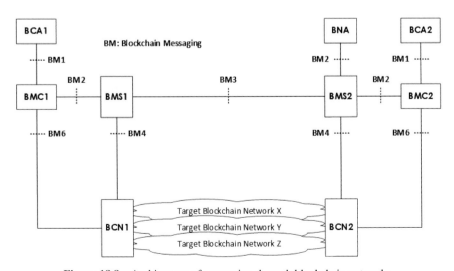

Figure 18.8 Architecture of messaging through blockchain networks.

support direct interaction with a BMC. BCNs are the only entity that directly interfaces target blockchain networks.

- **Blockchain network application (BNA)**: A BNA only interacts with a BMS and usually resides in the cloud and/or in an application server. A BNA can be implemented as a 3GPP AF. Similar to a BCA, a BNA as an application, can act as a sender to send messages to receivers via a target blockchain network, and/or as a receiver to receive messages from a sender via the same or different target blockchain network.

18.4.2 Data collection and sharing via customized blockchain

In this scenario, it is considered that when using the blockchain for facilitating data collection and sharing between data providers (DPs) and data consumers (DCs), i.e., blockchain as an intermediate storage medium between DPs and DCs, one of the potential issues is that the existing blockchain networks already built-up/deployed may not meet the performance requirements as required by DPs/DCs. For example, the data on-chaining delay may be too large due to a heavy-weight/complicated consensus protocol. Accordingly, Figure 18.9 illustrates blockchain-enabled data collection and sharing architecture, where a data collection enabler (DCE) can customize underlying blockchain system and blockchain operations (e.g., to set up a new blockchain network with a customized/desired consensus protocol) in order to meet

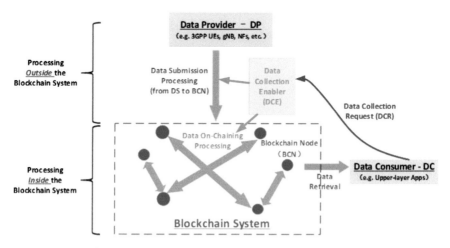

Figure 18.9 Blockchain-enabled data collection and sharing architecture.

the need of DPs/DCs. For example, the customized blockchain network may have very shot data on-chaining delay so that DPs may obtain the data from blockchain as soon as possible. Then, the DCE facilitates data exchange between DSs and DCs using the customized blockchain system and operations.

Data provider: DPs are referred to the entities that provide the data to be collected, such as various NFs in a wireless system. Using a particular UE-A as an example, various entities in the 3GPP system can be the potential DSs for providing data about UE-A.

- A base station or AMF as a DP can provide the current location of UE-A.
- UE-A as a DP provides the current data rate of UE-A.
- AMF as a DP provides the information on whether UE-A is reachable.
- UE-A itself as a DP provides its current radio signal strength of UE-A.

Data consumers: DCs are referred to the entities that need to use/consume the collected data. In the example of the Olympic Park, DCs include the upper-level live broadcast/webcast application software (e.g., either the application server and application clients hosted on UEs) and its users. For example, when a viewer/audience is looking for a desired anchor, she can send a search request, which needs to leverage real-time wireless data collected from the wireless system in order to discover the desired network anchor (e.g., at the desired location and with a good wireless connection). As another example, a viewer can query which network anchors are currently standing in the central square of the park. Such a request also needs to use real-time location data as well. Similarly, for a network anchor (who is webcasting a tennis final), she may need to send live invitations/ads to people who cannot enter the stadium but are the high-value viewers for her current streaming. These may also need real-time location data collected from the wireless system; for instance, a 3GPP access and mobility function (AMF) may answer the questions like which UEs are currently residing in a particular geographical area.

Blockchain system: Blockchain can be used as an efficient distributed sharing medium, which can bring superior advantages over traditional centralized storage, such as anti-tampering, traceability, high visibility, etc. Specifically, blockchain system can be used in a way such that the collected data from DPs could be stored in the blockchain for DCs to access. Typically, a blockchain system consists of numerous BCNs, which can be distributed in various places, such as in the cloud or at the edge of the network (e.g., co-located with a cellular base station, on a vehicle, etc.).

Data submission process: Data submission process is the process of delivering the data collected from a DP to a blockchain node. In the example of the Olympic Park, the real-time wireless data (e.g., the real-time geographic location of UE-A measured by this base station) of the network anchor A can be submitted by the base station to a blockchain node deployed in the 6G core network; in this example, the base station is the DP. This process mainly focuses on the procedure between the external DP and a blockchain node.

Data on-chaining process: This process happens from the time when the data is submitted and received by a blockchain node to the time when the data is successfully recorded on the blockchain and becomes visible to DCs. In fact, data on-chaining process takes place inside the blockchain system. Taking the example of the Olympic Park, when the real-time wireless data of the network anchor A is submitted by the base station to a BCN, the BCN will perform a series of blockchain operations (e.g., verifying the new blockchain transaction containing the submitted data, propagating the new transaction to other BCNs, executing a designated consensus protocol, creating a new block containing the new transaction) in order to append the submitted data to the blockchain and make it visible to DCs such as webcast applications. Such a data on-chaining process may cost a certain amount of time, which may be very sensitive to different data collection applications.

Data collection enabler: DCE is a network function providing the following services for DPs and DCs. In the Olympic Park scenario, network anchors are DPs while viewers/fans are DCs.

- DCE receives a data collection request from a DC, processes the data collection request, discovers potential DPs from the wireless system, and creates a customized blockchain system matching the data collection request.
- DCE can collect the data collection requirements of DCs, such as which wireless data needs to be collected, and how long the delay of the data on-chaining process can be tolerated, etc. Then, DCE can customize the processing of the blockchain system according to the specific needs as described in the data collection requirements. For example, a customized blockchain processing could execute a specific/selected consensus protocol in order to achieve a much lower minimum data on-chaining delay as needed by a DC/DP.

References

[1] 3GPP TS 23.501 V16.4.0 (2020-03), "System architecture for the 5G System (5GS); Stage 2 (Release 16)," March 2020.

[2] 3GPP TS 23.288 V17.5.0 (2022-06), "Architecture Enhancements for 5G System (5GS) to Support Network Data Analytics Services (Release 17)," June 2022.

[3] 3GPP TS 26.531 V17.0.0 (2022-06), "Data Collection and Reporting; General Description and Architecture (Release 17)," June 2022.

[4] https://www.forbes.com/sites/michellegreenwald/2020/12/10/live-strea ming-e-commerce-is-the-rage-in-china-is-the-us-next/?sh=1f3d446a65 35

[5] N. B. Somy et al., "Ownership preserving AI Market Places using Blockchain," arXiv, 2020.

[6] V. Hillman and V. Ganesh, "Kratos: A secure, authenticated and publicly verifiable system for educational data using the blockchain," in 2019 IEEE International Conference on Big Data (Big Data), 2019.

19

Blockchain-enabled Infrastructure Monitoring in 6G

Based on the work in [1], in this chapter, we introduce the notion of blockchain-enabled infrastructure monitoring solutions for future telecommunications networks. We first provide the rational and related work. Subsequently, we introduce the blockchain architecture and protocols. Finally, we provide some insights into important performance capabilities. The protocol and architecture discussed here can be applied in conjunction with the ledger methodologies outline in the previous chapters.

19.1 Rational and Prior Art

19.1.1 Introduction

There are several means to augment networking capabilities and ensure scalability for 6G systems. One possible approach is for mobile operators to collaborate and share infrastructure.

This has recently occurred in several regions around the world. For instance, there was a recent merger between O2 and Virgin Media [2]; there is a tower sharing agreement between UK's telco providers O2, Vodafone and Three [3]; there is also the case of KDDI and Softbank in Japan to share the RAN in rural areas; similarly; China Telecom and China Unicom share parts of their infrastructure saving an apparent $13.2 bn [4].

Sharing the telco infrastructure is clearly part of operational practices around the world, providing technical and financial advantages. However, current sharing agreements are very bespoke and typically between very few operator participants. With a trend toward disaggregation in telecoms, the transition from 5G to 6G will require more scalable solutions to infrastructure sharing.

Both 3GPP and O-RAN allow for disaggregation of hardware and software of RAN and thus enables a multi-vendor environment. The achieved openness, however, comes at the price of significantly increased integration costs and of course cybersecurity issues. For instance, [5] outlines the lack of a single accountable supplier as one of the important challenges for Open RAN.

This motivates the use of blockchain technologies which facilitates to establish trust among naturally non-trusting entities, in this case competing operators with hardware from different vendors. In 6G, transparency and the ability to monitor networking resources in a trusted manner among all the stakeholders will be vital.

In the case that an SLA is violated, the actual party at fault can be held accountable, and all the penalties should be applied and paid for automatically without any delay. For instance, if a specific router in the RAN is faulty, the respective party should be identified, billed and called for repairs. Using blockchains, all of that can be automated.

In here, we thus introduce and discuss a blockchain-based solution which is known as blockchain-enabled accountable and transparent (BEAT) infrastructure sharing through smart contracts residing on permissioned distributed ledgers (PDLs). The proposition is to manage access via rigorous access control mechanisms where only PDL-authorized members have access.

As discussed throughout this book, the advantage of PDLs is that they are immutable and can host executable smart contracts codes which get deployed and executed when triggered. This allows the SLAs between operators as well as vendors and, indeed, the entire supply chain to be run via automated smart contracts.

The PDL nodes required to instantiate such solution are typically installed on the various network devices; for instance, via embedded code, or on bare-metal, or on virtualized environments (VMs, K8s). The nodes monitor the infrastructure and traffic flow. Using blockchains allows one to automate the process, even if there are surges in network usage or cascading faults in the network.

19.1.2 Related prior art

At the time of writing, the idea of using blockchains to facilitate resource sharing is a fairly new and emerging topic. Some notable prior art is discussed below.

Some high-level approaches to spectrum sharing in 5G using distributed ledgers were introduced in [6] and [7] where, for instance, coalition algorithms for sharing of unused spectrum have been introduced. The interesting concept of tokenization for spectrum, infrastructure, and service pricing has been introduced. In addition, automated smart contract protocols have been presented. The studies are visionary but lack architecture details.

Yet another blockchain-enabled resource reservation and slicing broker approach is presented in [8] which is based on prior art in [9]. The authors propose that the tenants (i.e., the OTT players) request network services from the mobile operators on a per-need basis. Importantly, the SLAs for resource allocation are recorded to the ledger by means of a smart contract. However, the actual resource usage at a device is not recorded, and the problem of accountability in network sharing is not addressed. The extension of the notion of network slice broker (NSB) of [9] is expanded in [10]; it provides a blockchain-focused architecture for network slice auctions, in which infrastructure providers allocate network slices through an intermediate entity which then allocates resources to tenants. However, the notion of accountability has not been considered.

The authors of [11] and in [12] proposed an inter-operator network sharing architecture for small cells. Specifically, the network sharing SLAs between mobile operators are stored as smart contracts on a distributed ledger. Furthermore, [7] introduces a blockchain-enabled unlicensed spectrum sharing approach; however, falls short of introducing a viable architecture.

Solutions to enable accountability at the administrative-domain (AD) level have been introduced in AudIt [13], which is a network traffic monitoring and auditing protocol. In AudIt, the service providers report their QoS parameters, but not at device and component level. Another related solution has been presented in [14] and is referred to as FAIR, i.e., a forwarding accountability for Internet reputability protocol.

19.2 Blockchain-Native Architecture

19.2.1 High-level architecture

The blockchain-enabled resource sharing architecture is shown in Figure 19.1. It is enabled by the following actors

- **Network users**: There are three types, i.e., 1) *Network Owners*, which is a set of participants that are the actual owners of the infrastructure; 2) *Network Tenants*, which is the party leasing the infrastructure from the network owners; or 3) *a combination of both* in that they own infrastructure and also lease it so as to serve their clients.

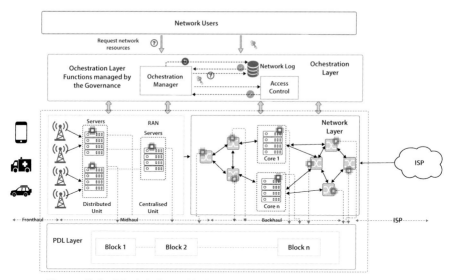

Figure 19.1 Blockchain-enabled network resource sharing architecture [1].

- **Device vendors**: They typically provide network devices, such as switches and routers.
- **Governance**: It typically refers to network governance which is formed by the consortium of the network users and may include their representatives. It is up to the network users to decide the specific strategy by which governance representatives are chosen. Governance is utmost important as it takes management decisions for access control, dispute resolution, among others. Governance members ought to have control over their own devices only and not over anybody else's devices. That ensures that in the case of a malicious user in the governance, only one vote will be compromised.

To provide additional operational efficiency and security, the architecture contains three operational layers: the orchestration, network, and PDL layers which have also been depicted in Figure 19.1.

19.2.2 Orchestration layer

The orchestration layer presides over network resource requests from tenants, akin to the ETSI's management and orchestration layer (MANO). This layer is governed and managed by the PDL, overseeing network operations and allocation decisions such as establishing network access, determining lease duration, setting prices, and granting privileges. The orchestration layer is managed by the governance of the network.

Shown in Figure 19.2, the orchestration layer boasts three main components:

1) The *orchestration manager*, which acts as a gatekeeper for incoming requests and boasts features such as the universal view akin to the software-defined mobile network orchestrator (SDM-O) discussed in [15] and the SDN-Server of [16]. Upon a network participant joining the network, the orchestration manager assigns credentials and keeps a record, allocating a node ID to a device. This node ID is distinct from Layer 2/3 addresses as the devices may change their IP addresses anytime whereas the node ID must remain the same.
2) The *access control*, a verification entity that maintains a database to keep records of credentials and responds to access control confirmation queries from the orchestration manager.
3) *Network log* is a database to maintain network resource logs.

The orchestration manager allocates network resources through stringent access controls, with the first function being to install network SLAs as smart contracts on the PDL. Two different types of SLAs are installed on the PDL, a) the resource orchestration SLA and b) the QoS monitoring SLA.

a) The *resource orchestration SLA* (RO-SLA) is the initial agreement between network users (e.g., an owner and tenant) and is executed at the start of the service. The governance installs RO-SLA at the earliest (e.g., at the time of PDL formation) and executes it with every network

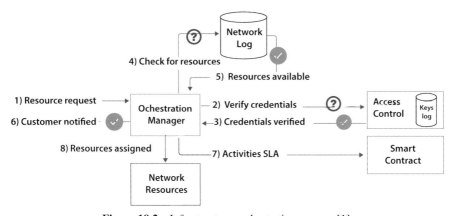

Figure 19.2 Infrastructure orchestration process [1].

request. RO-SLA maintains resource allocation details, such as route identity and QoS parameters agreed upon.

b) The *QoS monitoring SLA* (QM-SLA) this is an SLA for quality monitoring which records the per flow data to the PDL.

19.2.3 Network and PDL layers

General infrastructure and network resources such as networking instances, switches, routers, form the network layer. These sources are generally dealt with by above-discussed orchestration layer. Orchestration is vital since network resources have a limited capacity to forward network traffic whilst attaining prior agreed service levels.

When the tenants request network resources, the orchestration manager will check with the access control entity if the tenant has an agreement in place already. If an agreement is present, the orchestration manager shall verify the status of the network from the network log. That involves verifying the current load on each path of the network and on each networking instance.

If the network however has resources available, the orchestration manager will send a confirmation message to the tenant. That triggers a smart contract to be executed to initialize the SLA and then orchestrate the network resource for the tenant.

In the event that the capacity is not available, the tenant has to wait for the resources to become available and then execute the smart contract.

Stakeholders must know the performance and usage of the network components at a very fine-grained level. Such performance metrics are required for future SLA compliance and accountability of the sharing agreement.

Last but not least, the infrastructure usage is recorded at the infrastructure level and transparently shared with smart contracts at the PDL Layer. Every device ought to be installed with a PDL node and be able to execute smart contracts.

Jointly, the PDL-enabled infrastructure instances form the overall permissioned distributed ledger system.

19.2.4 Functioning of smart contracts

A tenant's ultimate goal is to secure service levels that align with their customers' expectations. However, service quality can be compromised due to various factors such as a congested pathway or malfunctioning network devices. In such scenarios, tenants are entitled to compensation without any complications. However, all stakeholders –network operators, vendors and supply chain – tend to point the fault at each other to evade paying penalties. Hence, proposed is the mechanism that records service data which cannot be denied by any party.

The proposed solution utilizes smart contracts to record said information to the PDL. For every flow, both the source and destination are recorded. PDLs are immutable, meaning data recorded to them cannot be erased nor modified. Additionally, PDLs are transparent, allowing all consortium participants to view flow source and destination information on the PDL.

To address the issues of scalability and privacy, it is proposed to record hashed data per flow to the PDL. Specifically, the *node ID*, *source IP address*, *destination IP address* and *timestamp* are recorded for packet i and node j. The following data D is then written to the smart contract: $D_{ij} = SHA3(node\_ID_j; src\_IP_i; dst\_IP_i; ts_i)$.

19.2.5 Trusted execution environments

The algorithmic PDL framework needs to be protected such that all stake-holders of the PDL trust the outcome, no matter which owners/tenants infrastructure is used. That is because the owner has no control over this virtual machine, which thereby enables secure and trustworthy data recording. On the other hand, both the Packet Processor and the PDL node are installed on operator and/or vendor-controlled devices, whom tenants may not trust them as owners could tamper with data.

Some device owners may, in addition to this, behave maliciously. For example, they may intentionally drop a packet and claim that the packet was sent from the source and was dropped in the network.

It is generally difficult to dispute such claims due to the best-effort nature of today's internet. To circumvent these really difficult issues, it is proposed to use fully trusted execution environments giving access to each PDL member.

19.3 Underlying Blockchain PDL Protocol

Above blockchain-based architecture design ensures that malicious behavior is extremely unlikely. That is because tenants are part of the PDL and thus known to the governance and other PDL users. Also, all activities are recorded to a PDL which allows for posterior verification. However, majority quorum is an issue in any blockchain. For instance, a dominant user with more than fifty percent of networking assets could theoretically influence

PDL operations. To this end, an interrogation protocol was introduced in [1] that is built on the two key elements of localized record maintenance and forwarding proof. It is the combination of the two that ensures future auditability.

19.3.1 Forwarding proof

Accountability is managed through the *receipts* equation given before, i.e. $D_{ij} = SHA3(node\_ID_j; src\_IP_i; dst\_IP_i; ts_i)$. These receipts are recorded at the source and the destination of the packet. In the event of an SLA violation, the device owners/vendors will be required to prove that they have allocated the devices from the source to the destination, as agreed in the SLA.

Receipts recording to the PDL through a smart contract at every device is not feasible due to PDL performance considerations. To this end, *forwarding proof* is suggested which is a lightweight mechanism for network users to show that they have allocated the SLA-agreed devices throughout the service. The forwarding proofs are stored in local storage and produced *on-demand* to the governance and are not exchanged until a dispute occurs to save the network bandwidth. Since PDLs are inherently transparent and permissioned, one does not need to use any intensive computation techniques to create proofs. The only objective is to identify the network user who has abused the system.

For the *ith* packet, Node ID is *N*, source ID is src_ID_i, destination ID is dst_ID_i and receive timestamp is tr_i. Here, source and destination are node's direct neighbors and may not be the final source and destination of the packet. The forwarding proof P_i can be calculated as: $Pi = N + src\_ID_i + dst\_ID_i + tr_i$. Note that receipt timestamp tr_i is the time when the received proof is recorded to the internal storage. This is different from the packet timestamp above which is the timestamp of the packet received at the device.

19.3.2 Localized record maintenance

Two different types of storage for record keeping are maintained, i.e., a short-term storage called the *proof buffer* and a long-term storage called the *report generator.*

- **Proof buffer**: Packet buffer is a short-term volatile storage that stores the forwarding proof for a governance-defined time called the *threshold time*. This threshold time is dependent on the PDL network priorities and available resources. The proof is kept in a local storage for a threshold time, and after this time elapses it can be overwritten by newer proofs.

- **Report generator**: For the integrity and compliance monitoring of the PDLs, governance should get periodic reports of the network users. Network devices generate large amounts of data, which makes it very difficult to keep all the data in the device for a long time. The report generator is a long-term nonvolatile storage that saves the packet count only. For every incoming packet, the software will increment the counter by 1, and at the end of service provisioning, it will send the report to the governance. The notion of periodic smart contract reports had been standardized in ETSI ISG PDL 11 [17] and has been discussed in the PDL part of the book. Given *src_ID* and *dst_ID* as source and destination identifiers respectively and are node's direct neighbors and may not be the final source and destination. The node N will store record R as: $R =$ (*src_ID*; *dst_ID*; *number_of _packets*).

19.3.3 PDL-based interrogation protocol

If a tenant or customer believes that they are not assigned devices as per agreed SLA and their performance is affected (e.g., throughput or latency degradation), they can ask the governance to initiate the *interrogation protocol*.

Once the dispute is launched, governance will initiate the interrogation protocol and ask all the devices on the route to send their proof buffers. If the proofs match with the governance records, it means that the devices were assigned honestly, and there was a problem with service quality in the network.

When the governance confirms that all the devices are assigned as per the SLA, further investigations of throughput degradation due to problems such as link failure and packet drop/loss should be carried out. Note that service degradation due to other copiously discussed factors such as packet loss and delay or devices intentionally dropping packets are out of scope.

Network users can still be dishonest, as they can install false replicated forwarding proofs on multiple devices and paths. For instance, one path A (the agreed path) can store the same data as another path B (path sent). Forwarding proofs are generated by all devices; therefore, if a network user is being dishonest, neighboring devices on the route also report their proofs with the corresponding timestamps. By matching their source and destination device identities, it can be verified which device has in fact forwarded the traffic.

19.3.4 Performance results

An important aspect is the SLA deployment latency. Remember that there are two different types of SLAs are involved: a) resource orchestration SLA (RO-SLA), that is, SLAs that allocate the resources; and b) QoS monitoring SLA (QM-SLA). It was found that both deployment latencies can be neglected.

For example, the RO-SLA resource orchestration SLA took a minimal time of mean 3.98 seconds; this is illustrated in Figure 19.3. A more in-depth performance analysis is conducted in [1].

19.4 Security Considerations

Designing a system for 6G using PDLs is not trivial. For this reason, in permissioned distributed ledgers, the governance oversees the network operations such as the allowed number of users and participants' misbehavior.

Most of the challenges can be resolved with the compliance strategies implemented by the governance. However, some considerations require further design attention, such as transaction throughput and scalability. These are discussed here.

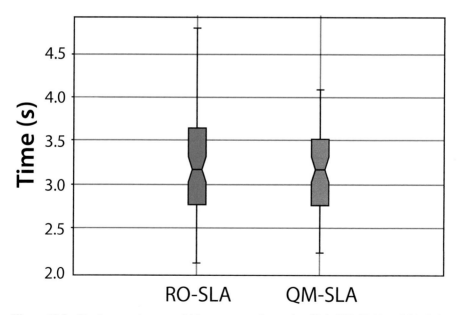

Figure 19.3 Deployment latency of (a) resource orchestration SLA (RO-SLA) and (b) QoS monitoring SLA (QM-SLA) [1].

19.4.1 Intra-PDL denial-of-service (DoS)

Every PDL allows a particular number of transactions per second (TPS), which are generally higher in PDLs (e.g., 20,000 TPS [18]) than in permissionless ledgers (e.g., Ethereum mainnet which has a TPS of approximately 15). This means that if many devices send data simultaneously, it can cause congestion at the ledger or DoS for incoming transactions.

Therefore, whilst designing a PDL network, it is important to adopt a PDL-type (e.g., Hyperledger Fabric), which can cope with the network's requirements. PDLs have a high transaction throughput and stringent access control mechanisms so that only the number of users that the underlying PDL system can cope with are allowed by the governance. Also, access can be denied when the network reaches a certain load threshold.

19.4.2 Denial-of-capability (DoC) attack

The permissioned nature of PDL makes inter-PDL DoS attacks unviable. However, general DoS attacks (e.g., DoS due to outside network users) are still possible. That is, malicious users can send an inflated number of requests to the orchestration manager, thus causing congestion.

Several solutions to combat DoS exist and can be used to mitigate the problem. For instance, one could opt for the capability-based solutions [19]. In such systems, the requesting traffic is limited to a small channel, and the rest of the bandwidth is dedicated to authorized traffic for general usage. During the requesting period, users will be assigned a token that allows them to access the network on the main channel. Based on criteria and user behavior, a user can be assigned a token for a longer time duration.

This is a viable approach because the protocol will need to communicate with its client only at the setup time. This will involve a small number of communications between a client and the network; also, the clients are likely to be legitimate and safe to be assigned tokens long terms. Limiting the connection requests to a dedicated channel will allow only the authorized traffic (from clients such as OTT) to further communicate with the orchestration manager.

However, the requesting channel is still open to unauthorized users to send requests. A large number of connection requests flooding the request channel can cause congestion at the requesting channel. Consequently, legitimate users are unable to send the connection request to the network.

This is identified as a "Denial-of-Capability Attack" by Argyraki et al. [20] and they argued against their viability in combating the DoS attack. However, other research works argue Argraki et al.'s argument and propose enhancements to solve the problem at the requesting channel, such as stateless-filtering [21] and puzzles [22]. One can easily implement these solutions to solve the problem of DoC attacks.

19.4.3 Malicious devices

All the devices record the data to the PDL and then the data is replicated across the network nodes (i.e., network devices). If a malicious device starts sending false and irrelevant data to the PDL, the system can get overwhelmed by the number of requests and increase the data sizes inside the routers exponentially.

To combat this problem, the proposed protocol maintains a node ID for all the nodes in the network. In the case of misbehavior, with said node IDs the governance can take appropriate actions and block future access of such nodes. Indeed, such an enforcement requires standardization which has been carried out in ETSI PDL.

19.4.4 Integrity of data

Smart contracts do not have any built-in means to verify the integrity of the data. Hence, it is vital to ensure that the data recorded by network devices is valid. The trusted execution environment ensures that the correct data is recorded to the PDL. However, the network device feeds the data to the packet processor and if this device is malicious, it will provide false information to the PDL.

This is one of the reasons the use of governance-controlled permissioned distributed ledgers ought to be advocated. In a PDL, the members are entitled through access control mechanisms and affected parties can report such misbehavior to the governance, which can take subsequently disciplinary actions and blacklist the node and may impose penalties.

19.4.5 Colluding participants

In a blockchain-enabled architecture network users can collude with each other. In such a case, dominant network users can behave maliciously toward other tenants. For instance, it could reject their transactions.

To solve such collusion problems, a regulatory authority [e.g., Ofcom in the UK or the Federal Communications Commission (FCC) in the USA] could also be a part of the PDL network governance. The role of the regulatory authority is as an observation entity only and it should be contacted only in the event of disputes. The regulatory authority neither takes part in consensus nor controls any device.

References

[1] T. Faisal, M. Dohler, S. Mangiante, and DR Lopez, "BEAT: Blockchain-Enabled Accountable and Transparent Infrastructure Sharing in 6G and Beyond," IEEE Access, 2022.

[2] Virgin Media and O2 Blockbuster Merger Provisionally Approved, May 2021, [online]. Available:https://bbc.in/3oh8PpX.

[3] O2 Three and Vodafone Agree New Deal to Enhance Rural Coverage, May 2021, [online]. Available:https://bit.ly/33N3u02.

[4] L. Hardesty, SoftBank KDDI add Nokia to Their Vendor List for Shared 5G Network, Oct. 2021, [online]. Available:https://bit.ly/3bitJPM.

[5] C. Gabriel and R. Komany, Open RAN: Ready for Prime Time? The Operator's Prespective, Oct. 2021, [online]. Available:https://bit.ly/3jQ3cOA.

[6] T. Maksymyuk, J. Gazda, M. Volosin, G. Bugar, D. Horvath, M. Klymash, et al., "Blockchain-empowered framework for decentralized network management in 6G," IEEE Commun. Mag., vol. 58, no. 9, pp. 86-92, Sep. 2020.

[7] T. Maksymyuk, J. Gazda, L. Han, and M. Jo, "Blockchain-based intelligent network management for 5G and beyond," Proc. 3rd Int. Conf. Adv. Inf. Commun. Technol. (AICT), pp. 36-39, Jul. 2019.

[8] J. Backman, S. Yrjola, K. Valtanen, and O. Mammela, "Blockchain network slice broker in 5G: Slice leasing in factory of the future use case," Proc. Internet Things Bus. Models Users Netw., pp. 1-8, Nov. 2017.

[9] K. Samdanis, X. C. Perez, and V. Sciancalepore, "From network sharing to multi-tenancy: The 5G network slice broker," IEEE Commun. Mag., vol. 54, no. 7, pp. 32-39, Jul. 2016.

[10] L. Zanzi, A. Albanese, V. Sciancalepore, and X. Costa-Perez, "NSBchain: A secure blockchain framework for network slicing brokerage," Proc. IEEE Int. Conf. Commun. (ICC), pp. 1-7, Jun. 2020.

[11] A. Okon, N. Jagannath, I. Elgendi, J. M. H. Elmirghani, A. Jamalipour, and K. Munasinghe, "Blockchain-enabled multi-operator small cell network for beyond 5G systems," IEEE Netw., vol. 34, no. 5, pp. 171-177, Sep. 2020.

[12] B. Mafakheri, T. Subramanya, L. Goratti, and R. Riggio, "Blockchain-based infrastructure sharing in 5G small cell networks," Proc. IEEE CNSM, pp. 313-317, Nov. 2018.

[13] K. Argyraki, P. Maniatis, O. Irzak, S. Ashish, and S. Shenker, "Loss and delay accountability for the internet," Proc. IEEE Int. Conf. Netw. Protocols, pp. 194-205, Oct. 2007.

[14] C. Pappas, R. M. Reischuk, and A. Perrig, "FAIR: Forwarding account-ability for internet reputability," Proc. IEEE 23rd Int. Conf. Netw. Protocols (ICNP), pp. 189-200, Nov. 2015.

[15] M. R. Crippa et al., "Resource sharing for a 5G multi-tenant and multi-service architecture," Proc. 23th Eur. Wireless Conf., pp. 1-6, 2017.

[16] M. Jiang, D. Xenakis, S. Costanzo, N. Oassa, and T. Mahmoodi, "Radio resource sharing as a service in 5G: A software-defined networking approach," Comput. Commun., vol. 107, pp. 13-29, Jul. 2017.

[17] Nov. 2021, [online]. Available:https://bit.ly/3qGIZiq.

[18] C. Gorenflo, S. Lee, L. Golab, and S. Keshav, "FastFabric: Scaling hyperledger fabric to 20000 transactions per second," Int. J. Netw. Manag., vol. 30, no. 5, 2020.

[19] T. Anderson, T. Roscoe, and D. Wetherall, "Preventing internet denial-of-service with capabilities," ACM SIGCOMM Comput. Commun. Rev., vol. 34, no. 1, pp. 39-44, 2004.

[20] K. Argyraki and D. Cheriton, "Network capabilities: The good the bad and the ugly," ACM HotNets-IV, vol. 139, pp. 140, Nov. 2005.

[21] A. Yaar, A. Perrig, and D. Song, "SIFF: A stateless internet flow filter to mitigate DDoS flooding attacks," Proc. IEEE Symp. Secur. Privacy, pp. 130-143, May 2004.

[22] B. Parno, D. Wendlandt, E. Shi, A. Perrig, B. Maggs, and Y.-C. Hu, "Portcullis: Protecting connection setup from denial-of-capability attacks," ACM SIGCOMM Comput. Commun. Rev., vol. 37, no. 4, pp. 289-300, Oct. 2007.

20

Metaverse in the 6G Era

In this closing chapter, we examine the role of 6G to support the emerging metaverse. We first provide an introduction to the concept of the metaverse. We then explain the link between the metaverse and blockchain technologies. Thereupon, we discuss networking requirements based on the used XR devices; we dwell on the need for 5G and 6G telecommunications systems due to the need to offload XR content in real time. We finish the chapter by discussing open challenges.

20.1 Introduction to the Metaverse

20.1.1 Overview

The concept of a "metaverse" – a virtual world that is fully immersive and interconnected – has been around for decades. The term itself was first coined by Neal Stephenson in his 1992 science fiction novel "Snow Crash," in which the metaverse is a virtual reality-based successor to the internet.

In the early days of the internet, the idea of a metaverse was mostly limited to science fiction and the dreams of tech enthusiasts. However, as technology advanced, the possibility of a metaverse became more tangible.

In the mid-2000s, virtual worlds such as Second Life and World of Warcraft began to gain popularity, providing early examples of what a metaverse could look like. These virtual worlds were primarily used for socializing and entertainment, but they also had in-world economies where users could buy and sell virtual goods and services.

In recent years, advancements in virtual and augmented reality technology have made the metaverse seem even more plausible. Companies such as Facebook and Google are investing heavily in virtual reality and augmented reality technologies, with the goal of creating fully immersive and interconnected virtual worlds.

The blockchain technology is also playing a big role in the development of metaverse. With the decentralized nature of blockchain, it allows the ownership of virtual assets and the creation of in-game economies, which are important features of metaverse.

However, there are still many challenges to be overcome before the metaverse can become a reality. These include issues with connectivity, latency, and data privacy, as well as the need for a standardized framework for building and connecting virtual worlds.

Despite these challenges, many experts believe that the metaverse is inevitable and will have a significant impact on society. Some predict that it will become a new form of social interaction and commerce, while others see it as a way to enhance education and training or even as a tool for solving real-world problems.

It's important to note that the concept of metaverse is in a very early stage of development, and it is still uncertain what form it will take in the future. It's an exciting time for the potential of this technology and it will be interesting to see how it develops over time.

20.1.2 The "Metaverse" Origin

As said above, "Snow Crash" is a 1992 science fiction novel by Neal Stephenson. In there, the author introduced the concept of the metaverse which is a virtual reality-based successor to the internet. The novel is set in a near-future version of the United States, where the internet has been replaced by the metaverse, and people can enter a virtual reality world using a device called a "metaverse deck."

The story follows the protagonist, Hiro Protagonist, who is a hacker and a pizza delivery driver. Hiro is drawn into a conflict between the mysterious and powerful L. Bob Rife, the creator of the Snow Crash virus, a drug and a computer virus, and Y.T., a teenage skateboard courier who becomes embroiled in the conflict. Together, they uncover a conspiracy involving the Snow Crash virus, which has the ability to infect both the physical and virtual worlds, and the plans of Rife to use the virus to gain control of the metaverse.

The novel is considered a classic in the cyberpunk genre, and it is known for its exploration of themes such as the impact of technology on society, the nature of virtual reality, and the role of corporations in the future. It is also known for its satirical and often humorous tone, as well as its complex and nuanced characters.

One of the most notable aspects of the novel is the concept of the metaverse, which is a fully immersive and interconnected virtual reality world. In "Snow Crash," the *metaverse serves as a successor to the internet and it's described as a place where people can interact, conduct business, and even experience a sense of community*. This idea of the metaverse was a significant influence on the development of virtual worlds and online communities in the years that followed the novel's publication.

Overall, "Snow Crash" is a thought-provoking and entertaining novel that explores the potential consequences of advanced technology and the impact it could have on society. It is a must-read for anyone interested in the concept of the metaverse.

20.1.3 The "Metaverse" Origin

The metaverse is often described as being immersive, spatially persistent, and highly interactive:

- **Immersive**: The metaverse is a fully immersive experience, meaning that users are fully immersed in a virtual world and can interact with it in a realistic way. This is achieved through the use of virtual reality and augmented reality technology, which can create a sense of presence and realism in the virtual world.
- **Spatially persistent**: The metaverse is spatially persistent, meaning that the virtual world exists independently of the users who are experiencing it. This allows for a sense of continuity and permanence in the virtual world, where changes made by one user will still be visible to others.
- **Highly interactive**: The metaverse is highly interactive, meaning that users can interact with the virtual world and with other users in a variety of ways. This includes the ability to move through the virtual world, manipulate objects, and communicate with other users in real-time. The high level of interactivity allows users to engage with the virtual world in a way that feels natural and intuitive.

Additionally, the blockchain technology can play a big role in the metaverse, allowing for decentralized ownership of virtual assets and creating in-game economies. It also allows users to be in control of their personal data and privacy.

20.2 Blockchain and the Metaverse

20.2.1 How both relate

The metaverse and blockchain are closely related; indeed:

- **Decentralization**: One of the key features of blockchain technology is its decentralized nature, which allows for the creation of a peer-to-peer network where transactions can be recorded and verified without the need for a central authority. This can be applied to the metaverse, allowing for the decentralized ownership of virtual assets and the creation of in-game economies, where users can buy and sell virtual goods and services.

- **Digital identity**: Blockchain technology allows for the creation of user-centric digital identities that are secure and verifiable, which can be used in the metaverse to create a sense of presence and authenticity for users.

- **Smart contracts**: Blockchain technology also allows for the creation of smart contracts, which are self-executing contracts with the terms of the agreement written into code. Smart contracts can be used in the metaverse to facilitate transactions, such as the exchange of virtual assets and the payment of in-game currencies.

- **Verifiability**: Blockchain allows for the verifiability of transactions, which can be important in the metaverse, especially when it comes to the ownership of virtual assets. For example, blockchain can be used to create a verifiable record of who owns a particular virtual item, which is important for maintaining the integrity of the in-game economy.

- **Privacy and security**: Blockchain technology can provide a high level of security and privacy for users in the metaverse. With blockchain, users can be in control of their personal data and keep it private. Also, with blockchain, the data stored in the metaverse can be secured and tamper-proof. In addition, redactable blockchain and distributed ledgers [1] can even enable users to modify their on-chain data and guarantee "the right to be forgotten."

Blockchain technologies can thus be used to create a decentralized, secure, and verifiable infrastructure for the metaverse, which can be used to facilitate transactions, create digital identities, and maintain the integrity of the virtual world.

20.2.2 Secure digital identity in the metaverse

A digital identity in the metaverse is a virtual representation of a user, which can be used to create a sense of presence and authenticity in the virtual world. Digital identities in the metaverse can be used for a variety of purposes, such as accessing different parts of the virtual world, purchasing virtual goods and services, and participating in social activities.

Blockchain technology can facilitate the creation of digital identities in the metaverse by providing a secure and verifiable way to create and manage them. Blockchain-based digital identities can be self-sovereign, meaning that users have full control over their digital identity and personal data. They can also be decentralized, meaning that they are not controlled by a central authority.

One example of a blockchain that can facilitate digital identities in the metaverse is Ethereum. Ethereum allows for the creation of digital identities using smart contracts, which can be used to record and verify the identity of users in a decentralized and tamper-proof way. Additionally, Ethereum also allows users to create and manage virtual assets, and assets can be linked to the user's identity, which can be used to enable ownership of virtual assets and enable in-game economies.

Another example is EOSIO, a blockchain protocol that is designed for high performance and scalability. EOSIO enables the creation of digital identities that are secure and verifiable, allowing for the creation of a secure and verifiable ecosystem for the metaverse.

Additionally, other blockchains such as the IOTA or Holochain, which are designed for specific use cases, could also be used to facilitate digital identities in the metaverse. But it is important to note that the development of digital identities in metaverse is still in early stages, and it's still uncertain which blockchain technology will be the best for this purpose.

20.2.3 Virtual asset ownership in the metaverse

Asset management in the metaverse refers to the ability to create, transfer, and manage virtual assets within a virtual world. Virtual assets can be anything from in-game currency, virtual real estate, unique items, and even virtual representations of physical assets like art and collectibles.

Blockchain technology can facilitate asset management in the metaverse by providing a decentralized, secure, and verifiable way to create and manage virtual assets. By using blockchain, virtual assets can be linked to a user's digital identity and can be transferred, tracked, and traded in a decentralized and tamper-proof way.

One example of how blockchain can facilitate asset management in the metaverse is through the use of non-fungible tokens (NFTs). NFTs are a type of digital asset that are unique and cannot be replicated; they can be used to represent virtual assets in the metaverse such as virtual real estate, virtual art, and virtual collectibles. NFTs can be created on the Ethereum blockchain, which allows for the creation of digital assets that are unique and verifiable, which can be used to enable ownership of virtual assets and enable in-game economies.

Additionally, other blockchains, such as EOSIO or TRON, also have the capability to facilitate asset management in the metaverse. For example, EOSIO has a high level of scalability and it can facilitate the creation of virtual assets at scale, while TRON has a high level of transaction throughput that can facilitate the transfer of virtual assets at high speed.

Asset management in the metaverse is an important aspect of the metaverse, as it enables the creation of in-game economies, where users can buy and sell virtual goods and services. This can add a new dimension of social interaction and commerce to the metaverse, making it more engaging and interactive.

20.2.4 Metaverse in-game economics

In-game economics refers to the economic systems within video games and virtual worlds, where players can buy and sell virtual goods and services, or players can even earn in-game assets (e.g., cryptocurrency) via play-to-earn (P2E) games. In-game economies can include virtual currencies, virtual goods, virtual services, and even virtual labor. These economies can be used to create a sense of immersion and engagement for players, and can also be used to generate revenue for game developers and publishers.

Virtual asset ownership is a key aspect of in-game economics. Virtual assets can be anything from virtual currency, virtual land, unique items, and even virtual representations of physical assets like art and collectibles. These assets can be bought, sold, traded, and even rented within the game. Virtual asset ownership gives players a sense of ownership and engagement in the game, which can lead to more immersive and engaging gameplay.

Blockchain technology can facilitate in-game economics by providing a decentralized, secure, and verifiable way to create and manage virtual assets. By using blockchain, virtual assets can be linked to a user's digital identity and can be transferred, tracked, and traded in a decentralized and tamper-proof way. This allows for the creation of in-game economies where players can buy and sell virtual goods and services, such as virtual currency, virtual land, and virtual goods.

For example, virtual economies based on blockchain technology can create a new level of immersion and engagement for players, as they will be able to own and trade virtual assets in a more secure and verifiable way. Additionally, it can also allow game developers and publishers to generate new revenue streams through the sale of virtual assets, and it can also create new opportunities for players to generate income through the sale of their own virtual assets.

It's important to note that the development of in-game economics in the metaverse is still in early stages and there are still many challenges to be overcome. However, the combination of blockchain technology and the metaverse has the potential to create new opportunities for creating, managing and exchanging virtual assets, which can lead to new forms of social interaction and commerce, as well as new revenue streams for game developers and publishers.

20.3 The Metaverse in the 6G Era

20.3.1 Connecting the unconnected

Over past decades, the telco industry has truly enabled connectivity of the unconnected. Initially a simple means of telephony, the smart phone has evolved into a social media gateway in our hands. From above, we understand that the role of telecoms in the metaverse era will be similar if not more pronounced. Indeed, from a telco point of view, the metaverse can be viewed to have the following properties [2]:

1. The metaverse is a virtual space that embraces a **social element**. It is not just a place where users spend time alone or with a selected few, but rather it aims to replicate the social interactions that occur in the real world. The metaverse allows for users to interact with one another in a human-like manner, through the use of avatars that can make eye contact, convey body language, and even engage in physical gestures like shaking hands or hugging.
2. In addition to its social aspect, the metaverse also has a strong **virtual narrative**. Some view the metaverse as existing solely in a virtual world, which can be accessed through VR headsets, such as Fortnite.

Others see it as being rooted in the physical world, but with digital overlays experienced through AR or MR, such as in the game Pokémon Go. Regardless of the method of access, the metaverse enhances social interactions and experiences through persistent virtual content. The metaverse can be accessed through various XR devices, including VR headsets, AR glasses, and even through 2D screens using WebXR technologies.

3. Finally, the metaverse is being **accelerated by means of cutting-edge technologies** such as Web 3.0, blockchain, NFTs, 5G, digital twins, AI, and XR devices. While the metaverse could technically exist without these technologies, their incorporation greatly accelerates its growth and expansion. These technologies allow for new forms of social interactions, transactions, and digital assets management in the metaverse.

Let us discuss the importance of VR and AR in more details in the subsequent section.

20.3.2 Metaverse VR and AR devices

Augmented reality (AR) and virtual reality (VR) are closely related to the metaverse, as they are both technologies that can be used to create immersive and interactive virtual experiences. One can think of AR and VR as proxies or portals between the physical world and the metaverse.

Today we have keyboards and touchscreens that all require interactions that need to be learned at some point. From a user experience point of view, however, the emerging metaverse devices yield a unique opportunity for more intuitive interactions and consumption of digital content and information.

As proxies, these devices need to translate information from the physical world into the virtual, but also back from the virtual world into the physical:

- The former – sensing the physical environment – is done through an exploding ecosystem of sensors which in their entirety form the Internet of Things (IoT). In the context of the metaverse, the IoT relies on Lidar sensors, cameras, volumetric capture devices, haptic suits and gloves, neural wristbands, or even Neuralink-like devices.
- The latter – the ability for us to consume the virtual metaverse content – is enabled by an exploding ecosystem of VR, AR, MR (which, together with haptics and other sensory interaction, is sometimes grouped into XR) as well as holographic projection devices.

VR technology involves creating a fully immersive and interactive virtual environment, where users can see, hear, and interact with a digital world as if they were physically present in it. This technology can be used in the metaverse to create a fully immersive virtual world that users can enter and explore. It involves spatially isolating computer-generated simulations of three-dimensional environments that can be interacted with in real-time through head-mounted displays (HMDs) and game controllers. VR devices have enjoyed a solid growth in both enterprise and consumer segments with popular products being Oculus Quest 2, Varjo VR-3, Playstation VR, Valve Index, and HP Reverb G2.

AR technology involves overlaying virtual elements onto the real world, allowing users to see and interact with digital information in their physical environment. It provides a composite view between physical and virtual worlds by superimposing a computer-generated image on a user's view of the real world. Popular AR gear is your mobile phone running apps providing AR filters as found in Instagram, Snapchat, and TikTok. Purpose-made AR devices are HoloLens 2, Lenovo's ThinkReality, and Nreal. There is even Mojo Vision and InWith, which work on AR contact lenses.

AR requires spatial persistence, meaning that if a user moves in the physical world, the virtual overlay should be anchored in the real world. For instance, if an AR user walks away from a physical table on which a digital vase with flowers is placed, these ought to get smaller with increasing physical distance between the user and the table.

VR emerged first because it can be achieved by rendering environments in a controlled manner with limited compute power. Compute capabilities and optics have evolved, however, and AR is catching up quickly. These technologies are the closest we have today to supporting the social engagement element of the metaverse.

All of the devices mentioned above have one important requirement in common to achieve device desirability in terms of comfort and weight at reasonable cost: they require performant, reliable, and secure networks. The goal is to offload as much of control and compute tasks possible away from the devices onto the edge. The devices need to be connected to the lowest possible latency, as well as an edge server where, for example, the graphics are rendered in real-time and then streamed to the HMD like in a video conference.

While the device ecosystem is still at its infancy, the XR ecosystem is already moving in this direction with technologies such as Boundless XR and

CloudXR. These emerging multi-access edge computing (MEC) capabilities make it possible to offer much more immersive experiences: VR headsets can show content at a much higher level of detail (LOD) and AR headsets can handle much more complex real-world interactions. However, this comes at a price.

Notably, data needs to be sent back and forth between AR/VR devices and the edge cloud within milliseconds, at (almost) bounded latency and at a high data rate. A reliable, secure and low-latency wireless connection to XR devices is thus paramount.

The only technology proven to achieve such limitless connectivity is cellular technology, i.e., 5G and soon 6G.

20.3.3 5G and 6G networking requirements

There are numerous wireless connectivity technologies today: the most popular being Bluetooth, Wi-Fi, and cellular technologies. Bluetooth lacks range, rate and reliability. Current generations of Wi-Fi offer the required rate but suffer from congestion and thus high latencies once several XR devices are connected simultaneously; Wi-Fi 7 promises to address the congestion issue but is nowhere near the range and global coverage offered by cellular technologies. Also, it does not offer any service level agreements (SLAs) that can be provided using 5G's emerging slicing concepts which is vital for many enterprise applications.

5G offers rate, range, reliability, latency and so much more. Indeed, the average uplink/downlink (DL/UL) data rates provided by 5G today are 200 Mbps/30 Mbps per user. Depending on the choice of scheduler, radio bearer configurations and radio conditions, the achievable latencies are in the order of 10 ms for frequency range 1 (FR1, i.e., below 6 GHz) and 5 ms for FR2 (above 24 GHz, i.e., mm-wave bands). Reliability can today be in the order of 99.99% with five to six nines of reliability achievable over the coming years.

Does that suffice for XR? If a user moves his/her head using VR, the new immersive visuals need to be projected within 20 ms (ideally below 10 ms) to avoid motion sickness. In AR, less than 20 ms is required to ensure that virtual objects appear spatially anchored in the environment for a single-user experience, and significantly less than that for a multi-user AR experience. On-device smart processing techniques, such as asynchronous time wrap (ATW) that reuses old content with the new head position, help to relax these latency requirements by a factor 1.5–3×.

Regarding the required data rates to facilitate edge-cloud XR processing, we differentiate between three scenarios — low, medium, and high offload for XR:

- In pure *VR*, the optimal target is to render most if not all content in the edge-cloud. Such a high offload scenario requires download/downlink (DL) rates which are proportional to the resolution of the rendered environment. Per a recent GSMA study [3], the rates are 30 Mbps for a 2K H.264-encoded stream and up-to 800 Mbps for an 8K H.266 encoded stream. The uplink (UL) rates are insignificant, i.e., well below 2 Mbps, as only HMD orientation and some other user-generated control via for example haptic gloves need to be transmitted.
- In *AR*, different spatially aware tasks need to be completed by the system, thus giving the opportunity to invoke three offload scenarios that are summarized in Figure 20.1. The DL rates range from 20–80 Mbps and the UL rates from 10–40 Mbps, depending on which tasks are offloaded to the edge-cloud.

In terms of latency requirements, a GSMA study differentiates between different degrees of XR interactions: weak interactions (like broadcasts) have a generous end-to-end latency budget of 10–20 s; moderate interactions (like an XR video conference) require 200 ms; and strong interactions (online games or engaging sports games) are ideally delivered at less than 20 ms. Clearly, the first embodiments can be delivered using 5G but the more stringent latency (and rate) constraints will require 6G.

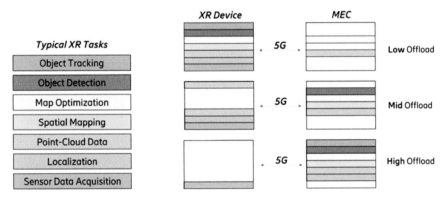

Figure 20.1 Illustration of the low, medium and high offload scenarios between AR devices and an edge-cloud for a typical AR compute task execution [4].

In terms of lightweight and accessible XR devices, this is achieved as more tasks are being offloaded to the edge-cloud. Indeed, the more is offloaded, the lower the requirements on processing capabilities and energy storage. Both help with the form factor, with the experienced weight and therefore the overall consumer price. First measurements indicate that low offload reduces device energy consumption threefold; mid offload fourfold; and high offload by more than sevenfold [5]. This is a tangible reduction and directly translates into an improved user experience.

Edge-cloud support is vital to scale XR and is therefore one of the fundamental technologies to enable the metaverse by making XR devices economically affordable, lightweight yet powerful, and connected with sufficient battery lifetime. A challenge with edge-cloud is how much can truly be offloaded to the edge, at the same time maintain the KPIs for the applications, and deliver an acceptable QoE to the end users regardless of if they are consumers playing games or enterprise users delivering the sophisticated next product in the metaverse. This means we should expect to see more edge-cloud type solutions in operator networks around the world where content gets closer to the RAN by using a UPF with local breakout.

Standards and standardized interfaces will ensure interoperability within this increasingly complex metaverse ecosystem. Having the metaverse run on a common blockchain operating system, such as Ethereum, does not suffice. Interoperability is required across blockchain families, across physical and virtual worlds, and across other important technologies underpinning the metaverse, such as haptic devices. Various standards initiatives deal with such standards today, such as MPEG (ISO/IEC), 3GPP, ETSI ARF, VR-IF, OpenXR, and Open AR Cloud.

Last but not least, it is important to ensure that large content developer communities around the world are able to easily integrate advanced XR capabilities into consumer and enterprise applications. It requires 5G-native APIs to be offered to the developer community, and ideally be embedded into SDKs of specific platforms. These APIs will help developers improve the quality of experience of their XR applications.

20.3.4 New business case for telcos?

Blockchains in the metaverse may offer a new way for telcos to monetize their assets in the 6G era. To exemplify this, let us examine the community-driven metaverse platform Sandbox. It has a lot in common with the non-blockchain games Minecraft and Roblox. The huge difference is that any creator in Sandbox can natively monetize assets and gaming experiences!

This is made possible through the transactional SAND utility token which is based on an ERC-20 Ethereum utility token of which there is a finite supply of 3 billion SANDs. The entire Sandbox platform is based on the Ethereum blockchain. That means that any asset generation, game moves, market places or anything else done in Sandbox automatically generates value since based on the underlying value token SAND.

The economic value of blockchain-based platforms is thus natively baked into the metaverse, whereas the value of traditional platforms is added posteriorly through a payment portal (e.g., PayPal).

This novel approach paves the way for creating assets and even experiences to attain economic value and thus make them tradable. It signals the birth of entirely new economic models, putting creators at the center and ensuring that any developed foreground intellectual property (IP) becomes monetizable.

And as long as the monetary tokens are based on the same blockchain, e.g., Ethereum, the generated assets can be traded across application platforms! Web 3.0 thus enables a form of "digital aura" with immutable content provenance across many different applications, as long as they are based on the same blockchain. For example, a creator can list a new digital garment on the Ethereum-based non-fungible token (NFT) site Opensea and trade assets into and out of Sandbox as well as any other metaverse based on Ethereum.

The resulting creator economy will be powerful! This is exemplified in Figure 20.2, which is structured into three parts:

1. the underlying traditional technology ecosystem on the lower IaaS part of the figure;
2. traditional metaverse examples on the right-hand side; and
3. Web 3.0-based metaverse examples on the left-hand side.

The traditional technology enabler segment is composed of device and component vendors, connectivity providers and platform players – the examples shown are non-exhaustive. The traditional way of building a metaverse experience is shown through the examples of Fortnite, Minecraft, and Roblox. They are traditional since the economic value through payment opportunities has been added posteriorly (and is handled through centralized payment/ownership gateways).

The new way forward is enabled with blockchains: Here, a new set of interdependent layers is emerging composed of the:

- blockchain layer;

- value layer; and
- the application layer.

The blockchain layer is comprised of the blockchain infrastructure; examples are Ethereum, Cardano, EOS, etc. The value layer is comprised of specific tokens running on these blockchains, payment wallets, token/currency exchanges as well as NFT marketplaces. The application layer hosts the actual metaverse applications, such as Decentraland or Sandbox.

Important to note is the order of the layers, the application layer cannot exist without the value layer!

For example, the Sandbox metaverse cannot exist without the SAND token which – in turn – cannot exist without the underlying Ethereum blockchain. Therefore, any economic activity in the Sandbox metaverse leads to economic gain. This is very different to the traditional approach where services and applications can exist (and even often only emerge as market winners) without payment built in.

Could that be the answer to building value generation natively into our 5G and emerging 6G networks? Indeed, one of the unsolved challenges in telecommunications is to build economic value natively into the infrastructure and thus move away from ARPU-centric business models. The metaverse and underlying blockchains could be the answer.

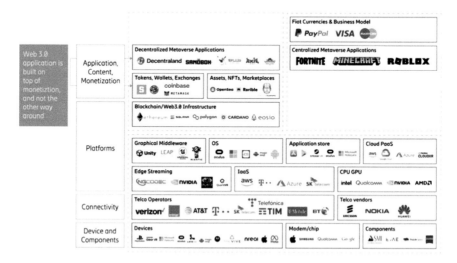

Figure 20.2 Illustration of the inversion of the value chain [6].

20.4 Metaverse Challenges and Opportunities

20.4.1 Current and potential challenges

As discussed throughout this chapter, there are several challenges that need to be overcome before the metaverse can become a reality:

- **Technical challenges**: Creating a fully immersive and interactive virtual world requires advanced technology such as virtual reality and augmented reality. These technologies are still in the early stages of development and there are still many technical challenges to be overcome, such as issues with latency and data privacy.

- **Connectivity**: Creating a seamless and immersive metaverse requires a high level of connectivity, which can be difficult to achieve. There are many different types of networks and devices that need to be connected and integrated, and there are also issues with bandwidth and data storage that need to be addressed.

- **Standardization**: There are many different virtual worlds and platforms being developed, and there is currently no standardized framework for building and connecting these worlds. This can lead to fragmentation and a lack of interoperability between different virtual worlds.

- **Business models**: The metaverse is still in early stages, and there is still no clear business model for how it will generate revenue. It is unclear how companies will monetize the metaverse and how users will pay for services and content.

- **Legal and regulatory challenges**: The metaverse raises many legal and regulatory challenges such as the ownership of virtual assets, virtual property rights, and governance. There is still a lack of clear regulations and laws governing the metaverse, which can create uncertainty for companies and users.

- **Privacy and security**: The metaverse will generate large amounts of data and personal information, which needs to be secured and protected. Ensuring data privacy and security in the metaverse is a complex and challenging task.

- **Human–computer interaction**: The metaverse is a highly immersive and interactive environment, and it requires new ways of human–computer interaction, which are still in early stages of development.

These are some of the current and potential challenges that need to be overcome in order to create a fully immersive and functional metaverse. However, as technology continues to advance and the metaverse becomes more tangible, solutions to these challenges are likely to be developed.

20.4.2 Future outlook

The future outlook of the metaverse is still uncertain, as the concept is still in its early stages of development. However, many experts believe that the metaverse has the potential to become a major platform for social interaction, commerce, and entertainment in the future.

As technology continues to advance, it is expected that the metaverse will become more immersive and interactive, allowing for more realistic and engaging virtual experiences. The integration of virtual reality and augmented reality technology is expected to make the metaverse more accessible and user-friendly, which will make it more appealing to a wider audience.

The use of blockchain technology in the metaverse is also expected to become more prevalent, as it can facilitate the creation of decentralized, secure, and verifiable virtual worlds. This can lead to the creation of new forms of social interaction and commerce, and it can also generate new revenue streams for companies and individuals.

The metaverse is also expected to have a significant impact on various industries such as entertainment, education, and business. The metaverse can be used to create new forms of entertainment, such as virtual reality gaming, and it can also be used to create virtual classrooms and virtual offices, which can be used to improve education and business productivity [7, 8, 9, 10].

References

[1] https://docbox.etsi.org/ISG/PDL/Open/0018_redactable_DL/PDL-00
    18_redactable_DLv003.docx
[2] https://www.ericsson.com/en/blog/2022/4/why-metaverse-needs-5g
[3] https://www.gsma.com/futurenetworks/wiki/cloud-ar-vr-whitepaper/
[4] https://www.ericsson.com/en/blog/2022/4/why-metaverse-needs-5g
[5] https://www.ericsson.com/en/reports-and-papers/ericsson-technology-r
    eview/articles/xr-and-5g-extended-reality-at-scale-with-time-critical-
    communication

[6] https://www.ericsson.com/en/blog/2022/9/metaverse-blockchain-5g

[7] https://www.ericsson.com/en/blog/2022/7/10-metaverse-use-cases

[8] https://www.ericsson.com/en/blog/2022/8/metaverse-education-from-u niversity-to-metaversity

[9] https://www.ericsson.com/en/blog/2022/9/metaverse-blockchain-5g

[10] https://www.ericsson.com/en/blog/2022/10/metaverse-challenges-and-opportunities

21

Concluding Remarks

Blockchain technology and telecommunications networks have the potential to revolutionize the way we interact and conduct business. Blockchain, with its ability to securely and transparently record transactions, can be used to create decentralized platforms for everything from digital identity verification to supply chain management. This technology can also be used to create new business models, such as tokenization of assets and micropayments, that were previously infeasible.

5G and later 6G networks, on the other hand, will provide the high-speed, low-latency, and highly reliable connectivity needed to support the growing number of connected devices and the increasing demand for data. This will enable new use cases such as virtual and augmented reality, as well as the Internet of Things, to reach their full potential.

Together, blockchain and 5G/6G have the potential to create a more secure, efficient, and equitable digital economy. The marriage of both technologies has formed the central part of this book. In contrast to similar publications in the field, we have focused on a standardization route which we believe ensures up-take, scale and market viability.

Indeed, *Part I* of the book lays the foundation for understanding the core concepts and technologies that enable blockchain systems, with a focus on permissioned distributed ledgers (PDLs). It begins by offering an overview of blockchain technology, explaining its key features, such as decentralized consensus, immutability, and cryptographic security. The section highlights the benefits of using blockchain for creating trust and ensuring secure data storage and transfer in various applications.

The next chapter dives into smart contracts, which are self-executing agreements built on blockchain platforms. These contracts are capable of automating complex transactions and processes, thereby increasing efficiency and reducing human intervention. Smart contracts are particularly significant for PDLs, as they empower organizations to develop and deploy decentralized applications (dApps) that leverage the unique features of blockchain technology.

In Chapter 4, the book addresses the critical issues of scalability and interoperability that have hindered the widespread adoption of blockchain technology. It discusses various solutions and techniques, such as sharding, side chains, and off-chain computations, which aim to improve the performance of blockchains while maintaining their core benefits. The section emphasizes the importance of addressing these challenges to ensure the success of blockchain technology in real-world applications.

Chapter 5 introduces permissioned distributed ledgers (PDLs) as a promising solution for many of the challenges faced by public blockchains. PDLs combine the security and trust features of blockchains with the control and privacy offered by traditional databases. By allowing only authorized participants to access the network, PDLs can enhance scalability and interoperability while maintaining the desired levels of privacy and security for organizations and industries.

In conclusion, Part I of the book provides a solid foundation in blockchain technology, smart contracts, scalability, and interoperability challenges. It presents PDLs as a viable solution that addresses these challenges while retaining the benefits of blockchain technology. This section sets the stage for a deeper exploration of the blockchain ecosystem, standards, and the role of PDLs in the 6G era in the subsequent parts of the book.

Part II of the book delves into the broader ecosystem surrounding blockchain technology, discussing the governance, technical standards, alliances, regulatory aspects, and research and development projects that shape the blockchain landscape. This section offers valuable insights into the various components that contribute to the adoption and growth of blockchain technology and PDLs.

Chapter 6 examines the blockchain governance standards, which play a crucial role in ensuring the effective functioning, security, and trustworthiness of blockchain systems. The chapter highlights the importance of establishing clear governance models and frameworks to facilitate decision-making, manage conflicts, and coordinate upgrades in the blockchain network.

In Chapter 7, the focus shifts to blockchain technical standards, which are essential for promoting interoperability, scalability, and security. Standardization helps in creating a unified approach to developing and implementing blockchain solutions, fostering collaboration among stakeholders, and driving adoption across different industries.

Chapter 8 explores the various blockchain alliances, such as the Enterprise Ethereum Alliance, Hyperledger, and R3, which bring together organizations, developers, and researchers to collaborate on the development of blockchain technology. These alliances play a vital role in promoting knowledge sharing, joint research, and the creation of industry-specific solutions that leverage the advantages of blockchain and PDLs.

Regulation and compliance are addressed in Chapter 9, where the book discusses the current regulatory landscape and the challenges faced by policymakers in creating an environment that supports innovation while protecting users and ensuring stability. This chapter emphasizes the importance of striking a balance between fostering growth and maintaining security, transparency, and privacy.

Finally, Chapter 10 showcases various blockchain R&D projects that are pushing the boundaries of what is possible with blockchain technology. These projects explore innovative applications, develop new consensus algorithms, and investigate ways to improve the scalability and efficiency of blockchain systems, ultimately contributing to the advancement of the technology and its potential use cases.

In summary, Part II of the book provides a comprehensive overview of the blockchain ecosystem, highlighting the importance of governance standards, technical standards, alliances, regulation, and R&D projects in shaping the future of blockchain technology and PDLs. This section emphasizes the interconnectedness of these components and their role in driving the adoption and evolution of blockchain technology in various industries.

Part III of the book delves into the specific standards needed for the successful implementation of permissioned distributed ledgers (PDLs), covering aspects such as PDL application governance, reference architecture, smart contracts, distributed data management, offline operations, and ledger interoperability. This section emphasizes the importance of these standards in ensuring that PDLs can meet the requirements of various industries and applications.

Chapter 11 discusses PDL application governance, focusing on the rules and processes that dictate how PDL-based systems should be developed, managed, and maintained. This chapter highlights the significance of creating robust governance models that address the unique challenges and needs of PDL-based applications, ensuring that they operate securely, efficiently, and transparently.

In Chapter 12, the book introduces reference architecture as a critical component for designing and implementing PDL systems. Reference architectures provide a standardized blueprint that can guide organizations in developing scalable, secure, and interoperable PDL-based solutions, facilitating the seamless integration of these systems with existing infrastructures.

Chapter 13 revisits smart contracts in the context of PDLs, elaborating on the specific requirements and challenges associated with developing and deploying smart contracts on PDL platforms. The chapter emphasizes the importance of creating standards and best practices for developing secure, efficient, and interoperable smart contracts that can meet the diverse needs of various industries.

Distributed data management is explored in Chapter 14, where the book discusses the challenges and opportunities associated with managing data in PDL-based systems. This chapter highlights the need for standardized approaches to data storage, access, and sharing, ensuring that PDL systems can provide secure, efficient, and reliable data management capabilities.

Chapter 15 covers offline operations, which are essential for ensuring that PDL systems can continue to function even when network connectivity is limited or unavailable. The chapter discusses various strategies for enabling offline transactions, data synchronization, and dispute resolution, emphasizing the importance of developing robust mechanisms that can maintain the integrity and reliability of PDL systems in offline scenarios.

Finally, Chapter 16 addresses ledger interoperability, a crucial aspect of PDL implementation that enables seamless interaction between different PDL systems and traditional databases. The chapter explores various approaches to achieving ledger interoperability, such as cross-chain communication and standardized APIs, highlighting the importance of overcoming interoperability challenges to unlock the full potential of PDLs.

In summary, Part III of the book emphasizes the critical role that standards play in ensuring the successful implementation of PDLs across different industries and applications. By addressing the unique challenges associated with PDL application governance, reference architecture, smart contracts, distributed data management, offline operations, and ledger interoperability, this section sets the stage for exploring the integration of PDLs into the 6G era in the final part of the book.

Part IV of the book focuses on the application of blockchain technology in the context of 6G networks. This section explores the potential use cases and benefits of integrating PDLs with 6G technology, highlighting the revolutionary possibilities that emerge from the intersection of these two advanced technologies.

Chapter 17 introduces the concepts of 5G Advanced and 6G, explaining the evolution of wireless networks and the key features that distinguish these next-generation technologies. The chapter sets the stage for discussing the potential synergies between blockchain technology and 6G networks, emphasizing the role of PDLs in enabling new, innovative applications.

In Chapter 18, the book explores the application of blockchain technology for data sharing in 6G networks, discussing how PDLs can facilitate secure, private, and efficient data exchange between various entities. The chapter highlights the potential of PDLs in enabling new business models and opportunities that were previously impossible or impractical, such as data marketplaces and decentralized data sharing platforms.

Chapter 19 addresses the application of blockchain technology in the 6G radio access network (RAN). The chapter explores how PDLs can be leveraged to optimize RAN operations, enhance network security, and enable new services, such as dynamic spectrum sharing and decentralized infrastructure management. This section highlights the potential of PDLs in driving the evolution of the RAN architecture and enabling more efficient, resilient, and adaptable networks.

In Chapter 20, the book examines the role of blockchain technology in the metaverse, particularly in the context of the 6G era. The chapter discusses how PDLs can facilitate the creation of decentralized, secure, and interoperable virtual worlds, enabling users to own, manage, and exchange digital assets across various platforms. The section emphasizes the potential of PDLs in revolutionizing the way we interact with the digital world and the metaverse.

In summary, Part IV of the book offers a compelling exploration of the intersection between blockchain technology, particularly PDLs, and 6G networks, highlighting the transformative potential of these technologies when combined. By examining various use cases, such as data sharing, native AI, RAN optimization, and metaverse applications, this section emphasizes the importance of further research and collaboration to fully unlock the potential of PDLs in the 6G era.

Blockchain and telecommunication systems are two of the most exciting technological advancements of our time, and the combination of these technologies holds the potential to create a more connected, efficient and equitable world. As these technologies continue to evolve and mature, we can expect to see new and innovative use cases emerge, changing the way we live, work and interact with each other.

Thank you for reading this book!

Index

About the Editors

Dr. Mischa Dohler is currently VP Emerging Technologies at Ericsson Inc. in Silicon Valley, working on cutting-edge topics of 6G, Metaverse, XR, Quantum and Blockchain. He serves on the Technical Advisory Committee of the FCC and on the Spectrum Advisory Board of Ofcom.

He is a Fellow of the IEEE, the Royal Academy of Engineering, the Royal Society of Arts (RSA), the Institution of Engineering and Technology (IET), and a Distinguished Member of Harvard Square Leaders Excellence. He is a serial entrepreneur with 5 companies; a composer and pianist with 5 albums on Spotify/iTunes; and is fluent in several languages.

He is a frequent keynote, panel and tutorial speaker, and has received numerous awards. He has pioneered several research fields, contributed to numerous wireless broadband, IoT/M2M and cyber security standards, holds a dozen patents, organized and chaired numerous conferences, was the Editor-in-Chief of two journals, has more than 300 highly-cited publications, and authored several books. He is a Top-1% Cited Innovator across all science fields globally.

He was Professor in Wireless Communications at King's College London and Director of the Centre for Telecommunications Research from 2013–2021, driving cross-disciplinary research and innovation in technology, sciences and arts. He is the Cofounder and former CTO of the IoT-pioneering company Worldsensing, cofounder and former CTO of the AI-driven satellite company SiriusInsight.AI, and cofounder of the sustainability company Movingbeans. He also worked as a Senior Researcher at Orange/France Telecom from 2005–2008.

Dr. Diego R. Lopez joined Telefónica in 2011 as a Senior Technology Expert and is currently in charge of the Technology Exploration activities within the GCTIO Unit. Before joining Telefónica he spent some years in the academic sector, dedicated to research on network services, and was appointed member of the High-Level Expert Group on Scientific Data Infrastructures by the European Commission.

Diego is currently focused on applied research in network infrastructures, with a special emphasis on virtualization, data-driven management, new architectures, and security. Diego acted as chair of the ETSI ISG on Permissioned Distributed Ledgers from its start until the end of its second term, and is currently chair of ETSI ISG ZSM on network service automation, and of the Network Operator Council ETSI ISG on network function virtualization.

Dr. Chonggang Wang is currently a Principal Engineer with InterDigital Communications. He has more than 20 years of experience in the fields of wireless communications, networking, and computing, including research, development, and standardization. His current research interests include future wireless systems, blockchain and distributed ledger technologies, decentralized and pervasive intelligence, and quantum internet. He participates in industry standardization activities with ETSI, IETF/IRTF, 3GPP, oneM2M, and IEEE. He is Vice Chair of ETIS ISG on Permissioned Distributed Ledgers (PDL) and a member of NextG Alliance Research Council. He is the Founding Editor-in-Chief of the IEEE Internet of Things Journal and is currently the Editor-in-Chief of IEEE Network – The Magazine of Global Internetworking. He is a Fellow of the IEEE for his contributions to internet of things enabling technologies.